Telling Border Life Stories

NUMBER EIGHTEEN

Rio Grande/Río Bravo: Borderlands Culture and Traditions

Norma E. Cantú, General Editor

A list of titles in this series is available at the end of the book.

TELLING BORDER LIFE STORIES

Four Mexican American Women Writers

Donna M. Kabalen de Bichara

TEXAS A&M UNIVERSITY PRESS | College Station

Second printing, 2019

This paper meets the requirements of ANSI/NISO Z39.48-1992
(Permanence of Paper)
Binding materials have been chosen for durability.
♾

LIBRARY OF CONGRESS CATALOGING-IN-PUBLICATION DATA

Kabalen de Bichara, Donna M.

Telling border life stories : four Mexican American women writers / Donna M. Kabalen de Bichara. — 1st ed.

p. cm. — (Rio Grande/Río Bravo: borderlands culture and traditions ; no. 18)

Includes bibliographical references and index.

ISBN-13: 978-1-60344-804-8 (cloth : alk. paper)

ISBN-13: 978-1-62349-819-1 (paper)

ISBN-13: 978-1-60344-950-2 (e-book)

1. American prose literature—Women authors—History and criticism. 2. Autobiography—Women authors—History and criticism. 3. American fiction—Mexican American authors—History and criticism. 4. Biographical fiction, American—Southwest, New—History and criticism. 5. Mireles, Jovita González, 1904-1983. Dew on the thorn. 6. Jaramillo, Cleofas M. Romance of a little village girl. 7. Wilbur-Cruce, Eva Antonia. Beautiful, cruel country. 8. Ponce, Mary Helen. Hoyt Street. 9. Mexican American women authors—Southwest, New—Biography—History and criticism. 10. Mexican American women in literature. 11. Self in literature. 12. Group identity in literature.
I. Title. II. Series: Rio Grande/Río Bravo ; no. 18.

PS366.A88K33 2013
818›.54030992870896872—dc23
2012031602

Contents

Acknowledgments

Through my participation as a member of the advisory board of Recovering the U.S. Hispanic Literary Heritage Project I have come into contact with texts that have been lost and recovered. The Recovery Project has focused on the preservation and dissemination of texts from the colonial period until 1960, and three of the narratives that form part of the present study are recovered texts: Jovita González's "Early Life and Education" and *Dew on the Thorn,* and Cleofas Jaramillo's *Romance of a Little Village Girl.* Upon reading the life stories these women had to tell about their memories concerned with Texas and New Mexico, I began looking at other spaces, those of Arizona and California, in an effort to find additional narratives created by Mexican American women who write about life experiences prior to 1960. After I began reading the texts written by Eva Antonia Wilbur-Cruce and Mary Helen Ponce, I found that these four women had much to say to those of us who live between two or more worlds.

Closer to my personal experience, although I am not Mexican American, I do come from a multilingual family in Cleveland, Ohio, where my paternal grandfather spoke to my father in Arabic and my maternal grandmother always spoke in Slovak to my mother and her siblings. Little did I dream that I would leave the United States after marrying a man who is from Mexico. My husband and I live in the sprawling metropolis of Monterrey, Mexico, where we have raised our three children who are dual nationals. In essence, for forty years I have lived, as have my husband and children, on the border of two worlds. Therefore, I do share that experience with the four Mexican American women authors that I have chosen to study here. My husband Roberto and my children—Monica, Roberto, and Denise—have to a great degree taken part in this endeavor. I have shared my thoughts with them, and they have generously given me time to work on what I believe is an essential project—the recovery of memory and women's voices in literature. What better place to find these voices than in autobiographies that emanate from the margins, from border spaces.

Throughout the course of this project I have had the support of a number of areas at the Tecnológico de Monterrey in Monterrey, Mexico. Therefore, I extend my sincerest gratitude to the Center for Studies of Memory, Literature, and Discourse, the Department of Humanities Studies, and the School of Business, Social Science, and Humanities for their intellectual and material support. My colleagues in the Department of Humanities Studies: Alicia Verónica Sánchez, for meeting with me every week, for your continuous encouragement given with a smile and sense of peace; Blanca López de Mariscal, for your generous spirit and example; Judith Farré Vidal, María Eugenia Ramos, Beatriz Mariscal Hay, Claudia Reyes Trigos, and Inés Sáenz Negrete, for your willingness always to share knowledge and experience; Robertha Leal and Hector Villarreal, for your technical expertise; Carolina Garza Amparán, my undergraduate assistant—this would not have been possible without your help in reviewing the technical aspects of drafts for each chapter of this book.

Portions of chapters 2, 3, and 4 have appeared as "The Border Autobiographies of Cleofas Jaramillo and Frances Esquibel Tywoniak: Cultural Memory as a Dynamic Process," in *Interpreting the New Milenio* (Cambridge Scholars Publishing, 2008); and as "Eva Antonia Wilbur-Cruce (1904–1998)," in *The Greenwood Encyclopedia of Latino Literature, Vol. 2*, ed. Nicolás Kanellos (Greenwood Press, 2008).

Telling Border Life Stories

Introduction

Contemporary Mexican American autobiography began to be recognized as a "distinct genre" with the publication in 1988 of a special issue of the *Americas Review*.[1] This publication focused on "U.S. Hispanic Autobiography," and the works of writers such as Oscar Zeta Acosta (*The Brown Buffalo*), Ernesto Galarza (*Barrio Boy*), Richard Rodríguez (*Hunger of Memory: The Education of Richard Rodriguez*), Gary Soto (*Living Up the Street*) and Anthony Quinn (*The Original Sin*) were deemed as important contributors to the development of the genre. Of particular interest in this collection of essays is Genaro Padilla's study entitled "'Yo sola aprendí': Contra-Patriarchal Containment in Women's Nineteenth-Century California Personal Narratives," which includes references to nineteenth-century women such as Apolinaria Lorenzana, María de las Angustias de la Guerra, Eulalia Pérez, María Inocente Pico de Avila, Rosalía Vallejo de Leese whose autobiographical utterances involve self-identification and "gender related issues" that deal with the woman's realm of experience.[2] The narratives provided by these women form part of the Bancroft Collection of the University of California.[3]

In a more recent discussion of contemporary trends in the development of Mexican American autobiography, Charles Tatum has presented a list of twenty-six works that he says have contributed to Chicana/o canon building. In his lecture "Voces únicas: Trends in Contemporary Chicana/o Autobiography," delivered in 2006 at the International Conference on Chicano Literature, he mentions the works of Acosta, Galarza, Rodríguez, and Soto. Of this list of works, which is not an exhaustive one, Tatum points to autobiographies written by the following women: Gloria Anzaldúa, Norma Cantú, Gloria López-Stafford, Pat Mora, Cherríe Moraga, Sheila Ortiz Taylor, Sandra Ortiz Taylor, and Mary Helen Ponce. In addition to this list he also includes *This Bridge Called My Back: Writings by Radical Women of Color*, an anthology that includes life writing by women of color.

It is important to note that a number of scholars have undertaken the study of autobiographies, work that entails the life narrations and writing of Mexican Americans who express their experiences during the

Transition period (1848–1910), the Interaction period (1910–42), and the Chicano period (1943–present).[4] As I have mentioned, Padilla's archival work in the Bancroft Library of the University of California Berkeley has resulted in the uncovering and analysis of narratives concerned with early Mexican American life experiences. His 1993 text, *My History, Not Yours: The Formation of Mexican American Autobiography*, involves a close look at the works of Mariano G. Vallejo's "Recuerdos históricos y personales tocante a la alta California," Juan Seguín's *Personal Memoirs*, and Rafael Chacón's "Memorias." These narratives provide documentation of the Mexican "discursive response to American conquest" prior to and after the signing of the Treaty of Guadalupe Hidalgo in 1848.[5] Padilla's text includes a detailed discussion of the women whose testimonials were recorded by the Bancroft field team, and he also presents analysis regarding the importance of *Romance of a Little Village Girl* by New Mexican author Cleofas Jaramillo. Here he emphasizes Jaramillo's "desire to inscribe her own experience" (197) through her life story. It is through the "discursive response" evident in these narratives, then, that alternative histories become evident; thus Mexican American autobiography can be seen as situated "outside the formal boundaries scholars have traditionally reserved for autobiography as a singularly self-disclosing text" (29).

Besides these early California memoirs, those autobiographies involving the lives of women prior to the Chicano movement are of special importance. The autobiography of Olga Beatrice Torres, *Memorias de mi viaje*, written in 1913, presents an account of the author's family members as they flee the Mexican Revolution and later settle in El Paso, Texas. Another recovered autobiography, *The Rebel*,[6] written in the 1920s, is a narrative written by Leonor Villegas de Magnón, who was originally from Mexico but then became a border activist in the area of Laredo, Texas. In her text the author narrates her support of the Mexican Revolution as a member of the Junta Revolucionaria and as founder of the Cruz Blanca, which offered care to the revolutionary forces in Mexico and the United States. Jovita González is considered one of the "escritoras méxico-americanas pioneras en la producción literaria generada en el sur de Texas."[7] In addition to portions of her writing that were published in *Folklore Publications*, she also coauthored *Caballero: A Historical Novel*, as well as a brief autobiography, "Early Life and Education," and the autobiographically informed novella, *Dew on the Thorn*.

An early New Mexican autobiographical account written in Spanish is that of María Esperanza López de Padilla. In poems such as "Simplicidades" and "María Esperanza," which are included in *Los pobladores Nuevo mexicanos y su poesía, 1889–1950*, she emphasizes everyday life through references to cultural traditions and objects within nature. She also recalls her childhood and the poems recited by her father and other members of the community. Other female authors who write from the area of New Mexico include Fabiola Cabeza de Baca Gilbert (*The Good Life*; *We Fed Them Cactus*), and Nina Otero-Warren (*Old Spain in Our Southwest*). All of these women wrote texts that combined information regarding folklore and the cultural life of Hispanic New Mexico, as well as personal life history.

In addition to these early narratives, of particular interest are two texts that focus on the lives of young girls who grew up just prior to and during the early years of the Chicano period. The first of these is Eva Antonia Wilbur-Cruce's autobiography, *A Beautiful, Cruel Country*. This narrative focuses on life in the border region between Arizona and Sonora. Although Wilbur-Cruce was born in 1904, she would not begin writing her autobiography until much later in life. In a second autobiography, Mary Helen Ponce's *Hoyt Street*, the author draws the reader's attention to her childhood and early adolescence as she grows up in the Mexican American barrio of Pacoima, California. This text, which began as a collection of stories, eventually evolved into a narrative that focused on family and friends, social practice, and cultural contact between Anglos and Mexican Americans.

The above-mentioned works certainly have contributed to the Mexican American literary repertoire. However, because they present semipublic and public discourse concerned with everyday aspects of women's experience, they are often considered as peripheral to the canon of Chicano literature. As noted by Ramón Saldívar, the "reasons for the continued exclusion of women writers from the history of Chicano narrative are as complex as are the reasons for the sexism of any other literary tradition."[8] It is precisely because of the historical exclusion of texts written by Mexican American women that I undertake a reexamination of a corpus of five autobiographical works. "Early Life and Education" and *Dew on the Thorn* by Jovita González (1904–83) deal with life experiences in Texas and were written probably during the period from 1926 through the 1940s; both texts were published in 1997. *Romance of a Little Village Girl*, which focuses on life in New Mexico, was written by Cleofas Jaramillo (1878–1956) when the author was in her seventies and was first published in 1955. *A Beautiful, Cruel Country*, by Eva Antonia Wilbur-Cruce (1904–98), introduces the reader to history and a way of life that developed in the cultural space of Arizona. This text was created over a ten-year period and published in 1987, eleven years before the author's death. *Hoyt Street*, authored by Mary Helen Ponce (b. 1938), began as a research paper during the period of the autobiographer's undergraduate studies (1974–80), and was published in its present form in 1993. It is important to note that my choice of autobiographical texts is based on the date of birth of each writer. That is, for the purposes of the present study, I examine the way in which each of these four women present life experiences that took place prior to the Chicano movement.

By listening once again to the voices that speak through these border autobiographies, and on the basis of a close analysis and interpretation of each text, I attempt to provide an in-depth study of a corpus of narratives emanating from specific geographical and cultural spaces within the United States—Texas, New Mexico, Arizona, and California—areas that are tied historically to conflicts between Mexico and the United States.

As the reader may recall, the period 1845–48 marks the beginning of an important juncture in the history of Mexico and the United States. This time frame corresponds to America's project of Manifest Destiny, which had to do with the idea of a national destiny designated by providence to occupy the whole of the continent. Territorial expansion had its beginning as far back as the Louisiana Purchase in 1803, and one of the expansionist aims in the War of 1812 was the conquering of Canada. Furthermore, as a result of the Adams-Onís Treaty of 1819, the United States also received territorial rights to Spanish Florida. As suggested by John S. D. Eisenhower, in addition to early western exploratory expeditions that took place during the Jefferson administration, "in the course of the next four decades other expeditions followed, and Americans became aware of the 'Oregon territory' occupied jointly by the United States and Britain.[9] They also learned of the lands to the southwest, under the shaky control of Spain until 1821 and thereafter under that of Mexico. Migrations of American settlers to the west were well under way as of 1844, when the annexation of Texas, long an objective of American diplomacy, became an acute issue in the United States."[10]

Texas' independence from Mexico and its annexation to the United States in 1845 were key factors that contributed further to conflict between the two nations, and ultimately war in 1846.[11] The war between Mexico and the United States resulted in Mexican cession of half its territories. The region acquired by the United States included what would become the present-day states of, California, Nevada, New Mexico, and Utah, as well as portions of Arizona, Colorado, and Wyoming.[12]

It is precisely the result of this history of conflict and its social and cultural effects on both Mexicans and Americans in these regions that are of interest here, especially in terms of the way information regarding these aspects are registered within the literary text. As Raymund A. Paredes has noted, "Mexican-American literature began to exhibit a distinctive character in the last third of the nineteenth century, a generation after the Treaty of Guadalupe Hidalgo ended the Mexican War and transformed over 80,000 Mexicans into residents of the United States."[13] It was through the literary text, and, as I argue in this book, particularly the autobiography, that early and later generations of Mexican Americans gave voice to a cultural memory that referred to those changes wrought by history and changing borders.

What I propose, therefore, is that the voices of autobiographers such as González, Jaramillo, Wilbur-Cruce, and Ponce are especially relevant because they speak of life experiences that took place well before the advent of the Chicano movement.[14] That is, those autobiographies provide the reader with information regarding history, social practice, and ideological perspectives that contribute to the preservation of a distinct cultural heritage that involves the spheres of New Spain, Mexico, and the United States.[15] This, I believe, is their contribution to the Mexican American literary tradition.

In order to discern the distinct notions concerning the autobiographical form, and as a first step in approaching this group of texts, I begin my discussion in chapter 1 with a survey of perspectives concerning the genre of autobiography. For analytic purposes I have divided this overview into three phases. In the first phase of critical perspectives I examine the work of two theorists, Wilhelm Dilthey and Georg Misch, both of whom emphasize the importance of the representative male life as a means of arriving at historical truth. In the second phase I consider authors such as Georges Gusdorf, Francis R. Hart, Karl Joachim Weintraub, William Spengemann, and James Olney. In this section I highlight the problematic of representation within autobiography and the complication faced by the autobiographer as he or she attempts to provide a certain truth with regard to the self. In the third phase of criticism, I choose to concentrate on poststructuralist and postmodern points of view presented by theorists such as Elizabeth Bruss, Louis A. Renza, Mary

G. Mason, Estelle C. Jelinek, Janet Varner Gunn, Domna C. Stanton, Sidonie Smith, Shari Benstock, and Francois Lionnet. In this portion of my discussion I focus on the ways in which poststructural and postmodern criticism contributes to an understanding of those strategies that underlie the life writing of women, particularly in terms of the way self-disclosure in relation to others takes place within the narrative.

Theory regarding the European roots of autobiography, although relevant, cannot be considered as complete. Indeed, if we are to delve into the deeper meaning of the writings of Jovita González, Cleofas Jaramillo, Eva Antonia Wilbur-Cruce, and Mary Helen Ponce, it is of crucial importance to take on the task of broadening earlier notions of autobiography by reviewing Chicana/o scholarship on this subject. Therefore, I examine the perspectives of Chicana/o critics such as Genaro Padilla, Juan Velasco, and C. Alejandra Elenes as a first step in my attempt to enrich previous discussion of the autobiographical genre; here I am especially interested in their views on life writing that emanates from border spaces. Furthermore, I look at those definitions of autobiography that are alluded to in the writings of Chicanas such as Gloria Anzaldúa, Cherríe Moraga, Pat Mora, and Norma Cantú. My purpose in this direction is to challenge what I consider to be a limited and exclusionary view regarding the genre of autobiography.

In addition to a critical analysis of these theoretical undertakings, I present my own definition of "border autobiography," a term I suggest more closely defines the multi-structurality of the texts created by González, Jaramillo, Wilbur-Cruce, and Ponce. Because I am interested in the communicative function of each autobiography, the final section of the first chapter focuses on the publication history of each work. I also explore the individual autobiographer's intention in writing her life story as well as the question of whom she intends to address through her text.

The next three chapters are based on an operational model that takes into consideration both discursive and semiotic perspectives that function as the organizing principles of a critical analysis and interpretation of the corpus. Those broad areas to be examined include historical references, as well as social practice, cognitive schemes, and ideology, all of which are evident within each text. Chapter 2 involves two sections; the first is concerned with narrative discourse. My approach in this direction begins with a definition of "discourse" based on Foucault's notion of the term as a "general domain of statements," which often responds to certain regulatory practices. Within this chapter I also propose that narrative can be understood as both a textual and cultural phenomenon. From a textual perspective I consider Gérard Genette's definition of various aspects of narrative, such as chronological deviations. I also work with definitions of narrative suggested by Gerald Prince and Mieke Bal. In terms of the text as a cultural phenomenon I refer to Donald Polkinghorne's view of narrative as the means by which individuals invest experience with meaning. Furthermore, so as to clarify the development of the life course evident within each narrative, I present a chronotopic analysis of those life experiences highlighted within the autobiography; special emphasis is placed on the symbolic spaces in which they occur. This portion of my discussion is based on Bakhtin's definition of the "real-life chronotope," particularly the way in which autobiographical "self-consciousness" is organized around memory concerned with ancestral ties. The second section of chapter 2 examines the descriptive discourse of each text, with special emphasis on the concepts of "land" and "home." For this portion of the chapter I refer to the Neuchâtel School and the concept of natural logic as defined by Jean-Blaise Grize, Jean Michel Adam, and André Petitjean. Here my discussion centers on the effect of descriptive discourse within the text.

A textual analysis of each narrative based on cultural semiotics is the focus of chapter 3, where my interpretation is informed by Yuri Lotman's definition of culture as nonhereditary memory that is shared by a community or social group. I assert that the corpus of works considered here can be defined as a semiosphere of border autobiographies. My discussion in this direction is derived from Lotman's concept of the semiosphere as an abstract space in which cultural systems exist as a semiotic continuum. As a means of arriving at a deeper understanding of the recollections of each autobiographer, I center on Lotman's perception of cultural memory as a mechanism through which certain types of communication or texts are conserved and transmitted. As I point out, each text is multifaceted and can be perceived as a space where cultural memory is registered, as a generator of meaning, as heterogeneous, and therefore as polyglot. Within this chapter I also discuss the concept of border or boundary. Again I take my lead from Lotman's usage of the term "border" to designate not only physical or geographical limits, but also the function of the text as a filter or translator of external messages. Furthermore, as a means of venturing into the meaning of historical references evident within each text, I also examine the notion of cultural explosions and their effects on individual semiotic spheres. In the final section of this chapter I draw attention to memory as it is related to "other" cultural groups that form part of the heterogeneous representation of life in the border autobiography.

Because I am interested in what discourse reveals about collective practice, individual female identity, and individual women's position within a cultural collectivity, chapter 4 stresses the way in which discursive production and mechanisms of power and ideology are represented within the narrative. Therefore, my textual interpretation in this chapter focuses on cultural practices and ideological systems that are evident in each text. I initiate my discussion with references to the definitions of "ideology" presented by Michel Foucault, John B. Thompson, and Olivier Reboul. Of particular relevance to my analysis is Foucault's project concerning the politics of discourse, especially in terms of the way societal control of discourse production affects the writing of the four female authors I point to here. I also refer to Thompson's perspective regarding the operation of narrativization, and to Reboul's notion of "diffuse" ideologies as they are used to justify prevailing power structures and the way they figure in each life narrative.

In this chapter I draw attention to the social legacy that the autobiographer intends to preserve through the written word. Pierre Bourdieu's notion of *habitus* and the "cultural field" inform my analysis along these lines as I attempt to interpret the effect of social practice on the female subject. In order to discern the way in which the autobiographer enters into dialogue with the reader, the second section of this final chapter examines the imaginary formations evident within each text. Here my discussion is based on the work of Michel Pêcheux who has suggested that discourse is always pronounced from a particular position or place within a social formation. He notes three structural elements—A and B as producers and receivers of discourse, and R as a discursive referent. Therefore, I ultimately attempt to map out the autobiographer's perception of self and the way she addresses others—that is, her family and the Anglo reader of her text. I also concentrate on her perspective regarding referents such as male and female authority figures. Finally, my reading and interpretation of each text involves an examination of the female subject's response to sexual ideology.

This book involves a multi-structured interpretive analysis of five works: "Early Life and Education," *Dew on the Thorn*, *Romance of a Little Village Girl*, *A Beautiful Cruel, Country*, and *Hoyt Street*. Through a detailed examination of these texts concerned with life in Texas, New

Mexico, Arizona, and California, I intend to demonstrate that the concept of the border autobiography provides a critical framework for understanding the meaning generated in the works of four Mexican American female writers. The border autobiography presents the voice of the female writer who has chosen to write about her life, the life of her family and other members of society, and those elements of history that have affected the community, as well as her knowledge about social practice. Thus, I propose that an exploration of both narrative and descriptive discourse and a semiotic analysis of history and cultural memory evident within each text provide a window into understanding the way each autobiographer presents herself, her family, a cultural community, and the cultural "other." This study is ultimately an attempt to highlight social practice and discourses perceived within the text and which reveal an alternate form of knowledge that critiques the marginalized, border position of women within a patriarchal society.

Chapter 1

Memory and Historical Remembering

The Art of Autobiography and Theoretical Perspectives

The corpus of texts created by Jovita González, Cleofas Jaramillo, Eva Antonia Wilbur-Cruce, and Mary Helen Ponce are heterogeneous in terms of their narrative form, and all of the narratives involve life writing by a female subject who writes from a border position. That is, the autobiographer presents notions of her ethnic self as situated within the symbolic border space between Mexico and the United States. In addition, these texts also involve references to common sociocultural practices as well as a historical past, which involves the present-day states of Texas, New Mexico, Arizona, and California, geographical areas that were at one time under the rule of New Spain, Mexico, and then the United States.

As pointed out by Sidonie Smith and Julia Watson in *Reading Autobiography*, "[W]hen 'life' is expanded to include how one has become who he or she is at a given moment in an ongoing process of reflection, clearly the autobiographical story requires more explaining."[1] Because these texts involve complex form and content, they certainly require an extensive explanation, one that is related to the following questions: In what way do theoretical notions regarding autobiography evolve, and how do these various perspectives contribute to a more thorough understanding of the group of texts considered for the present project? What particular autobiographical elements are evident in these texts and in what way do these elements open windows into understanding the meaning of these works? Is it necessary to determine a definition that is more specific with regard to the type of literature that comprises the present corpus? As a means of addressing these questions, the present analysis will focus on the history of criticism of autobiography based on the theoretical criteria of a number of key writers, with special emphasis on the contributions of Chicana/o perspectives.

Three Phases of Critical Perspectives concerning Autobiography

One of the most important aspects of the autobiographical form of writing has to do with memory as it is registered within the text. In *Memory, History, Forgetting*, Paul Ricoeur asserts that a distinctive feature of memory is the presence of those "marks" or "*sémeia*, in which the affections of the body and the soul to which memory is attached are signified."[2] Because autobiography is a type of self-referential writing that signifies different types of memory, it is pertinent to consider two questions that Ricoeur sets before the reader: "Of what are there memories? Whose memory is it"? (3) These questions, I believe, are especially relevant as we try to comprehend the various perspectives concerning autobiography that I review here. I would like to point out that my goal is not an exhaustive survey of theory concerned with the genre. Rather I have chosen those sources that highlight a variety of definitions of the genre and how these might be related to the concept of border autobiography that I define later in this chapter. As we shall see, each phase of criticism suggests a shift in emphasis that varies from an early focus on the memories of "great men" and the historical significance of the exceptional life, to the creative aspect of memory, and finally to new notions on memory as it is related to self and collective invention in the borderlands.

Autobiography as a Historical Document and Basis for Knowledge

Early notions of the genre of autobiography refer to the writer as someone involved in a process of self-discovery and who is deemed an outstanding figure within society. In traditional studies of autobiography, elements such as history and subjectivity are seen as "stable elements in the story of one's life. Texts that affirm this stability, or that can be construed as affirming it, form the 'tradition' of autobiography."[3] For example, the traditional autobiographical text conforms to what Gilmore defines as the "Augustinian lineage," where the autobiographical subject would be a man who is white, probably heterosexual and of an elite status.

The ideas of Wilhelm Dilthey and Georg Misch provide a framework regarding early perceptions of autobiography. In his work on autobiography, "The Historical Relevance of Autobiography and Biography" in

Pattern and Meaning in History,[4] Dilthey gives autobiography a preponderant position within history as it is related to the development of society. For example, he suggests that autobiography can be seen as "the germinal cell of history" and as the "highest and most instructive form in which the understanding of life comes before us. Here is the outward, phenomenal course of a life which forms the basis for understanding what has produced it within a certain environment."[5] Of importance is Dilthey's use of the word "phenomenal" and the idea that a particular autobiography is of interest because it presents us with the course of a life that serves as an outstanding example, a model to follow, within the context of a historical period. In fact, as a historian, Dilthey proposed the use of autobiography as a means of writing about history, as "the root of all historical comprehension" (86).

For Dilthey, then, autobiography provides insight for appreciating the historical past: "The power and breadth of our own lives and the energy with which we reflect on them are the foundation of historical vision. It alone enables us to give life back to the bloodless shadows of the past . . . it makes the great historian" (87). Thus, it is by examining the individual life, and those historical elements that were responsible for its formation, that we are able to understand the human world. Because it is the "phenomenal course of a life" that interests Dilthey, his theorizing focuses on autobiographies that present different phases of the lives of Augustine, Rousseau, Goethe, and Bismarck as "typical forms." He suggests that by tracing the development of their lives, one is able to find the "particular combination of characteristics common to them all" (94); these characteristics would be of interest to future generations who presumably would model their lives after this type of man. The importance of the autobiography for Dilthey, then, is its informative function; that is, society would achieve instruction by reading about the life of a great man whose life portrayed those characteristics that were "common" to other great men.[6]

From this viewpoint, the great feat of the autobiographer is his capacity to find the "threads" of his life and set them down in writing as a coherent whole. Insight into the individual subjectivity of experience, however, is considered by Dilthey as narrow. He instead suggests that the autobiography of the prominent individual is of importance in terms of the way it relates to universal history. Man looks back on his past and links together the different parts of his life, and it is the way that this life is linked together with other "great" lives throughout history that is of interest to Dilthey. It is by analyzing "individual contexts," especially those related to experience in areas such as religion, art, and politics, that the historian is able to delve into the structure of the world of history.

Also in line with Dilthey's thoughts are the perceptions of German philologist Georg Misch regarding the history of autobiography, which he defines in terms of the meaning of the word itself, that is, "the description (*graphia*) of an individual human life (*bios*) by the individual himself (*autos*)."[7] Misch's *History of Autobiography in Antiquity* presents autobiography as a genre in literature that is "special" and which "defies classification" (3–4). Indeed, for Misch, this type of literature is seen as a subcategory of biography. Just as Dilthey points to the connection between autobiography and history, Misch too argues that autobiography provides "documentary value for knowledge of the world and of man" (1). He also suggests that this type of writing involves psychological and moral perspectives of a particular period as "an original interpretation of experience" (4).

Like Dilthey, Misch refers to the "great" or ancient autobiographies that are considered models. For example, he particularly emphasizes Plato's "Seventh Epistle" as well as Isocrates's autobiographical "oration in court," and the records of deeds evident in the documents of Emperor Augustus. Misch also sees the writings of St. Augustine, Rousseau, and Goethe as exemplary, and he praises Augustine's *Confessions* as the writing of an "*homme supérieur*," in which "the concentrated expression of the nature of an individual, an age, a race" is found (3). Once again, we find an exaltation of the great individual whose writing is a "manifestation of man's knowledge about himself" (8) as well as how his life is lived during a particular epoch in connection with the world that surrounds him. Misch, then, is concerned with "human life as actually lived by individuals, and . . . the social and historical 'world' in which they live" (8). Thus, autobiography is perceived as "always" representative of the period in which it is written; therefore, its function is as an "instrument of knowledge" (10), and not simply a medium through which self-awareness is expressed. Furthermore, Misch asserts that any autobiography that deals with the average way of life is considered to be inferior in quality.

It is clear that according to the definitions of autobiography presented by both Dilthey and Misch there is no room for the voices of those who do not contribute to the accumulation of historical knowledge within a particular (and we must assume hegemonic) society. For example, because autobiography must be "representative" of the sociocultural period in which it is written, the subject of this type of life writing would necessarily reflect a way of life that is considered to be superior; thus life writing was not to be concerned with the "average life." On the basis of these notions of exclusion, it becomes obvious that the female voice of the autobiographer who writes from a doubly marginal position, as a woman and as a Mexican American, would not be considered as worthy of study from the perspective of Dilthey and Misch. As we shall see, it is the next generation of critics who offer a more creative perspective regarding the autobiographical form, as they consider elements other than those which point to the "representative" life of a "great man" who contributes to knowledge of a historical period.

Autobiography as a Literary Text and as Art

As we have seen, early notions of the autobiographical form were concerned with the autobiographer's experience as the basis for understanding a particular world; that is, the written word of the text was important because it reflected the expressions of an exceptional individual within a given historical time period. With the second phase of criticism, there is a notable shift in emphasis from the historical, or the "*bios*," to that of individual consciousness of the subject of the autobiographical text, which is now perceived as a literary form and therefore as art.

According to Smith and Watson, the theoretical considerations that most affected this change were those concerned with class consciousness as determined by Marxist views, which focused on the relation between individual consciousness and broad economic forces. The authors also note the effect of Freud's psychoanalytic theory, which suggests a struggle between the "self" and "forces occurring outside conscious control."[8] It is because of this struggle that the possibility of attaining "conscious control" over individual identity or experience is seen as impossible; therefore, speaking "truth" in autobiography is considered unattainable. For example, in *The Psychopathology of Everyday Life* Freud suggests that our everyday usage of language includes errors in speech, reading, and writing as well as "faulty recollections"; these are not coincidences or accidents, but rather they reveal something that has been repressed into the unconscious.[9] It is precisely the subtleties of unconscious purposes evident in language usage that contribute to what is considered the creative aspect of the autobiographical form in this second phase of theorizing.

For example, James Olney suggests that Georges Gusdorf's essay "Conditions et limites de l'autobiographie" is a key work in the study of autobiography, especially in terms of the genre with its focus on the study of the "I." As Olney notes, "it was this turning to *autos*—the 'I' that coming awake to its own being shapes and determines the nature of autobiography and in so doing . . . opened up the subject of autobiography specifically for literary discussion, for behind every work of literature there is an 'I' informing the whole."[10] Gusdorf understands autobiography as a genre that is "solidly established" and "traceable to a series of masterpieces" of the Western tradition (28). Although he suggests that the purpose of autobiography is the achievement of self-knowledge through the interpretation of an entire life, he further notes the importance of the genre as more than a presentation of historical objectivity, or even as solely a literary mode. Rather, it is the anthropological function of the autobiography, where inner consciousness is projected into an exterior space, that is important.

In spite of the limiting aspects of Gusdorf's definition and his suggestion that autobiography is based on the historical consciousness and individualism expressed in a series of Western masterpieces, he also notes that autobiography involves the possibility of "composing" and "reconstructing of life across time" (38); therefore, he suggests the idea of the reconstruction of a personal history, but one that involves creative nuances. Gusdorf perceives autobiography as "a new spiritual revolution: the artist and the model coincide, the historian tackles himself as object" (31). The change that Gusdorf points to concerns private rather than public history, and it is autobiography that can be seen as "the mirror in which the individual reflects his own image" (33). From this very gendered perspective, each "man" has a history, one that is worthy of narration. The subject becomes his own witness and expresses a "more profound sense of truth as an expression of inmost being . . . not as he was, not as he is, but as he believes and wishes himself to be and to have been" (45). What becomes evident then is the conception of creativity in terms of the narratives concerned with the possibility of arriving at a sense of truth about self.

Francis Hart considers autobiography as the "plurality of mimetic and formal value," and he is concerned with three key elements that form what he has termed the "anatomy" of autobiography: a) the mimetic question concerning the way in which there is an interplay between history and fiction; b) a concern with the "purposive form and experimental development" of the autobiographical act; and c) the question of the "elusive" intention of autobiography to present "truth" to a particular audience.[11] He also defines three types of autobiography: the confessional, the apology, and the memoir. All three are seen as personal history, history where "the autobiographer recognizes, interrelates, and attempts to manipulate toward some truth or integrity his relationships with his recoverable past, with his formal or technical options, and with his rhetorical and psychological intentions" (226). However, Hart also notes that although truth telling is an intention of autobiography, it is generally elusive and represents instead interplay between an attempt at truth telling with regard to the past and those options for writing chosen on the basis of the author's intentions. Hart also suggests that the autobiographer selects the type of "I" to present to the reader; that is, the "I" may be an "inductive invention" or an "intentional creation" used as a means of affecting a particular response from the reader. Therefore, it is important to recognize and interpret the autobiographer's various intentions as they "interact and shift" within the narrative. This interaction and shifting of intentions is of particular importance for understanding the corpus of texts considered in this book. Indeed, as I discuss in the following chapters, it is precisely the various intentions of the autobiographer that contribute to the creation of a multilayered text.

Karl J. Weintraub's study of the autobiographical mode focuses on man's need to understand his own sense of being and life, and he traces this aspect in his exhaustive analysis of autobiography beginning with antiquity through the eighteenth century. As Weintraub points out, he is interested in the "proper form of autobiography wherein a self-reflective person asks 'who am I?' and 'how did I become what I am?'"[12] It is pertinent to note that Weintraub's perspective coincides with both Gusdorf and Hart who also note that the retrospective standpoint allows the author to impose interpretative meaning on the past. Thus, all three authors conceive of the creative, plural or interpretative aspect of autobiographical writing, yet there are limits, as the title of Gusdorf's essay suggests, to this creative or revolutionary type of writing; that is, from all three perspectives, autobiography is connected to historical consciousness.

William C. Spengemann's discussion of the genre acknowledges two approaches to understanding what he calls "the boundaries of autobiography."[13] As he mentions, one school of thought insists that autobiography must to some degree offer "a factual account of the writer's own life . . . based on historical rather than fictional materials" (xii). He goes on to explain that in contrast to this view are those critics who "assert the right of autobiographers to present themselves in whatever form they may find appropriate and necessary" (xi). Here Spengemann is obviously referring to the conflict between fact and fiction in autobiographical writing.

Of particular interest as well is his definition of the poetic autobiography that has to do with the use of allegorical or metaphorical language as the basis for poetic expression that does not necessarily emphasize biographical facts, but rather fictive elements. This classification allows us to observe the different types of autobiography, or, as Hart has noted, the "wide plurality" of this literary form. Spengemann's insight regarding poetic autobiography opens the definition of the genre to include elements not strictly concerned with *bios*, or the course of a life, but rather with the dramatized personae and the fictive metaphor as the basis for the narrative. His concept of "the fictive metaphor" is of particular interest for the present study, especially in chapter 4 where my analysis of *Dew on the Thorn*, an autobiographically informed narrative, focuses on the use of the fictional form that is used creatively to address the problematic of the female role within a cultural field marked by patriarchy.

In *Metaphors of Self*, James Olney defines autobiography as "a single, radical and radial energy originating in the subject center, an aggressive, creative expression of the self, a defense of individual integrity."[14] In this definition Olney is apparently emphasizing the notion of the "self" and the construction of self-representation within language, yet he modifies this definition as he suggests that rather than try to define what he perceives as the invisible self, it is more productive to look "sidewise to an experience of the self, and try to discover or create some similitude for the experience that can reflect or evoke it and that may appeal to another individual's experience of the self" (29). The metaphor, or this "sidewise" look, provides a connection between what the writer creates and what the reader relates to in the process of reading. Indeed, as Olney suggests, "metaphor is essentially a way of knowing," and it is through the metaphor that the image of self is presented and which "[makes] available new relational patterns [and] simultaneously organizes the self into a new and richer entity" (31–32).

Later, in "Autobiography and the Cultural Moment," Olney defines autobiography as life writing, as self writing, and as "the most rarified and self-conscious of literary performances."[15] Here "autobiography" refers to the unfinished process of "being" and "existing." It does not simply refer to a particular number of years of one's life, but rather to the "spirit" or "vital principle . . . the act of consciousness, or transcendent reality, or a certain mode of living, a certain set of personality and character" (239). What becomes apparent here is the parallel between the definition of poetic autobiography presented by Spengemann and Olney's amplification of what can be considered as autobiography; that is, both perspectives point to the creative aspect of life writing.

A close examination of these definitions of autobiography provides us with several insights. Although these critics generally coincide in their perception of autobiography as art, what seems to be limiting this creative possibility of the genre is a continued adherence to the notion of autobiography in relation to individual greatness, especially as evidenced in their reference to canonical works by writers such as Augustine, Rousseau, Montaigne, and Goethe. In terms of the contribution of women, Weintraub makes reference to two works, *The Life of Teresa* and *The Life and Religious Experience of Celebrated Lady Guion*. These works follow the tradition of a chronological description of life experience, yet it is important to point out that they do not portray the life stories of the average woman, of the individual personality immersed in everyday social practices. In their writings these religious mystics speak of an extraordinary religious experience and move from a recounting of sinful life to the experience of conversion, and finally to a way of life devoted to God.

Although this second phase of theoretical views stands out in terms of an emphasis on the creative aspect of the autobiographical form, we find that the major limiting factor is a continued emphasis on fact and truth. This mirrors those aspects evident in the first phase of theoretical perspectives mentioned previously, in terms of an emphasis on the model individual as part of the ideally developed civilization that underlies the "grand narratives" referred to by Lyotard. It is this line of thinking that is ultimately responsible for marginalizing other types of life writing, especially those works by women who write life stories concerned with the everyday tasks of the home sphere, of family relations, and cultural practice. A number of these narrowly defined aspects of autobiography are addressed in the third phase of theoretical analysis.

New Notions of Autobiography

It is during the final thirty years of the twentieth century that another shift in critical analysis concerning autobiography becomes evident. In this period, dominated by poststructuralist and postmodern views, the text is seen as a textual object where a weaving of self-referential codes is evident. Of particular importance is the influence of critics such as Derrida and Foucault. Derrida's notion of "differénce" sets the tone for questioning language, thought, and meaning which are not fixed, and he asserts instead that there are multiple layers of meaning at work in language, which is constantly shifting. Derrida also questions the concept of consciousness, which is based on the idea that we are present to ourselves. Indeed, he notes that "the center is not the center," but rather "a point of departure" where we find "repetitions, substitutions, transformations, and permutations [that] are always taken from a history of meaning [*sens*]."[16] Because of this sense of shifting center, because "we cannot grasp or show the thing, state the present, the being-present, when the present cannot be presented, we signify, we go through the detour of the sign. We take or give signs. We signal. The sign, in this sense, is deferred presence."[17] From this perspective, then, the autobiographical "I" is a sign, but it can never exactly be present to itself since the center of the "I" is not really a center, and self-presence is a fiction.

Of further importance is Derrida's rejection of *logocentrism*, a term used to explain that spoken words definitively represent objects, concepts, and meanings in the real world. Indeed, for Derrida, knowledge of the world is always mediated. As Smith and Watson note as well, both Derrida and Lyotard critique "universalized 'master' narratives" and they question "the firmness of generic boundaries between fact and fiction."[18] This sense of fluid generic boundaries is relevant as it contributes to what I define as the border autobiography later in this chapter.

Foucault's view regarding discourses is pertinent particularly because his discussion focuses on notions of power and their effect on the self. For example, he states that "in every society the production of discourse is at once controlled, selected, organised and redistributed according to a certain number of procedures, whose role is to avert its power and its dangers, to cope with chance events, to evade its ponderous, awesome materiality."[19] It is precisely this perspective, which emphasizes the prohibitions and limits placed on discourse, that will be a key focus of my discussion in chapter 4 where I discuss the limits imposed upon the female as a speaking subject. Bakhtin's influence is also notable in this period, specifically in terms of his view concerning the dialogic nature of language and its relation to a living context; that is, he suggests that culture constitutes the indispensable context of a literary work. Bakhtin also argues that the autobiographical "I" speaks in terms of "a multitude of concrete worlds, a multitude of bounded verbal-ideological and social belief-systems."[20] Other areas, such as postcolonial, ethnic, and feminist studies, also have had an effect on perspectives regarding autobiography in this period.

Published in 1976, Elizabeth Bruss's *Autobiographical Acts: The Changing Situation of a Literary Genre* points clearly to changing notions of self writing, and Bruss notes the rigid definitions of the genre, such as the one presented by Roy Pascal who critiques the fact that most autobiographical writing does not successfully represent "the whole man" and therefore does not demonstrate "moral responsibility" on the part of the autobiographer in fulfilling the task demanded by the genre.[21] Ultimately, an important question for Bruss is what autobiography really captures, whether it is truly able to record information or whether much of what is contained in autobiography is created. She finally suggests that from a twentieth-century perspective, autobiography focuses more on "indeterminacy" than on "fact." Her emphasis, then, is on how autobiographical narratives demonstrate changes in terms of their literary form and function as well as in terms of references to various "cultural systems."[22]

In a later essay, "Eye for I: Making and Unmaking Autobiography in Film," Bruss defines autobiography in terms of truth, act, and identity values which determine its inclusion within the genre. Truth-value involves the way autobiography coincides with documentary evidence regarding the "veracity" of those events presented in autobiographical material. Of particular importance is her conception of act-value, which provides a definition of autobiography as "a personal performance, an action that exemplifies the character of the agent responsible for that action and how it is performed" (299–300).[23] Identity-value has to do with the author, narrator, and protagonist as "conjoined" or as "the same individual occupying a position both in the context, the associated 'scene of writing,' and within the text itself" (300). It is Bruss's notion of autobiography as a performative act, then, that sets the stage for this third phase of theoretical perspectives. Autobiography is not simply an act of truth telling and historical documentation of life, but rather an act that, depending on its purpose, will find the autobiographer choosing certain aspects of his or her life to emphasize, while others will "recede into a background" (*Autobiographical Acts* 12).

Louis A. Renza also examines the notion of truth in autobiography in his important article "The Veto of the Imagination: A Theory of Autobiography," with several questions concerning the possibility of the "indeterminate mixture of truth and fiction" or "fact rather than self-invention."[24] In response to these questions, Renza argues that autobiography, which he considers as a formal genre, is "neither fictive nor nonfictive, not even a mixture of the two . . . [but rather] a unique, self-defining mode of self-referential expression" (295). Particularly interesting is Renza's idea of the "spirit of anarchism" that can be perceived in autobiographical works in which "the writer blends the exclusive sense of self disclosed through his act into an exclusive, though collective, 'minority'" (290). Renza's definition takes into account that "self presence" is constructed with the reader's expectations in mind, thus autobiography is seen as an act that presents other possibilities, such as the anarchic spirit that projects an intention other than self-representation. That is, the autobiographical "I" may actually become a "revolutionary self" that is determined "to resist linguistic usage that is phenomenologically occupied by a given social establishment" (290). This notion of language as related to resistance is of interest for the present study, and will be discussed in more detail in chapter 4 as I explain the way in which the autobiographer uses her writing as a means of contesting the constraints placed on women within a Mexican American patriarchal society.

Challenging Horizons of Expectations: Self, Community, and Culture

It is during the early 1980s that a number of feminist literary critics present important theoretical studies on autobiography as a means of "deconstruct[ing] the patriarchal hegemony of literary history, poetics, and aesthetics, and to reconstruct histories, criticism, and theories from a different perspective."[25] One of these studies is Mary G. Mason's article "The Other Voice: Autobiographics of Women Writers," which focuses on the history of women's autobiography, with an emphasis on works dating back to the fifteenth century. In her article Mason critiques early history of the genre, with its "strict classifications," as being obsessed with the Western notion of self and for most often refusing to consider early women's autobiography due to its lack of "self-disclosure." Mason argues that the autobiographical speaker becomes a performative subject by means of the act of "self-narrating," which marks the moment when the "essential, original, coherent autobiographical self" becomes evident.[26]

Mason further asserts that the "self is not a documentary repository of all experiential history running uninterruptedly from infancy to the contemporary moment" (108). Therefore, her study, based on the lives of four women—Margaret Cavendish, Duchess of Newcastle, Dame Julian of Norwich, Margery Kempe, and Anne Bradstreet—suggests that rather than focusing on self, the early life stories of women can be seen as recording and dramatizing "self-realization and self-transcendence through recognition of another" (235). It is due to this recognition of others that Mason sees the works of these women as relevant, not only in the fourteenth century but also in the twentieth century. That is, within these texts a sense of "self-discovery of female identity" is evident. This type of autobiographer, rather than exalting the "I," perceives the personal self in harmony with the "public community" and therefore capable of understanding another consciousness.

Estelle C. Jelinek's study *Women's Autobiography* defines the genre of autobiography as one of "disclosure," and she, like Mason, critiques the fact that historically the genre has been defined on the basis of what critics consider "good" autobiography. She emphasizes, however, that the subject of women's autobiography has to do with feelings, the spouse, domestic activities, interpersonal relations, and in some instances religion. Thus, the central focus of works written by women is not necessarily the "I." In her discussion of autobiographical texts written by women, Jelinek further echoes Mason's sense of women's writing as focusing on what is considered personal life, such as "domestic details, family difficulties, close friends, and especially people who have influenced them."[27] Again what is emphasized is the fact that women's autobiography normally does not "mirror the establishment history of their times" (8). Instead women tend to focus their writing on others rather than on their own work and they downplay their participation in public life, worldly activities, and their professions.

Janet Varner Gunn's perspective broadens those presented by Mason and Jelinek as she asserts that "autobiography is a mode of fictional and historical narrative," an "instrument of self reading" rather than a formula for writing.[28] Her discussion broadens those presented by Mason and Jelinek by emphasizing the autobiographer's reading of self, not as a private act but rather as a cultural reading of self, given that self-knowledge is "grounded in the signs of one's existence that are received from others" (31). Varner Gunn, then, is highly critical of the historical emphasis in theoretical criticism that excludes the cultural dimension of the "autobiographical act" and focuses solely on self writing as a private act.

Domna C. Stanton's "Autogynography: Is the Subject Different?" presents autobiography as a genre that is "at the very center of modernist concerns," and she proposes a gendered definition of autogynography as "autobiographical writing by women."[29] Stanton criticizes the body of critical writing that has accumulated over the years with almost no reference to women's autobiographies. As part of her commentary, Stanton presents autogynography as having "a global and essential therapeutic purpose to constitute a female subject" (39), and she defines the "referential status of the signature . . . as a name that comprised various semes of gender, ethnicity, or class that evoked various cultural and literary associations" (141). Thus it is precisely due to woman's "different status in the symbolic order" and the way in which the feminine subject "asserts itself discursively" that androcentric criticism has normally excluded women's autobiography. Stanton's article essentially questions previous theorizing on autobiography that privileges the texts by men and therefore, because of a particular gendered "horizon of expectations," has resulted in the marginalization of autobiography written by women.

In the first chapter of *Poetics of Women's Autobiography: Marginality and the Fictions of Self-Representation*, Sidonie Smith reiterates Stanton's view regarding the marginalization of women's writing in the history of critical theory of the genre of autobiography. For example, she criticizes the "restrictive, prescriptive, and inappropriate" criteria evident in the writings of Misch and Weintraub as responsible for promoting "male" norms for the reading of autobiography. She also refers to the "revisionist psychoanalytic theory" proposed by Nancy Chodorow, which asserts that "the process of individuation differ[s] for men and women."[30] Indeed, as Smith clarifies, Chodorow suggests that "feminine personality . . . comes to be based less on repression of inner objects, and fixed and firm splits in the ego, and more on retention and continuity of external relationships."[31] Ultimately Smith comments on the importance of retrieving from the "gaps in literary history" those autobiographies written by women and which "challenge the naïve conflation of male subjectivity and human identity."[32] In defining autobiography to include "any written or verbal communication that takes the speaking 'I' as subject of the narrative" (17) she proposes the inclusion of letters, diaries, journals, and oral histories as part of what is considered as autobiography.

Along similar lines, Benstock's article entitled "Authorizing the Autobiographical" focuses on traditional attitudes regarding autobiography in which those aspects of women's self writing that stresses "womanhood" have not been taken into account. From Benstock's standpoint autobiography can be understood as the textual space where layers of "socioideological horizons interact and enter into dialogue."[33] She further posits that autobiographical writing also includes "a repeated but untranslated, unconscious message [that] is directed at the culture from the position of the Other, by those who occupy positions of internal exclusion within the culture—that is by women, blacks, Jews, homosexuals, and others who exist on the margins of society" (16). Thus, women's autobiography, particularly the self writing of women who are members of minority groups where the self is "decentered—and often . . . absent altogether" (20), takes into consideration that which is outside of self, whether it be the everyday elements and "scenes" of life or the lives of others as they interact with the self.

Complementing these views regarding the autobiographical form, Leigh Gilmore offers a feminist theory with regard to the production of autobiography in her text *Autobiographics: A Feminist Theory of Women's Self-Representation*. Gilmore's particular notion of self writing is presented in terms of "autobiographics," which she designates as those aspects of self-representation that are not limited by the "legalistic" and "ecclesiastical" constraints on the definition of self that derived from the writings of Augustine. Indeed, autobiographics has to do with self-invention and "is concerned with interruptions and eruptions, with resistance and contradiction as strategies of self representation" that take place in the margins of hegemonic discourse.[34] Because her analysis is a feminist one, she critiques the limits of autobiography as she argues that "women's self-representation describes territory that is largely unmapped, indeed unrecognizable, given traditional maps of genre and periodization" (5). Autobiographics, then, involves a process of "self-restoration" and it is the means of constructing a space from which women can present that which has been forgotten.

In resonance with these perspectives that challenge definitions of autobiography as more than simply a narration of the "I," Françoise Lionnet's *Autobiographical Voices: Race, Gender, Self-Portraiture* sees this "self-reading" and "self-writing" as an attempt to represent life, particularly in terms of those elements that point to "deep symbolic and cultural value."[35] Having been born in Mauritius, schooled in France, and now living in the United States, Lionnet can be seen as a *métisse*, thus it is precisely her definition of *métissage* that is of interest here; that is, the "braiding of cultural forms through simultaneous revalorization of oral traditions and reevaluation of Western concepts [that] has led to the recovery of occulted histories" (4).[36]

In Lionnet's discussion of authors such as Maya Angelou, Zora Neale Hurston, and Maryse Condé, as well as two female Francophone authors, Marie Cardinal and Marie-Thérèse Humbert, she describes their texts as "creative explosions," where there is an emphasis on the "broader generic configurations of autobiography" that can be seen as "nonhierarchical modes of relation." Indeed, for Lionnet, *métissage* is defined not only as a concept but also as a practice that "is the site of undecidability and indeterminacy, where solidarity becomes the fundamental principle of political action against hegemonic languages" (7). From this perspective, the autobiographical subject can take on the role of cultural observer who is involved in autoethnography, and writing therefore takes on anthropological dimensions concerned with the preservation of culture through the written word. This project of "creative explosion," for example, is clearly evident in texts such as *Canícula*, where Norma Cantú uses a collage of photographs, autobiographical data, and references to cultural traditions to make up what she at first calls "fictional autobiography" and refers to as "ethnographic."[37]

Lionnet's reference to *métissage* "as undecidability and indeterminancy" can clearly be related to Gloria Anzaldúa's concept of a new *mestiza* consciousness. Here she points to a "racial, ideological, cultural and biological cross-pollination, an 'alien consciousness' [that] is presently in the making—a new *mestiza* consciousness, *una conciencia de mujer*. It is a consciousness of the Borderlands."[38] According to Anzaldúa, this new consciousness involves the collision of cultures and requires flexibility as the *mestiza* comes to grips with plurality and learns to "shift out of habitual formations . . . away from set patterns and goals and toward a more whole perspective, one that includes rather than excludes" (79).

With the perspectives of Anzaldúa, Cantú, and Lionnet as background, it becomes clear that traditional definitions of the genre of autobiography as writing concerned with the lives of great men is ethnocentric and exclusionary. That is, in addition to the autobiographical "I," we must consider the creative, cultural, and ethnographic aspects of the genre, and most specifically, the contribution of women in this area. Furthermore, Anzaldúa's notion of the new *mestiza* consciousness and Lionnet's definition of *métissage* are both relevant as we try to focus on the writing of women of Mexican origin. For instance, Louis Mendoza points to the importance of "alternative histories and literatures" in relation to "cultural negotiations."[39] He also notes the clear relation that exists between narratives that deal with both literary and historical elements. Indeed, he suggests that "[i]nasmuch as Chicana/o literature also narrates the historical experiences of Mexican men and women in the United States, it offers us yet another way of imaginatively reconstructing historical, cultural, and social relations" (20). This project of "creative explosion" or imaginative reconstruction of "historical, cultural, and social" elements is clearly evident in texts such as Cantú's *Canícula*.

In keeping with Mendoza's view, Genaro Padilla's *My History, Not Yours: The Formation of Mexican American Autobiography* defines autobiography from a Mexican American perspective. Indeed, rather than presenting a focus on the general aspects of autobiography, Padilla defines contemporary Chicana/o autobiography as a distinct genre involving the "socio-ideological problematics of autobiographical self-fashioning" and "a major articulation of resistance to American social and cultural hegemony."[40] He sees the genre as "outside the formal boundaries scholars have traditionally reserved for autobiography as a singularly self-disclosing text" (29). Padilla's analysis of the autobiographies of Mariano Vallejo, Eulalia Pérez, Rafael Chacón, and Cleofas Jaramillo is particularly important for understanding Mexican American autobiography, especially in terms of elements such as alternative history and resistance to the cultural and political hegemony of the United States. As Padilla notes, the Mexican American autobiography is noteworthy because it does not comply with the form of traditional life writing which focuses on reconstruction of the individual self. He also emphasizes the way in which Mexican American autobiography presents the individual life in close relation to the configuration of lives within a community.

Padilla sees traditional theories of autobiography as constraining and exclusionary and therefore in need of being "renegotiated," allowing for "alternate forms of self-representation" (30). Autobiography, then, can be seen as "historiography" or as "cultural ethnography" that introduces autobiography in terms of collective representation, or the self in relation to the community. That is, from his perspective the autobiographical form must include *cuentos* or folktales, *romances* (narrative ballads), and religious dramas such as the *pastorela*, as well as a recounting of personal life "matrixed within a family genealogy" (21). In his definition of autobiography, Padilla draws attention to the purpose that underlies Mexican American writing—that is, a "desire to reconstitute the self of an earlier presence," which can be represented in the "memory's imagination" (30).

Along similar lines, Juan Velasco argues that "Chicana/o autobiographical narratives become a way of transcending the main effect of oppression—their subjects' invisibility."[41] He points to the "multiplicity of voices created in those works" as a way of transcending the limitations of what he terms "the small 'I'" (322).[42] He further asserts that these narratives represent "a radical practice of writing, a process of life writing that links communal truth and personal narratives. This is achieved as the new 'I' created along with this writing implies a temporal axis of representation" in which the voice is simultaneously adopting the experience of the personal and the communal" (322). When taken in combination, this type of expression results in the formation of a new "I," or "a new voice for a higher sense of the cultural 'self'" (322). Velasco calls this type of expression "automitografía," defining it as an "autobiographical act [that] becomes the performative agent of transformation, as it reverses the forms of representation of traditional autobiography to connect with the cultural production of lo mexicano within the U.S." (322). Chicana/o autobiography, then, can be understood as a "process (crossing)" whereby the writer re-creates memories concerned with the construction of identity that gives voice to what has previously been silenced. Hence, in contrast to Dilthey's definition of the "I" of great men who give expression to their life story through the confessional form, the Chicana/o construction of identity involves the "'total Self' [that] is able to create a voice through which we can envision individual self-empowerment and community agency" (325). Indeed, as Velasco argues, Chicana/o autobiography documents "the postcolonial pain of the Mexican self in the United States, mutilated by the experience of internal colonialism" (325).

Like Velasco, C. Alejandra Elenes also emphasizes the importance of autobiographical narratives, especially those written by women where there is an emphasis on personal experience as the basis for "the construction of knowledge."[43] For example, in her discussion of the narratives created by Ana Castillo (*Massacre of the Dreamers*) and María Elena Lucas (*Forged under the Sun/Fojado bajo el sol*), Elenes emphasizes the autobiographical projects of marginalized women as they work toward "reclaiming their own subjectivity, through their struggles against multiple forms of oppression" (110). For Elenes, then, the life stories written by Castillo and Lucas demonstrate the capacity of the writer to examine and critique her social conditions. Thus, both Velasco and Elenes focus on autobiography as an act concerned with the expression of a personal and collective self involved in the process of cultural and knowledge production.

What becomes evident from an examination of a third phase of critical theory is a focus derived from poststructuralist views that are less interested in the formal structure of autobiography and instead place a greater emphasis on broadening the concept of the autobiographical form. Indeed, the theoretical panorama presented by these critics is particularly relevant in terms of their arguments concerned with women's autobiography and the type of knowledge and experience it presents. Because the present study deals with the autobiographies of women whose memory, knowledge, and experience are derived from more than one cultural sphere, and so as to more clearly understand the multilayered dimensions of this type of life writing, the following section is an attempt to present the definition of what I have termed "border autobiography."

The Border Autobiography

A major question posed by the above discussion is not simply how to determine which elements are pertinent in defining autobiography as a genre, but rather how are we to classify those texts that do not correspond or comply with the limits of the genre? As Derrida pointed out in his article "The Law of Genre," "as soon as the word 'genre' is sounded, as soon as it is heard, as soon as one attempts to conceive it, a limit is drawn . . . one must respect a norm, one must not cross a line of demarcation."[44] As I have mentioned, for Dilthey autobiography must necessarily be "representative" of the sociocultural period in which it is written, and the subject of this type of life writing, then, must also reflect a way of life that is superior to the "average life." On the basis of these lines of demarcation, it becomes obvious that the autobiography that represents the life of women of Mexican origin would not be considered significant since the female voice and her realm of experience do not coincide with what is considered historically pertinent and worthy of imitation.

One of the other limits or boundaries of autobiography has to do with what is included and what is excluded from the genre. Philippe Lejeune, for instance, argues that the memoir, biography, personal novel, autobiographical poem, journal, self-portrait, and essay are not to be included in the formal definition of autobiography because the author, narrator, and protagonist are not necessarily one and the same.[45] From this type of limitation, one would infer that a combination of any of these styles would also be unacceptable. It is this type of limitation with which Derrida takes issue: "If a genre is what it is, or if it is supposed to be what it is destined to be by virtue of its *telos*, then genres are not to be mixed . . . or, more rigorously: genres should not intermix. And if it should happen that they do intermix, by accident or through transgression, by mistake or through a lapse, then this should confirm, since, after all, we are speaking of "mixing," the essential purity of their identity."[46] Here Derrida questions the "transgression" of mixing different types of writing within a text, as well as the notion of how mixing affects the "purity" of what is being written in terms of its identity and position within the limits of a particular genre. This discussion regarding conformation with strict notions of the autobiographical mode also raises relevant questions. When life writing combines autobiographical elements of the self as well as information regarding the history of a family, of place, of particular cultural practices, under what generic definition are we to analyze them? How are we to classify those texts that involve intertextual references regarding oral tradition? In what way are we to consider texts that include history that does not focus on the dominant cultural group? In what way can we define the type of discourse that is evident in texts that represent what Derrida points to as "other trajectories," or those that do not conform to the law of genre?

As a means of answering these questions, the present section attempts to map the characteristics of "border autobiography" as a term that defines those texts that represent another type of trajectory—that is, one that involves the mixing of literary types or modes. Furthermore, the border autobiography as a different type of trajectory represents the intersection of more than one semiotic system or structure that is heterogeneous and historical in nature. For example, Yuri Lotman has suggested the dynamic quality of semiotic systems, and he points out that there are stages in this dynamic process of development that involve "the constant dragging of extra-systemic elements into the orbit [of what is considered] systemic, and the simultaneous expulsion of the systemic to the domain of the extra-systemic."[47]

Evan-Zohar calls this type of system a "polysystem," which he defines as "a multiple system, a system of various systems which intersect with each other and partly overlap, using concurrently different options, yet functioning as one structured whole, whose members are interdependent."[48] He notes, however, that it is the existence of the "repertoire" or "the aggregate of laws and elements (either single, bound, or total models) that governs the production of texts" (17–18) that will ultimately determine whether texts fall into canonized or non-canonized systems. Because of these laws, different strata exist within a system, and their meaning value is determined by those elements, texts, or patterns of behavior considered acceptable by the dominant or official culture. Any type of literature or behavior that is outside what is considered pertinent by the dominant culture can be seen as extra-systemic or irregular and may go undetected, especially if perceived as opposed to dominant elements of a system.[49]

This interaction between the systemic and extra-systemic creates a tension between the two, and as a result those texts that are not considered legitimate may be ignored because they represent or exist as alternative systems of knowledge that accumulate near the borders of the system or outside it entirely. It is of particular importance to note here that I am using the term "border" to refer not only to the geographical dividing line that exists between two countries or states but also in reference to the symbolic limits that separate the cognitive realms of different historical and sociocultural worlds.

What can we say about those texts that reflect more than one semiotic system, and what is their position within the literary repertoire? Evan-Zohar has suggested that it is the "language system—i.e., the aggregate of factors operating in society involved with the production and consumption of lingual utterances"[50] that determines the hierarchical position of literary repertoires within a particular system that has its own "elite." To be considered as part of this elite, literary works must be written in the dominant language, yet in all literary systems we find language being used in a way that does not correspond entirely to dominant forms. An example of this conflict between language systems can be found in Chicana/o literature where we find a mixing of English and Spanish. It is precisely this mixed language usage that corresponds to the overlapping of various semiotic spheres—New Spain, Mexico, and the United States—that represents the gradual "translation" of old world reality to that of the new, but without totally letting go of the past. That is, the literature of this semiotic space involves a conglomerate of knowledge from various world spheres.

The border autobiography, then, represents an alternate system of knowledge, one that is the result of the historical intersection of more than one semiotic system, and it therefore does not conform to the generic laws of the dominant system. First it can be seen as occupying a position outside of the dominant literary "repertoire" because it does not fit the traditional definition of autobiography. As we shall see in later chapters, this is particularly true in fictional narratives such as *Dew on the Thorn* in which the autobiographer's life informs the text and where there is a mixture of personal history, collective history, nonfiction, fiction, or intertextual narrations that refer back to oral traditions that do not bear directly on the identity of the author. It is precisely this mixing of genres that marks the border autobiography as a hybrid narrative form.

The position assumed by the autobiographer when writing is also a key aspect of the border autobiography. That is, she may prefer to remain closely connected to the ancestral country of origin by writing either in the language of that country or by writing about life experiences and cultural practices that correspond to that space. By adopting a position closely tied to the home country, the literary work of the autobiographer normally occupies a peripheral position until his or her literature finds its place in the dominant literary system. For example, the writer often chooses to give testimony about his or her ancestors as well as present-day family members. In his discussion of minority Canadian literature Milan V. Dimic sees this type of literary content as promoting the "continuity of referential modes" rather than focusing on future life experiences. As he notes, members of marginal cultures often yearn for their lost identity; therefore, this type of narrative content allows for the possibility of remaining in the life experience of the system of the home country which can be seen as a way of maintaining a sense of identity, albeit outside of the dominant culture.[51] As previously noted, the recovery of a lost or silenced identity is a central issue in those autobiographies written by women of Mexican descent. Here the autobiographical text stands in opposition to the erasure of individual and collective identity.

Another aspect in understanding the border autobiography has to do with groups of people living in a particular geographic space as citizens of a nation-state who suddenly come under the dominion of a different nation-state due to war and consequent treaties. Again, the concept of border in this case has to do with the geographical dividing line between two countries or states, but it also has to do with symbolic space. In his discussion of rites of passage, for instance, Van Gennep notes that "an individual or group that does not have an immediate right, by birth or specially acquired attributes, to enter a particular house and to become established in one of its sections is in a state of isolation."[52] If we broaden the notion of "house" to mean home or country, it becomes more relevant to understanding the sense of isolation that is often expressed, either explicitly or implicitly, in the border autobiography when an individual or group of people cross the physical boundary that separates one place, one country, from another. Crossing the border takes place, yet the person is not able to identify with, feel part of, or feel accepted by the new home country and what it symbolizes.

An example of this is the case of more than 80,000 Mexican citizens who inhabited the northern frontier of Mexico—that is, the present states of Texas and the areas of New Mexico, Arizona, California, Nevada, Colorado, Utah, and a portion of Wyoming. They did not leave their homeland, but as a result of the Treaty of Guadalupe Hidalgo and the cession of more than half of Mexico's territory to the United States, those Mexicans living in these areas were expected to accept American citizenship.[53] This resulted in the intersection of two systems—one related to a pre-Hispanic and Spanish past, and the other to an Anglo world sphere. Those who chose to remain in these areas, as well as their descendants and later immigrants, developed what can be considered as a border culture that reflects a way of life involving two fields of cultural identity and practice.[54] Therefore, as suggested by José Limón, we must consider both cultural groups together as the "Greater Mexico," or "all Mexicans, beyond Laredo and from either side, with all their commonalities and differences."[55] Indeed, as I shall point out in chapters 3 and 4, the intersection of the life spheres of Mexico and the United States has resulted in the emergence of narratives that contest the effects of this historical collision.

As we have seen, Dilthey and Misch emphasize the role of autobiography in constructing the history of a society within a given period. However, Dilthey also asserts, "Every life can be described, the insignificant as well as the powerful, the everyday as well as the exceptional. Different points of view can produce the interest to do this. A family preserves its recollections . . . everything human forms a document which conjures up one of the infinite potentialities of our existence."[56] Thus, Dilthey exalts the "historical individual whose existence leaves a permanent mark," especially if the life course is recorded in a biography, a form considered by this author as "a work of art" (90). In terms of this sense of history, and particularly that of Chicanas, Norma Klahn asserts that the autobiographical literary form that emerged as a result of the civil rights movement involves "the experiences of a people who identify as belonging to a particular imagined community."[57] I would argue that the value of the border autobiography has much to do with recollections that are valuable in terms of the recovery of personal histories that contribute to the broadening of a public history that has been responsible for silencing or marginalizing personal recollection, especially that concerned with "Greater Mexico." The border autobiography, therefore, is a historical document with deep symbolic and cultural value. As such, it is concerned with the diachronic and synchronic implications of transcultural memory, which involves self- and collective representation. This type of autobiography involves the use of discursive strategies of narration and description as the basis for presenting sociocultural practices as well as those principles responsible for generating such practices.[58] Just as the border autobiography is a narrative based on the semiotic space of two cultures, it also involves a type of border discourse, neither fits the traditional limits of the genre of nonfiction nor conforms to notions of historical writing.

The border autobiography, then, is life writing that represents "other" sociocultural and ethnic experiences that do not coincide with the dominant culture. This type of experience is often considered as a subculture and has the potential to alter the canonized repertoire, yet because it does not function as a model within the dominant culture, it is generally marginalized. However, because the focus of this type of text may involve discourse that refers to other cultural systems, the autobiographical "I" at times becomes what Renza has termed the "revolutionary self," which takes on the role of resisting the canonical system through self- and collective restoration.[59] I would argue, therefore, that because the border autobiography exists within the system of autobiographies as a "different option" or "other trajectory" it functions as a means of complementing the dominant culture. I agree with Walter Mignolo who has noted the need to "free literary studies from the claws of the canon and open it to the uncertainties of the *corpus*."[60] For him it is obvious that the testimonial narrative, sub-literatures, and popular culture should be taken into consideration, and the canon should be at the service of cultural creativity. Thus, I would suggest that the border autobiography, as one of the "uncertainties" of literary production, contributes to "cultural creativity" within literary systems.

As I have tried to demonstrate in my discussion here, the three phases of theoretical positions concerned with the definition of autobiography often point to conflicting notions regarding which texts should or should not be considered autobiographical. Indeed, because of the broad spectrum of writing that deals with the self, authors Sidonie Smith and Julia

Watson have chosen to use the term "life narrative" in referring to writing that concerns the life story, and they have defined fifty-two genres of this type of writing. Of this list, the types of life narrative that have something to do with the texts created by González, Jaramillo, Wilbur-Cruce, and Ponce are auto/biography, autoethnography, autogynography, bildungsroman, ethnic life narrative, genealogy, life narrative, memoir, and relational autobiography.[61] Each of the narratives considered for this project is written by a Mexican American woman who writes a life story involving an autobiographical "I" that presents her own sense of personal development and her recollections or memories of the past. In addition to this personal life story, each writer also includes genealogical and biographical information about family members and her relation to them, as well as the way in which they are inserted into the history of a larger community. Furthermore, each autobiographer makes specific references to a personal and communal sense of ethnic identity.

I would argue, therefore, that the texts written by González, Jaramillo, Wilbur-Cruce, and Ponce do not fit clearly into the definition of any single type of life writing mentioned by Smith and Watson. In addition, as I have mentioned previously, they also refer to the sociocultural systems of Spain, Mexico, and the United States. Of further importance is the way these narratives present an interweaving of life history with descriptions regarding geographical spaces and social, cultural, and religious practices, and the insertion of folkloric narratives, all of which point to a mythic and historical past that is recalled and inserted into the life of the autobiographer and the extended community to which she belongs.[62] On the basis of the heterogeneous information evident in each of these narratives, I assert that the concept of "border autobiography" more accurately describes the way in which the autobiography often crosses the borders or frontiers of various types of writing. That is, though a text may bear the mark of the genre of autobiography together with all its rules, the border autobiography involves what Derrida has called "remarkable supplements," which branch off into other areas.[63] From my standpoint, then, each of the narratives considered for this study can be defined as a border autobiography or multi-structured text that presents evidence of various literary, historical, and cultural elements that take shape in a space where different semiotic systems intersect and interact.

Because the border autobiography is a form of communication, it is pertinent to analyze the way each of the narratives considered for this study involves the author as an addresser who writes with a specific purpose and audience or addressee in mind. The task of this section, then, is to point out the ways in which the works of González, Jaramillo, Wilbur-Cruce, and Ponce demonstrate a communicative function.[64] The communicative task evident in these narratives is not simply to inform, but rather to have an influence on the addressee. Therefore, the following discussion also includes references to the emotive function of the text in which the speaker's attitude toward the various topics of the narrative is revealed. Furthermore, by presenting a brief history of publication of each work I attempt to address the following questions: Why does the author write? Whom does she address in her text? What is the speaker's attitude toward those topics she writes about in her text? Finally, why is the autobiographical genre the space where the marginalized, oppressed voices of Mexican American women emerge?

Jovita González's "Early Life and Education" and *Dew on the Thorn* are two recovered manuscripts that were published in Houston, Texas, by Arte Público Press in 1997.[65] As noted previously, these manuscripts are assumed to have been written during the 1920s and the latter part of the 1940s. They form part of the González de Mireles Papers, which were donated to Texas A&M University-Corpus Christi where they are part of the Special Collections and Archives Department. It was through the team effort of José E. Limón, Nicolás Kanellos of Arte Público Press, and the Recovering the U.S. Hispanic Literary Heritage Project that these texts were finally edited and published. Limón prefaces the brief recovered autobiography by González, who is considered to be a precursor of contemporary Chicana/o literature. He notes that González has left a book, "her book," and she "has also left us a brief unpublished autobiography."[66] Limón also presents the reader with an introduction to *Dew on the Thorn* that notes the importance of autobiographical, historical, fictional, and folkloric elements that make up the text. Here again is the mark of a hybrid of forms that make up a border autobiography, a hybrid that until recently was unknown to the general public.

The section of the text concerned with González's autobiography is entitled "Early Life and Education" and it is divided into two sections. The first section deals with her childhood, and the second section focuses on her educational experience and briefly mentions her marriage to Edmundo E. Mireles. The autobiographically informed narrative that follows is entitled *Dew on the Thorn*, a text that begins with references to New Spain and genealogical information regarding the Olivares family. The major portion of this narrative focuses on the family life of Don Francisco and Doña Margarita, as well as the romance between Rosita and Carlos. Of particular interest is the fact that the principal narrative of *Dew on the Thorn* is interrupted by the insertion of folkloric narratives that, according to Limón, incorporate the author's early writing as well as research she had undertaken during 1934–35.

In her brief autobiography, González addresses the reader with a question: "Why was my mother, a descendent of a Texas landowner, born in Mexico?" (ix). Her answer speaks clearly of the "fear of reprisals of the new conquerors" (ix). She then notes that the "*colonizadores*" in Texas returned to Mexico but that many, like her grandfather, once again return to the Texas "homeland." She ultimately tells the reader that she has "always felt at home in Texas" (xi) and that it is this emotive expression of her appreciation of Texas as home that prompts her to write. Indeed, in the second section of her autobiography, she tells the reader of her lifelong interest in the "legends and stories of the border" and she notes that the thesis she wrote for her MA, "Social Life in Cameron, Starr, and Zapata Counties," was "the result of that year's study and a lifetime of love and understanding for my people, the border people" (xiii).

Because her research focused on uncovering the oral and written tradition of those who lived in the borderlands, we can assume that her text functions as a channel of communication in which she enters into dialogue with those who, like herself, have an appreciation of Texas border life. However, she also addresses a reading public that has little or no knowledge of border life. Thus, her purpose in writing has to do with contesting those who, like her professor, Dr. Eugene C. Barker, judged the study of border life practices and folklore "an interesting but somewhat odd piece of work" (xiii).

González's response to Barker's remark is evident in the narrative content of *Dew on the Thorn*. With its references to border life and history as well as the inclusion of folkloric stories, this text can be seen, first of all, as intending to contribute to the conservation of González's own cultural heritage and that of people of Mexican descent living in the border regions of South Texas. However, *Dew on the Thorn* is addressed also to those Anglo-Americans and their descendants who were responsible for "a series of unfortunate circumstances which had made the Olivares [family] cling tenaciously to the traditions of their people, [and which] had also made them look upon all Americans with distrust and dislike."[67] Although the Olivares family is the autobiographically informed fictional family of her narrative, they stand as referents signifying all those original Mexican families who were Texas landowners and had been wronged by Anglo-Americans in the past.

The title page of *Romance of a Little Village Girl*, written by Cleofas Jaramillo and published late in the autobiographer's life (1955), makes no mention of its type. However, in the preface, the author tells the reader that she desires to revive the years of "one who lived a harmonious happy young life" and that "this quiet romance I will try to describe in the following pages of my autobiography."[68] Like González, Jaramillo first presents references to the New Spanish province and her genealogical background; she then goes on to write briefly about her childhood. The narrative continues with several chapters dedicated to her life as a married woman, as a mother, and finally as a widow. The final chapters of the narrative focus on her writing and the role she played in founding the Spanish Folklore Society. This text also includes sections that focus on the sociocultural practices of New Mexicans.

Romance of a Little Village Girl was originally published in San Antonio, Texas, by the Naylor Company in 1955. As Jaramillo mentions, she tried unsuccessfully to publish her manuscript in "Western universities," and "after holding it for several months, they would return it, saying they did not have the funds with which to publish it" (168). She then explains that she finally published the text at "a small private press here in my city" (168). Through references to the difficulties she encountered as she tried to publish her work, the reader becomes aware of the marginalization of Jaramillo's writing, which was not considered up to the standard of the dominant works produced by Anglo authors who wrote about life in the Southwest. Indeed, it is not until the later publication of this text in Albuquerque by the University of New Mexico Press (as part of the Pasó Por Aquí Series on the Nuevomexicano Literary Heritage) in 2000 that the text is finally given its proper position as a document that preserves the cultural heritage of New Mexico. In the forward of this edition, editors Erlinda Gonzales-Berry, A. Gabriel Meléndez, and Genaro Padilla laud the narrative as a "pioneering work in letters" from New Mexico. This edition also includes a detailed introduction—and analysis of both *Romance of a Little Village Girl* and Jaramillo's *Shadows of the Past*—by University of New Mexico scholar and Chicana literary critic Tey Diana Rebolledo.

Romance is a text that speaks to the cultural "other," to the "stranger" who may not be aware of the "romantic current" of life in New Mexico's villages, a way of life that is "invisible" to outsiders. Indeed, she chides those who wanted to read what she wrote simply to get ideas for their own writing. She then addresses those "smart Americans" who think they know about Spanish cooking and the Santa Fe festival (173–74). Her narrative, then, is meant to correct their misconceptions. Her purpose in publishing the text is stated explicitly in the preface: "This quiet romance I will try to describe in the following pages of my autobiography" (ix). This romance has to do with her "happy young life" as an example of the way of life in "our New Mexico," one that is "invisible to the stranger" (ix), a life that includes an appreciation of the "customs and traditions" of a beloved New Mexico.

In her prologue to *A Beautiful, Cruel Country*, Eva Antonia Wilbur-Cruce has termed her text "my memories." Indeed, as Wilbur-Cruce notes, her initial purpose involved a determination "to keep putting memories on paper."[69] In terms of its autobiographical elements, this text differs from Jaramillo's because it focuses primarily on what the autobiographer describes as "recollections of my early life in the border country along the creek" (1).[70] However, this text is similar to those written by Jaramillo and González in that it also presents the reader with genealogical history as well as history of the Arivaca Valley. Of further interest in this text are the references to traditional fiestas and narrative insertions regarding the diaspora and exodus of the Indians from this territory.

A Beautiful, Cruel Country was written over a ten-year period, and as the autobiographer explains in her prologue, the process of writing began when her friends Linda Newell and Kathryn Murphy visited Wilbur-Cruce's family ranch. After showing them around the ranch she told them about her childhood on the open range and her contact with the Papago Indians.[71] She then decided to write what became a fifty-page letter, initially addressed to her nieces and nephews who knew nothing of "country life" in the Sonora and Arizona Territory borderlands. Her friends encouraged the author to write more extensively, and ten years later she had a complete manuscript, which was ultimately edited and published by the University of Arizona Press in 1987 when Wilbur-Cruce was eighty-three. A reprint edition was published in 1991 and a digital edition was published in 2004. Thus, this work, which was initially begun as a private piece of writing for young members of the family, now joins other University of Arizona Press publications that are classified under women's studies. However, it is also important to note that the dust jacket of the 1987 hardback edition also points to the text as "a valuable primary source from a little-known region."[72]

In the prologue to her narrative, Wilbur-Cruce states that she writes "primarily to entertain, but also to share personal memories of that time" (xiii). Indeed, once she began writing, her motivation to continue grew out of a chance meeting with an old family friend, Federico Lara. After reminiscing about the past, "of the ways we had found to survive in that vast country," Wilbur-Cruce records her friend's commentary: "we are surrounded by new people who don't understand us, and we don't understand them, Evita" (xii). The author then informs the reader that it was this remark that fueled her determination "to keep putting memories on paper as well and as fast as I could" (xii–xiii).

For whom were these memories to be preserved? To begin with, she wrote hers so that family members might understand the joys and hurts of her personal past, the "old days," the way of life on the open range. Ultimately, however, she wrote "to evoke that beautiful, cruel land of solitude for others in a form more accessible and permanent than it can take in my own memory" (viii). Thus, she writes not only to her family, but to others, those "new people" who have no understanding of the history and way of life in the borderlands between Sonora and Arizona at the turn of the century. The author further notes that she also writes to let others know about and understand "the appalling racial hatred, so prevalent for so many decades—a poison with which we came in contact every day" (xiii). Wilbur-Cruce, like González and Jaramillo, begins her narrative with references to her early childhood and life in the "border country." The text makes reference to the early contact between Anglos, Indians, and Mexicans, which sets the stage for the problems of racism, or "poison" that must be revealed to young family members but also to those "other" readers who should know of these difficulties in the border country. The purpose of this narrative, then, coincides with those of both the González and Jaramillo texts, which also express an intention to inform the cultural "other" about life in the borderlands.

Hoyt Street by Mary Helen Ponce is an autobiography written from the cultural space of California. The title page of this book is clear: *Hoyt Street: An Autobiography*. Although the use of the term autobiography is explicit, a "Note from the Author" informs the reader that this narrative "began as a research paper for a folklore seminar."[73] It then took shape as a "social history of sorts," and ultimately became "my life story" (x). The autobiographer's life story, like the one presented by Wilbur-Cruce, focuses on the narrator's childhood, with special emphasis on the barrio of "the town of Pacoima." Ponce also presents the reader with family history, but here we find a family history of "Mejicanos" rather than those "who looked Spanish" (5, 15). This is a family history involving Mexican Americans, a personal history that begins with Ponce's father and mother, who were immigrants in the United States, and ends after the narrator turns thirteen and becomes a "bonafide teenager" (337).

Like the works of Jaramillo, González, and Wilbur-Cruce, Ponce's narrative has also been published by a university press. The first hardcover edition was published in 1993 by the University of New Mexico Press. In 1995 a translated version, *Calle Hoyt: Recuerdos de Una Juventud Chicana*, was published in New York by Anchor Books. A paperback edition of the English version was also published by Anchor in 1995. The most recent edition of the book was published in a paperback by the University of New Mexico Press in February 2006.

Ponce tells the reader that her writing not only focuses on what she remembers about her own life, but also on "communal history" (ix–x). Indeed, in "Notes from the Author," she asserts that "Mexican-Americans need to tell their side of the story in order to put to rest negative stereotypes" (ix–x). When she tells us that it is for the "hard-working decent, and honorable" (x) Mexican Americans that she writes, she is essentially stating that she is giving voice to those who have been silenced. Thus, it is the voice of her text that speaks to those who have stereotyped ideas about Mexican Americans. Furthermore, she writes with the intention of educating the cultural "other" about the culture of Mexican Americans as it exists in the barrios of large cities like Los Angeles and elsewhere in the United States.

Mary Helen Ponce's text also begins with a reference to a particular geographical space: "the town of Pacoima." Pacoima is introduced as the home of Mexican immigrants. She begins her text by presenting a picture of the "many men in the barrio [who] worked in agriculture" or as "troqueros" (3). The narrator then tells us about her father who is one of these many men. It is the use of phrases such as "people in Pacoima" together with "our house" and finally "my first memories are of the kitchen" that situate the reader in a world that Ponce intends to create: the world of a family that forms part of a community, a community where there is poverty but great dignity. Ponce, like González, presents the reader with a question: "Why write of Pacoima? . . . that place (they never referred to it as a town) is infested with gangs and drugs" (ix). In response she states that she has "no set answer" other than the fact that her childhood was a happy one. Thus, as she notes, "I persisted to write of what a friend calls my 'Macondo,' a reference to Gabriel García Márquez's mythical town" (ix). Like Wilbur-Cruce's determination toward writing, Ponce too presents a persistent voice that addresses those who would judge the immigrants and their children who lived and continue to live in the Mexican American barrio. This "autobiography, or life story," this "communal history," like those created by González, Jaramillo, and Wilbur-Cruce, stands as a document that preserves Ponce's history and that of women who have grown up in the borderlands.

Ultimately, as we reflect on the border autobiographies created by these four women of Mexican descent, it becomes clear that each narrative functions as a discursive device through which the autobiographer articulates her desire to speak of herself and for herself, as well as for those who form part of a particular cultural collectivity. Most importantly, these foremothers of later Chicana writers choose to present a feminist perspective regarding lived experiences as members of their cultural group. Therefore, an in-depth study of their narratives telling life stories related to specific geographical regions is pertinent. As suggested by Paula Moya, the life experiences of people of Mexican descent must be recovered because "their histories and accomplishments have been systematically ignored or distorted."[74] Moya argues that racial/cultural background and experience must be considered when trying to understand social relations. This view is clearly related to Alvina Quintana's reflections as presented in *Home Girls* where she points to her exposure to regional experiences—her own and those of her parents—and the way they have contributed to the multiple dimension of her identity.[75] I mention both Moya's and Quintana's perspectives to contextualize this book, which focuses on four women who choose to communicate and preserve personal and cultural memory through the genre of autobiography. Furthermore, these theoretical stances coincide with the present project where I argue the importance of examining cultural identity in relation to lived experience within the domains of specific social structures. That is, by examining the ways in which González, Jaramillo, Wilbur-Cruce and Ponce have documented their lives, the reader discovers a literary space where each writer presents her own sense of identity, as well as that of a cultural collective, that of the Mexican American community. In so doing, each writer crosses discursive boundaries by focusing on her difference as she situates herself, her community, and specific cultural traditions at odds with an Anglo-centric project intent on silencing those experiences that emanate from the border.

Chapter 2

Narrative and Descriptive Discourse

The Autobiographical "I" and Cultural Preconstructs Concerned with Space

The narratives created by González, Jaramillo, Wilbur-Cruce, and Ponce present the reader with four heterogeneous life stories. Each text presents various layers of meaning, the first of which has to do with narrative discourse that is concerned with the autobiographical "I" and the symbolic spaces she occupies during her life course. However, these border autobiographies not only present life stories through the voice of an autobiographical "I"; at another level each is concerned with the autobiographer in relation to a cultural collectivity. This level of meaning can be understood through an interpretation of descriptive discourse that refers to such topics as land, home, family genealogy, and education, as well as religious and cultural practice.

As we have seen, each of the authors considered here either explicitly or implicitly has a specific audience in mind as she writes. Her text may at once be directed to those who are closest to her or those who have little knowledge of Mexican American history and cultural practice. Each also seems to be addressing those readers who, like herself, have experienced the constraints of traditional roles assigned to women. Key to understanding each narrative text, then, is the identification and interpretation of the types of discourse to which it conforms. Émile Benveniste, for example, perceives discourse as "language put into action, and necessarily between partners."[1] In its simplest sense, discourse is conversation or information. However, as suggested by Foucault, discourse can be defined as "the general domain of all statements, sometimes as an individualizable group of statements, and sometimes as a regulated practice that accounts for a number of statements."[2] It is through the regulating practices of discourse (through knowledge) that we become who we are, and it is through "discursive formations" that certain already established identities or subjectivities are reinforced. It is precisely the "general domain of statements" regarding the life story of the female subject evident in the border autobiographies of Jovita González, Cleofas Jaramillo, Eva-Antonia Wilbur-Cruce, and Mary Helen Ponce that is of significance here.

The autobiographer presents her life story, first of all, through narrative discourse that is produced by the act of telling within the text. Therefore, of key importance is the identification of specific references to symbolic spaces where development of the autobiographical subject takes place. Here it is important to recall Foucault's assertion that discourse produces the subject.[3] Barthes also notes that the subject can be defined as an "effect of language," arguing that "all those outside power are obliged to steal language."[4] The Mexican American women writers considered here, for example, represent the voice of the cultural "other" situated outside the realms of power, a subject whose roles have been culturally assigned to her. Indeed, the observations of Geneviève Fraisse in "A Philosophical History of Sexual Differences" points to the traditional role of women: "marital dependency and subordination to the preservation of the species."[5] That is, women have been confined to roles of obedient daughters, wives, and mothers. This assigning of roles corresponds to what Foucault has determined as discursive or "tactical elements or blocks operating in the field of force relations."[6] Of further importance, then, is the way each autobiographer uses language as a means of responding to these limits.

With these ideas as background, the focus of this chapter involves an examination of the narrative and descriptive discourses evident in the texts of González, Jaramillo, Wilbur-Cruce, and Ponce, particularly in the way the autobiographical "I," as a "subject-in-process," presents her life course.[7] I will be most interested in looking at the way the autobiographer expresses herself from an assumed or appropriated type of discourse that has to do with those "force relations" that have historically situated her in the traditional roles of daughter, wife, and mother within the space of the home where the male figure takes on a dominant position.[8] The questions that guide my analysis are: What does each autobiographer choose to narrate? In what way has she chosen to narrate her life story? How does the female autobiographer represent herself within various segments and symbolic spaces of the narrative? What aspects of her world does she describe, and what is the purpose of choosing these aspects? Therefore, this chapter first highlights the use of narrative discourse and the way it reveals the development of the autobiographical subject. Second, I present an analysis of descriptive discourse evident in each text and what it reveals about concepts such as land and home.

Narrating the Autobiographical "I" and Life Worlds

The analysis of the corpus of texts I examine in this book is grounded in the study of narrative as both a textual and cultural phenomenon. From a textual perspective, narrative has been defined "as the representation of real or fictive events and situations in a time sequence."[9] The narrative text can also be understood as one in which "an agent relates ('tells') a story in a particular medium, such as language, imagery, sound, buildings, or a combination thereof."[10] Furthermore, as suggested by Barthes, the narrative process of relating or telling "is present in myth, legend, fable, tale, novella, epic, history, tragedy, drama, comedy, mime, painting, . . . windows, cinema, comics, news item, conversation."[11] This narrative process of telling is certainly evident in autobiography as it shares certain "fundamental features of narration that unite it with history and fiction, while separating it from the sciences."[12] It is precisely an examination of these "features" or strategies evident in the narratives of González, Jaramillo, Wilbur-Cruce, and Ponce that concerns us here.

With respect to the narrator, or the "I" presenting her life story, it is important to note that in referring to autobiography, Genette uses the notion of "the retrospective first-person."[13] This type of narrator is "autobiographical" and can be seen as one with the hero who, as suggested by Genette, is "more 'naturally' authorized to speak in his own name" (198). However, we cannot assume that the author is equivalent to the narrator and to the protagonist in each of the works considered here. Barthes, for example, asserts that "*who speaks* (in the narrative) is not *who writes* (in real life) and *who writes* is not *who is*."[14] In "Autor y personaje en la actividad estética," Bakhtin has also noted that "[t]he author must convert him/herself into *other* with respect to him/herself as a person, [and] should see with eyes of the other."[15] These ideas are in keeping with the perspectives of Paul de Man and James Olney, who have suggested that the subject can only be represented by means of figures of the self and therefore cannot be seen as equivalent to the author of the text. On the basis of these propositions, then, throughout my discussion I use terms such as "narrator" or "the narrating 'I,'" "autobiographer," and "autobiographical narrator," as well as "autobiographical 'I'" as a means of referring to the autodiegetic voice speaking through the narrative as the transmitter of the significance of those elements of the life story being recounted.[16] How are we to understand the relation between the autobiographical "I" and her life world? Foucault provides some insight into this matter when he suggests:

> The space in which we live, which draws us out of ourselves, in which the erosion of our lives, our time and our history occurs, the space that claws and gnaws at us, is also, in itself, a heterogeneous space. In other words, we do not live in a kind of void, inside of which we could place individuals and things. We do not live inside a void that could be colored with diverse shades of light, we live inside a set of relations that delineates sites which are irreducible to one another and absolutely not superimposable on one another.[17]

Here there is an emphasis on the "heterogeneous" spaces in which we live and the relationships experienced within those spaces. Interestingly, each of the works analyzed here presents the autobiographer's sense of self in relation to the larger family. Furthermore, in his discussion of the bildungsroman, Bakhtin points out that the biographical and autobiographical text present a sense of emergence that "is the result of the entire totality of changing life circumstances and events, activity and work."[18] As part of this process of change within a life, it is also important to consider the "threshold" or the "crisis and break in a life" and its effect on the person's life course as it is revealed through the narrative discourse of the text.[19]

My examination of this corpus of texts is first of all chronotopic.[20] That is, from a Bakhtinian perspective I examine the "path of life" and the process of development or "emergence" of the autobiographical subject evident in the "real-life chronotope." I would like to note, however, that the major portion of my analysis focuses on the way in which the autobiographical "I" develops or emerges within those heterogeneous spaces in which the life course takes place. As part of this I also analyze the way the autobiographical subject presents herself in relation to ancestors and family members in general, or what Smith and Watson have defined as "contingent others who populate the text as actors in the narrator's script of meaning."[21] That is, I am interested in the way "contingent others" coexist with and affect the self-identity of the autobiographical "I" during her process of development within various symbolic spaces, as well as certain cultural preconstructs evident within each text.

Jovita González's "Early Life and Education" and *Dew on the Thorn*

Although the recovered autobiography of Jovita González, who writes from the geographic space of Texas, is only five pages long, it is an important document in its own right, especially in terms of how it is related to the autobiographically informed text *Dew on the Thorn*. González divides her autobiography into two segments: "Early Life" and "Education." The autobiographical narrator begins the chronology of her text by emphasizing her place of birth: "I was born in Roma, Texas." However, although there is an initial reference to the autobiographical "I," and although this section is entitled "Early Life," the reader immediately encounters a discrepancy in the chronology of narrative events. That is, through retroversion the narrator subordinates her past history to that of an account of the life of her father, her grandparents, her mother, and a cousin of her father. This is further evident as the narration continues with a reference to the autobiographer's father, "Jacobo González Rodríguez a native of Cadereyta, Nuevo León México, [who] came from a family of educators and artisans."[22] Thus, from the very beginning of the narration the autobiographer takes on the function of informing the reader about data concerned with her family rather than simply focusing on self.

The chronology of the narrative continues its reference to the autobiographical narrator's family as she points to her father's educational journey: he "finished the equivalent of our high schools" (ix) and was later "sent by his superiors in Monterrey to become the director of the boy's school in Mier" (ix). The narrator once again subordinates her own life history to that of her grandparents as she mentions her paternal grandfather Pablo: "I did not know my grandfather . . . he died before I was born" (ix). As the chronology continues there is a brief reference to the narrator's mother, Severina Guerra Barrera, but it is through another instance of retroversion that the narrator focuses on her maternal grandparents, who "came from a long line of colonizers who had come with Escandón to El Nuevo Santander." She further explains that "one of my ancestors, Don José Alejandro Guerra had been surveyor to the Crown" (ix). It is interesting to note that this family history of contingent others also informs the first chapter in *Dew on the Thorn* as the narrator refers to the Olivares family and "Don Juan José, [who] had come in 1748 as Surveyor of the Spanish Crown."[23]

This same segment of the narrative moves from the marriage of the narrator's parents in Mier, Tamaulipas, to a retrospective deviation that explains that her "grandfather, with financial aid from his mother, the widowed Ramona Guerra Hinojosa, returned to Texas to regain or buy some of what had been their land."[24] There is no further information regarding the return to Texas by the narrator's ancestors and we are simply informed that this place in Texas was known as Las Víboras. The seeming omission of information here is taken up in more detail in *Dew on the Thorn* where the narrator points to the founding "of the towns along the Río Grande, Camargo in 1748, and Mier; Revilla and Dolores one year later."[25]

The chronology of the autobiography then moves quickly to the time when Jacobo González Rodríguez and Severina Guerra Barrera were married as the reader is told, "Homes were built, families grew, and the ranchers wishing a Mexican education for their boys looked for a teacher."[26] The teacher was Jacobo González who was "to bring Mexican education to the border boys" (x). Thus, this first part of the autobiography, rather than focusing on the autobiographical "I," emphasizes communal history as the narrator re-creates her own past in relation to that of her family's, situated in the border world initially known as Nuevo Santander.

Narration of the life course that focuses on family history is interrupted as the narrating "I" switches to a segment concerned with "the girls," who occupy a symbolic space reserved for women: "What about the girls? They were taught at home. We were fortunate to have with us, at intervals, Mamá Tulitas, our paternal grandmother. She brought to us fantastic tales from medieval Spain. Before our eyes passed Christian damsels wooed by Moorish Knights. Crusaders fighting for the Holy Sepulchre, the Cid receiving his spurs from *la infanta* doña Urraca, the unfortunate Delgadina '*que paseaba de la sala a la cocina*,' as she was followed by her infamous suitor. Perhaps more important was the Mexican version of Cinderella which we loved" (x). Here the narrator creates the context of what is considered to be a female space, which revolved around Spanish tales told by the paternal grandmother. These stories focus on a Catholic Spanish past that is transferred to the border space of Texas where the narrator's family has historical roots.[27] Careful attention to the semantics of this reference points to a group, "the girls," who are signaled at first by the pronoun "they." Initially, then, it seems that autobiographical González did not form part of that group until she uses words such as "we," "us," and "our," which ultimately signal her inclusion in this space.

The autobiographical "I" appears once again as she introduces the reader to an aunt: "I must add someone very special, mi Tía Lola, my mother's sister. As a young widow, she had come to live at Las Víboras Ranch. She was a handsome woman with a will of iron and a vast store of family history" (x). The autobiographer then notes, however, that family history was not considered good enough to serve as the basis for education and "my father and mother realized that my sister Tula and I were not getting the proper training girls in our family should have" (xi). She tells the reader that "we had learned to sew and crochet" (xi), yet she further clarifies "that was not enough either"; she ultimately explains that her father "decided they should move to San Antonio where we could be educated in English" (xi). Here the narrative subject can be seen as enmeshed in a way of life. That is, Las Víboras Ranch is the space of the father, a space that welcomed widowed aunts, a space that protected the female members of the family and encouraged an appropriate type of knowledge designated solely for women.

The father's decision to move to San Antonio would seem to be a logical ending to this segment of the life story, but it is interesting to reflect on the way in which the narrative sequence is interrupted: "Tía Lola and grandfather suggested mother should take us to Mier to see Mamá Ramoncita, our great grandmother" (xi). It is Mamá Ramoncita who will function as a source of information for these young girls with respect to knowledge about their own history regarding a specific geographic space: "Texas is ours. Texas is our home. Always remember these words: Texas is ours. Texas is our home" (xi). What becomes evident by the end of the first segment of the narrative is the existence of two types of experience that seem to be in opposition. That is, on the one hand, the life circumstances of the autobiographical narrator have been limited to those activities that seem appropriate for "girls," yet she is also in close contact with strong women: Tía Lola who had an "iron will" and Mamá Ramoncita "with her dark sharp eyes."

Indeed, both Tía Lola and the narrator's grandfather are instrumental in pointing the way to Mamá Ramoncita, who functions as a voice or source of knowledge that informs these young girls that there will be cultural conflicts once the family moves from the geographic space of Mexico to that of Texas. Thus, it is in this digression that we see a narrating "I" who encounters a source of knowledge that provides narrative anticipation of her future studies involving two conflicting worlds which are emphasized in the second segment of the autobiography, entitled "Education." This knowledge of history regarding disputed land rights also informs *Dew on the Thorn* when fictional Don Francisco's wife, Doña Margarita, echoes Mamá Ramoncita's words: "The *Americanos* may come. They may take the land, but our spirit, the spirit of the conquerors, will live forever. Texas is ours. We stay!"[28]

The second narrative segment of this real-life chronotope is organized around life events involving a threshold in the autobiographical subject's path toward education. González refers to her experiences first in San Antonio, Rio Grande City, and the University of Texas at Austin, and next the border areas of Webb, Zapata, and Starr Counties where she conducted research. She then refers to her life as the wife of Edmundo E. Mireles in Del Rio and Corpus Christi, Texas. What stands out in this section of the narrative is the repetitive use of "I," which takes on a more assertive tone. For example, within less than three pages of the text, there are numerous references to self, all of which have to do with a move away from the space of the father's home, where girls were educated in appropriate female activities, to a new space that emphasizes the autobiographer's work as a teacher, writer, and researcher.

Here the narrative "I" presents her personal history of life successes, as a "subject-in-process." Interestingly, the word "I" occurs eight times in the first portion of the autobiography, whereas in this second section "I" occurs thirty-six times as the narrator refers to herself and her achievements. The narrating "I" begins by telling the reader how she first had to learn English to be able to attend school in San Antonio: "With the aid of a dictionary and my father's constant help, I was able to be promoted at the end of the school year" and "by attending summer school I finished the equivalent of the high school course when I was eighteen."[29] This emphasis on the "I" and her more assertive role is further evident in references to González's work and successes in research and higher education: "I went to Rio Grande City . . . I was given a position at the city schools. Since I lived with my uncle and aunt, I saved all my money . . . that went to my college fund" (xii).

The narrative chronology continues with further recounting of personal successes. For example, the autobiographer notes, "The following fall I enrolled in the University of Texas" (xii). We then encounter a series of references to achievements that involved teaching. However, the climax to this development is evident in González's explanation of a later experience: "The summer of 1925 brought me a far reaching experience. I met J. Frank Dobie" (xii). Because Dobie was a folklorist, she suggests that he confirmed her own prior sense of the importance of the legends and stories of the Texas borderlands, noting that "he made me see their importance and encouraged me to write them, which I did, publishing some in the *Folk-Lore Publications* and *Southwest Review*" (xii). This history of personal success continues: "I was awarded the Lapham Scholarship to advance further research along the border and to study for my M.A. . . . As a result of the thesis [I wrote], and again through the recommendation of J. Frank Dobie, I was awarded a Rockefeller grant in 1934" (xii–xiii).

This list of actions and achievements of the narrating "I" is significant because it clarifies a "far reaching experience," one that suggests a female subject who has moved from the private home space reserved for female activity to a public space of research, writing, and publishing, activities normally reserved for men during this time period. This segment stands in contrast to the first part of the narrative as the narrating "I" uses the autobiographical mode to celebrate her own emancipation from a space or "field of force relations" that limited her intellectual potential.

The brief final segment of the autobiography refers to another change in life circumstances: her marriage to Edmundo E. Mireles. The chronology of this section points to a change in the use of "I," which becomes a "we" as she refers to her life in a space dominated by her husband. Here González recounts how she collaborated with her husband in organizing a Spanish program for elementary school and the writing of two sets of textbooks that were used to teach Spanish at the elementary school level in Texas. The narrative comes to an abrupt end as the narrator states, "Until my retirement I taught Spanish and Texas History at W. B. High School in Corpus Christi. We have been happy" (xiii). Of particular significance here is the editorial comment by José Limón with regard to this final information: "What she does not tell us in her autobiography is that in 1938–1939, while they were contemplating the move to Corpus Christi, she explored the possibilities of further graduate study toward a Ph.D. at Stanford, California, California-Berkeley or the University of New Mexico, but following what were likely complicated marital negotiations, she decided to go with him to Corpus Christi" (xxiv).[30] The implication of "We have been happy," together with the comment by Limón, is that the narrating "I" expresses the reality of a female subject in relation to others. The "I" makes a choice that situates her as part of a relationship, the marital "we." Indeed, as suggested by Chodorow, the masculine personality "comes to be defined more in terms of denial of relation and connection (and denial of femininity), whereas feminine personality comes to include a fundamental definition of self in relationship."[31] It is precisely the female "I" in relation to contingent others that marks each section of this autobiography. First we see the autobiographical subject surrounded by ethnic history and immersed in traditional Mexican family life, a symbolic space dominated by the father as head of the household. Then we are presented with the outstanding achievements of the "I," yet the narrator consistently refers to the help she received from her father, her grandfather, her uncle, Frank Dobie, Archbishop Droessars, and Bishop Capers, all of whom she notes aided her and opened doors for her studies and work. Although González expresses her achievements, she assumes a discourse related to the limitations imposed upon women, especially as they attempt to move beyond the space of the family. Ultimately the writer makes no explicit reference to her husband helping her, but rather focuses on a collaborative effort in the area of education, as she refers to "my husband and I."

As Limón has suggested, there is really nothing that would make the reader doubt the word of the autobiographer, but it is the "cultural imperative" of marriage that makes us question the sincerity of the words "We have been happy." The answer perhaps can be found in the major narrative of *Dew on the Thorn*, which presents the romantic love relation between Carlos and Rosita. Rosita, like the autobiographer of "Early Life and Education," is immersed in the space of the father's house, where his word is law. Rosita and Carlos are in love, but because of a misunderstanding Carlos is disgraced and Rosita is forbidden to consider him as a possible husband. Rosita obeys her father's orders, yet because this narrative is nostalgically romantic, the two lovers are finally reunited after Carlos's reputation is cleared. Thus, the narrating "I" of "Early Life and Education," like Rosita, follows the traditional path of womanhood, that of marriage with its promise of happiness. In the case of Rosita, the final reference to her situation focuses on Rosita's father, Don Francisco, who, "taking Carlos by the arm . . . led him to Rosita. He took the girl's hand and placing it in Carlos' eager hand said to her in a voice that trembled with emotion. 'My child, it is for you to cage him; it is up to you to see that he does not leave his nest again.'"[32] The last mention of Rosita in the narrative has to do with her marriage, and what stands out is her silence as her father places her hand in Carlos's. Thus Rosita submissively moves from the space of the father's home to that of her husband's.

It becomes apparent, then, that the implicit commentary embedded in both narratives reveals the limitations, the boundaries that link the female subject to what Beauvoir has called "*féminitude*" or the "culturally determined status of difference and oppression."[33] Indeed, the autobiographical "I" evident in the last segment of González's narrative can be compared to the narrator's initial subordination of the autobiographical "I" to that of familial history. This section implicitly expresses further subordination of the female subject's work, research, and writing to the work her husband has undertaken. The ultimate subordination of the autobiographer's activities to those of her husband's sphere of interest clearly demonstrates the tension between the subjectivity of the narrating "I" and the identities culturally assigned to her.

Cleofas Jaramillo's *Romance of a Little Village Girl*

Like "Early Life and Education," the autobiography of Cleofas M. Jaramillo re-creates the narrator's life course from childhood to adulthood in what can be considered a personal history that is situated in New Mexico, yet the text also evokes an ancestral history. Because this text is much more extensive than the one created by González, in addition to the narrator's life story, the narration includes insertions of historical elements and digressions that involve descriptions of land and home, to be discussed later in this chapter.

The narrator begins her account by focusing on the historical past of her family as she re-creates her own life story within the context of a larger narrative that points to Spain as the starting point of what would become a way of life of the Nuevo Mexicanos.[34] The chronology of the first two chapters of the narrative moves from the spaces of Old Spain to New Spain, and there is an emphasis on the past of "the Spanish race," with mention of Columbus and "[i]ntrepid Cortez, Coronado and Oñate and brave De Vargas and many other explorers and colonizers [who] followed after."[35] A sense of connection to the identity of these early settlers is expressed by the narrator as she mentions that "some of my ancestors, the Luceros, descendants of Pedro de Godoy, settled the little valley of Ojo Caliente, which had already been discovered by Sosa and by Cabeza de Baca" (3). It is through the use of "my ancestors" that the autobiographical narrator immediately situates herself with those contingent others who left "the comforts of their European abodes to come into this wilderness" (4), and she clearly assumes a discourse that declares the rights of the Spaniards to settle this land that was already inhabited.

This initial historical retroversion and the specific references to the narrator's "ancestors" that make up the first section of the narrative are similar to references concerned with the collective history evident in the text created by González. Both autobiographical narrators have chosen to refer to family history as it relates to a particular space, one that is closely linked to the sense of identity of the narrating "I" and her family ties to New Spain. In both instances the autobiographical "I" clearly asserts her authority as a writer as she tells the reader that she and her ancestors are "of" this land and therefore have a more thorough knowledge of the way of life that corresponds to this space, which pertains to those of Hispanic descent but not the *extranjeros.*

The initial chronology of Jaramillo's family history is interrupted as the narrator digresses into references to the independence of Mexico from Spain, which resulted in "the last phase of Spanish rule" as this territory came under "the stars and stripes of the United States" (69). Temporally, the first segment of the narrative begins by explaining that "the country had adjusted itself to the new changes" (10), and the autobiographical "I" situates herself in an idyllic setting: "I can still see myself, like a wild bird set free of a cage, running from one berry bush to another, filling my little play bucket, my heart beating with delight at the sight of beautiful mariposa lilies, blue bells, yellow daisies, feathery ferns—plucking some to trim the pretty sunbonnets mother made for me" (10). This focus on a romantic, ideal space is echoed in the way the narrator defines herself in relation to her family. She is the child of a man who "ran his combined dry goods and grocery store without help. He directed the work on his farms . . . he raised beef, sheep, pork and race horses. . . . He read his Bible and kept in it a record of the births and deaths of members of his family" (11). Her mother's activities consisted in "raising her family of five boys and two girls" and she "made her babies' layettes by hand" (11–13).

Thus, as was also evident in the "Early Life" narrative, the home involves different spatial realms which are based on gender. Indeed, as the narrator notes, "if [my] father and mother had a different idea about something, they talked it over in a nice way. If [my] mother could not convince my father as to how a thing should be done, she dropped the subject without arguing" (15). And what of the autobiographical "I"? Like her mother, the narrator recognizes her subjugated position in the space dominated by her father. She says little except to note that when her father decided to expand the store and invade space reserved for the family house, "we lost the east inside porch on the court, and with it went my swing that I enjoyed so much" (15). Both of these examples demonstrate the way in which the female is immersed within a discourse that limits the woman's right to speak out against male dominance within the home.

The chronology that focuses on the narrator's childhood is interrupted with descriptions regarding cultural traditions such as the "Indian Feast of San Geronimo" and "The Parish Feast Day." The autobiographer then presents a narrative segment that demonstrates once again her sense of subordination to the male members of the family, as she emphasizes the history of her father's education and that of her oldest brother rather than her own. Here we also find references that focus on separate spaces for girls: "I was just eight years old and was tutored in Cousin Inocencio's private school that year" (28). She notes as well how she learned to recite "Luisa and Maria's Lost Thimble," which reminds us of the tales that form part of the autobiographical narrator's childhood in "Early Life."

Emphasis on the life course continues as we are introduced to the space of the boarding school, which points to a new phase of the "subject-in-process." The autobiographical narrator tells the reader of the happiness she felt while doing her schoolwork. Here Jaramillo recounts her experience in an English-speaking convent school for girls, where she learned painting, embroidery, and knitting, or, as she notes, "art and fancy work of all kinds" (30). The kind of identity expressed by the speaking subject within this segment of the chronotope once again involves discursive formations that limit the type of activities taught at boarding school. These activities are meant to prepare young girls for life within the domestic sphere, an aspect that is further emphasized in a narrative insertion of a description of the narrator's aunt, Aunt Piedad: "[She] was the symbol of those days that have passed, when the ladies had a gracious living, having been brought up in the tradition of refined helplessness, to be waited on. She lived a leisurely life with her three daughters in her attractive home. Her pride was giving pleasure to them—buying them fine clothes, a fine carriage in which after their siesta, the house servant took them on a ride" (33). Thus, both the home space, with its examples of the narrator's mother and Aunt Piedad, and the confined space of the convent boarding school are symbolic spaces where the woman's sense of identity takes shape. Furthermore, this part of the life course is similar to moments of the early years in "Early Life," in which young girls listen to romantic, "pretty" stories that paint a picture of what life holds in store for them.

In a later portion of this chronotope the autobiographical "I" narrates her experiences within the space of Loretto. Here she notes that "each year my studies became more interesting. There I could spread out into all the branches of study I could take" (52). The narrator at first seems to be enjoying this academy, which provided the means of moving forward into further intellectual opportunity, yet this moment is followed by a comment regarding the fact that only one of the girls in her class was Spanish and the rest were American. She further laments that "I was neglecting my beloved language" (52). She recounts moments from her childhood and adolescence, and the "I" that is articulated seems to enjoy the new world being opened up to her in the Loretto Academy; at the same time, however, she is conscious of her close ties to the collective "we" of a Spanish identity. Again we find an autobiographical "I" mentally hovering between two spaces, between her experience of a "Spanish" past and an American present. That is, these overlapping spaces situate her in what Gloria Anzaldúa has defined as Nepantla, or that in-between space concerned with the process of self-discovery.[36]

The life experience of the narrating "I" in the second segment of this text presents another situation of liminality as she finds herself situated between the space of the father's home and that of her future husband. At this point in the life journey there is an emphasis on Jaramillo's last year in school, when she is being courted by Venceslao at the same time she continues her studies. Here there is an anticipatory remark by the narrator that does not take on full meaning until the final segment of the narrative: "I continued my music and the business course I had started, although not dreaming that I would ever make use of it. I took it merely because I wanted to learn all that I saw the other girls learning."[37] Not until later in the narrator's life story do we discover that this business course would become important as she will need to deal with her husband's debts after his death. Of particular importance here is the way in which Jaramillo represents herself—as a young woman who appropriates a discourse that locates the female subject within the domestic sphere only. Thus, from this assumed perspective, the business course was not expected to be an important aspect of her life.

Also continuing within this second segment is a romantic tone evident in the initial portion of the text. Here the narrator focuses on the "magic that wove an unexpected romance for the little village girl [that] started at a wedding feast" (57). This romance involves the narrator's cousin Venceslao Jaramillo: "This young man had begun to fill my mind, for each day I found in him more, his abilities, his social popularity and strong character" (67). Interestingly, however, within the span of two pages, she moves from a romantic contemplation of "this genteel young man [who] had become my ideal suitor and had changed my mind from becoming a nun or remaining an old spinster," to the moment when her parents receive a marriage proposal from Doña Ana Maria on behalf of her son.

The wedding proposal becomes a moment of crisis in the autobiographer's life as she expresses a conflict regarding the demands of a tradition that perceives marriage as a natural step for the woman. This part of the text reminds us clearly of the moment in *Dew on the Thorn* when Don Francisco places Rosita's hand in that of Carlos's. Of particular interest in *Romance*, however, is the autobiographical "I" and her commentary regarding her father's decision to respond favorably to the marriage proposal. Whereas Rosita of *Dew on the Thorn* remains silent, the narrator of *Romance* responds by questioning her father's decision: "What kind of answer had he taken? I had not been consulted" (71). Furthermore, in response to her mother's insistence on accepting the marriage proposal, she notes, "I wanted to spend at least another year with her, and even wanted a year at one of those fine colleges I saw advertised in my *Home Journal* magazine" (71). Taken together, these comments present an autobiographical subject immersed in a way of life that negates the possibility of choice for the woman; however, we do find the emergence of a voice that tentatively contemplates the possibility of further study.

In chapter 11, entitled "School Dreams Blossom into a Wedding," the dream of further study is subordinated to the demands of custom. The first lines of this chapter are also indicative of what the married woman's role would be: "The following week's mail brought me a cheerful letter: 'Be prepared to go to Denver with mother and me to buy your trousseau'" (73). How are we to read the narrator's selection of words such as "blossom" in the title of this chapter, and her use of the word "cheerful" to describe a letter that demands compliance to what is expected of her as she steps forward onto this new road in life? I would argue that although the autobiographer has previously questioned her parents' acceptance of her marriage to Venceslao Jaramillo, the use of linguistic markers such as "blossom" and "cheerful" can be read as an implicit expression of the autobiographical subject attempting to deal with the reality of her situation. Indeed, she tries to soften the tone of the letter by explaining, "It is a Spanish custom for the bridegroom to buy the trousseau and pay all the wedding expenses" (73). However, just as the narrator's mother had remained silent when she was unable to convince her husband of her point of view about changes in the house, so too does this young woman accept her subordinate position as she acts in accordance with roles assigned to her. She becomes the wife of Venceslao Jaramillo in 1898 in Taos, New Mexico, and moves to the symbolic space of her husband's home.

Like that of the narrator of "Early Life," this voice also speaks of the seeming happiness of her life course after marriage: "For a month we traveled, visiting different cities. In Los Angeles we had our wedding picture taken at a fine studio. Were we still tired from all the work and excitement that we looked so serious? It was so different from the smiling brides I now see in photographs. Nevertheless, we were just as happy" (81). It is when we consider the narrator's own question regarding the unsmiling, serious faces of her studio photographs, and the fact that she chooses "At the Home I Found Difficult to Call Home" as the title for chapter 13, that we perceive an autobiographical subject at odds with the reality of the new space she occupies, a space dominated by an agenda of everyday life that is set by her husband's involvement in a political career.

In a chapter entitled "Politics Are Fascinating," the autobiographical "I" once again subordinates Jaramillo's life to her husband's accomplishments: "That fall, Ven went stronger into politics, and at the next two elections he won the office as senator from Rio Arriba County." Ultimately she explains that "it was interesting to go to the legislature to hear the heated arguments when there was a good debate" (113), and she later remarks that "after meals our group of ladies sat around the pleasant lobby chatting, the men joining us after dinner in the evening" (113). Thus, as we have seen in "Early Life," here too the autobiographical "I" assumes a discourse that dictates that she be satisfied with taking her place alongside other women to chat and wait for the men to return from what are implicitly considered more relevant activities.

A crucial change in life circumstances of the autobiographical "I" becomes evident in the final segment of the narrative. Here we discover the voice of a more outspoken woman. At first this autonomy is muted as the narrator reveals that at her husband's death, "I felt something rush into my hand. Was this undescribable thing something of my husband's spirit that passed into me, through my hand? Was this what gave me the courage and strength needed?" (128). Like the narrator of "Early Life," who attributes much of her success to others, especially male figures who helped open doors for her academic and writing activities, this autobiographical "I" also attributes her strength to her husband.

In this section of the narrative we also find a woman forced to accept her role outside the space of the father's and the husband's home as she begins to function autonomously. This is no longer a narrative that focuses on the autobiographer's role as wife, mother, and homemaker. Instead this segment of the chronotope highlights the life course of a woman who has previously depicted herself as not being sufficiently intelligent, but who has ultimately taken on the task of sorting out the debts left by her husband. This woman, who had spent nine years in a secluded convent school and who had studied only one business course, demonstrates her capacity for intelligent action: "I immediately addressed the cards to farmers who lived in the near villages, giving them a list of the farm machines and setting the price five dollars cheaper. . . . I not only sold the new ones, but also sold all the old discarded ones under the shed. . . . I cleared for the estate three thousand dollars, adding the cash from the crops Sofio harvested that fall" (132).

Here we no longer detect the romantic voice evident in the first segment of the narrative. Indeed, as she situates herself in the autonomous space of this final section of the autobiographical chronotope, we find a voice of self-assertion, the voice of a woman who comes into her own sense of selfhood.

The final segment of the narrative focuses on a space where the autobiographical "I" is alone after the death of her daughter Angelina, who was brutally murdered. A chapter entitled "A Night of Horror" recounts this "ghastly" event, and description of the trial that followed is inserted in the text. Ultimately the narrator continues her life story as she focuses on how she began anew after these extreme life crises. We also find a newly defined autobiographical subject who continues work on a manuscript she had started years earlier. This was a manuscript encouraged initially by her daughter, a manuscript for "this new generation [that] knew nothing of our interesting old customs" (167). Jaramillo describes the texts that result from her effort: *Spanish Fairy Tales*, which consisted of "twenty-six stories translated into English and published in book form" (167), a cook book entitled *The Genuine New Mexico Tasty Recipes*, and a book on folklore, *Shadows of the Past*."[38]

By choosing to write these texts, the autobiographical "I" ultimately occupies a space that had initially been reserved for Anglos. Jaramillo's attitude toward this project is tentative at first, as she explains, "I had the material, but like a builder without experience, did not know how to put it together" (168). She comments further on the Western universities that were not willing to publish her text. Her response to this is strong and clear: "I decided to have it published by a small private press here in my city" (168). At this point we perceive a subject who assumes an authoritative stance, a woman who has progressed from a situation of timidity and silence to one in which she makes her voice heard within her city, her own space of achievement.

The final symbolic space of the chronotope involves an autobiographical "I" who takes further action, as she organizes "our Santa Fe Fiesta" and then founds the Sociedad Folklórica, which she tells the reader "brought me a feeling of considerable satisfaction because it has awakened much interest among our Spanish population in learning and appreciating our old traditions" (183). Although the action is taken by the individual "I," the contingent others or members of the Hispano community are also evident in references such as "our population" and "our traditions." Yes, the narrator has to an extent put aside her muted voice and taken on the voice of an autonomous, authoritative "I." Yet this autonomous "I" is still situated in relation to other members of the community and she continues to operate within a specific cultural space as she focuses on the life and customs of the Nuevo Mexicanos, thus writing herself and her people into history.

Eva Antonia Wilbur-Cruce's *A Beautiful, Cruel Country*

The temporal focus evident in the life course of Eva Antonia Wilbur-Cruce, narrated in *A Beautiful, Cruel Country*, is limited to a short three years of the autobiographer's early childhood—from three until five years of age—and her experiences in Arizona's Arivaca Valley.[39] The chronology of this narrative, however, also involves historical retroversion regarding the Cerro Colorado Mining Company and the Arizona Territory of the 1860s, as well as extensive allusion to memories regarding the displacement of the Indian population that had inhabited this area for centuries. Because of the historical presence of the Indians, and because this area was homesteaded by both Anglos and Mexicans, the text also illustrates cultural practices of these various groups.[40]

The initial narrative focus of this text is similar to both "Early Life" and *Romance*. That is, rather than centering on the autobiographical "I," we find references to a particular space: "our house sat at the foot of Pesqueira Hill, which rises in a northwesterly direction from the banks of Arivaca Creek."[41] As the narrator points out, it is this place, with its view of the Guijas Indian village and the vegetation that covered the *lomita* where she often took morning and evening walks, that is connected to "some of my clearest recollections of my early life in the border country along the creek" (1).

The first segment of the chronotope does not progress lineally as it also includes historical retroversions concerned with past family history. It is interesting to note that in the story of her childhood, this narrator does not immediately refer to having Spanish roots; she instead takes on the voice of a subject who is of Anglo and Mexican heritage. The first two chapters of the narrative sequence emphasize Wilbur-Cruce's Anglo grandfather, Wilbur, a Harvard-educated physician, and her Mexican grandfather, Don Francisco Vilducea, "The Man with the Bible." Thus, unlike the narrators of "Early Life" and *Romance*, who point to their Spanish ancestors as a means of making clear historical familial ties to the geographic space of Texas and New Mexico, the first reference to this narrator's family's Spanish ancestry is inserted near the end of the narrative in the chapter entitled "A Surprise! A Surprise," when the narrator refers to her paternal grandmother Rafaela's "Castillian ancestors" (251).[42]

In this chapter the narrator recalls fragments of a conversation between Grandmother Rafaela and her son, the narrator's father, as she berates him for not having educated his children regarding their Spanish background: "a disgrace . . . a terrible job . . . to fight the devil and you . . . Samaniego . . . Don Ignacio Pesqueira . . . Charles Poston . . . Governor Safford . . . Father Suastigui . . . royal blood" (250).[43] Within these fragments the autobiographer alludes to her Spanish ancestry. However, placing this information toward the end of the narrative seems to suggest a minimization of this aspect of the writer's identity; this stands in contrast to the "Early Life" and *Romance* narratives, which emphasize Spanish ancestry from the very beginning of their texts. Moreover, because this history is presented linguistically as fragments it suggests that the autobiographical "I" recognizes that her own identity is not based on a pure bloodline. Instead she expresses her own identity in terms of a hybrid sense of self, one that is based on Anglo, Mexican, and Spanish ancestry.

Many of the narrator's early recollections also center on what she sees and hears: "I see horn tips glistening in the sun above a swirling of dust; I hear the bawling of calves being branded and smell burnt hair" (42). She remembers her mother protectively carrying her away from an ant hill where she had been bitten by ants. She then recalls "the crest of a neighboring hill [where] I sit on the crook of my father's arm" (43). Here we find the beginning segment of a chronotope that presents the female child who is cared for by both parents, yet the narrating "I" later explains that for many things "I engaged the help of my father. After all, I was his favorite daughter. He had told me so, and by that token I chose him as my favorite parent" (46). Thus, we find the autobiographical "I" who situates herself somewhere between the protective space provided by the mother and the adult world of ranch life dominated by her father.

One of the first spaces the autobiographical "I" is introduced to by her father is the Cerro. Because their daughter is a mere three years of age at this point, the mother's response to this trip planned by her husband is a negative one: "She is much too young. She is a mere baby, and the Cerro is one of the worst mountains around here" (48). The narrator emphasizes how her father ignored his wife's reaction and "put me on the saddle with him" as they went off to explore the mountainous terrain. This example points clearly to discourse that emphasizes what Fraisse defines as "a domestic life based on the hierarchy of the sexes."[44]

What perhaps sounds like an adventure to be enjoyed with her father becomes a moment where the narrating "I" observes her father roping a sick calf that needed to be "doctored." Within this time and space the child undergoes a first step as a subject in the process of emergence, as her father instructs her to insert her finger into the animal's wound to remove the maggots that had infested it. She recounts that she followed her father's instructions: "I put my finger inside the wound and felt the maggots moving against the tip of my finger. I felt sick, retched, and vomited over my father's hand."[45] The narrator mentions that her father's response is to tell her not to feel so delicate; she then recalls, "I closed my eyes and tried it again. By now all the maggots were spilling out of the wound" (51).

The autobiographer continues her narration, and she emphasizes her father's response as well as her own thoughts: "'Good girl. That's the way to do it,' said Father. I guess I had toughened up. Good thing I did, for this was one task I had to do many, many times, month after month, year after year" (51). After this incident the father suggests going to find a water hole so they can wash up. The narrating "I" responds, "Yes, Pa" and she further comments, "I was silent. I felt sick inside. 'Toughen up, toughen up,' I thought" (51). Here the narrator spotlights a situation in which she is introduced to the father's realm, where she must obey his instructions and take in the knowledge that he offers her. Thus, the child who emerges from this experience is aware that toughening up has to do with learning to handle situations involving activities that normally pertain to the male sphere of experience.

Later in the chronotope the narrator comments briefly on the birth of her brother William and on Doña Tomaza's visit: "Doña Tomaza made a striking figure when she got down from the buckboard. She always wore a man's white shirt and a long black alpaca skirt that reached almost to the toes of her boots. Her long green gloves had a fringe on the sides . . . She had lived and worked all her life on a cattle ranch" (78). The description of Doña Tomaza is in direct contrast to the female space of childbirth, as Wilbur-Cruce notes, "Father led the way to the bedroom where Mother was lying in bed with her first male child in her arms" (80). This brief mention of the female space of childbirth is minimized, as the remainder of this narrative section refers to the way Doña Tomaza and Father taught young Eva to guard the gap and keep horses from straying.

We also find a second moment that contributes to the autobiographer's premature emergence into an adult world, when the autobiographical "I" recounts how her father placed her in the saddle of her horse Diamante, and then sent her out to guard the gap in spite of the fact that she was only four years old:

> One day Father went across the creek to bring in some cattle and left me alone guarding the gap. I was supposed to head off the herd and drive it into the corral as usual. It wasn't long until I heard hoofbeats and clattering horns. The herd appeared around the bend, and a mottled-faced steer ran straight toward the gap, the other cattle following him fast.
>
> No matter what Diamante and I did the steer kept coming on and before I knew it he had taken the gap. I galloped through to head him back and the other steers followed me. When Father came up the creek driving an old cow, all the cattle had disappeared. He was angry. (84)

Once again this young girl occupies another space, the open range where she is taught to guard the animals from escaping into the gap. The mere fact that she attempts this activity is laudable in itself, yet because of her young age she fails in her task, and she recounts how "Father uncoiled his rawhide reata and whipped me across my arms and back" (85). This critical space, the gap, is associated with the father's domain and his power over her. This is a space where, in the fourth year of her life, she must continue to absorb knowledge regarding ranch life imposed by the male parent:

> Mother pointed to my back and said, "Why?"
>
> "Well, she let the cattle go at the gap."
>
> "You expect a four-year-old child to head off a herd of longhorn steers? You are insane." Mother's voice was clear, cold, and strong.
>
> I had never seen her look so tall. (87)

At this moment the autobiographical subject represents herself as a child hovering between the protected space of the home, provided by the mother, and the rugged realm of the father's space. Of further importance is the way in which the girl is immersed in a discourse that deprives the wife of control over her husband's decisions. Both instances of the autobiographer's mother and her inability to stem her husband's decision—to take their daughter to the Cerro and to punish this young child by whipping her—stand as examples of the "field of force relations" in which "the man commands and woman obeys."[46] However, as the narrator recalls, her mother verbally takes her husband to task for his action, thereby overstepping the boundaries that have been set for her.

During the fall corrida we are introduced to another segment in the life story of this young child. The narrator initially points out that "Mother began the difficult job of bathing me. I fussed and fussed as usual. While she was brushing my hair I heard cattle lowing and calves bawling on the northern hill above the creek."[47] Thus, although the autobiographical "I" is within the home space and in her mother's care, she hears the outside noises of ranch life, and immediately after her bath she remarks that "Father came into the house and said that Diamante was saddled and ready. Moments later we were riding along the creek on the way to the place of roundup" (217). Once again, this child moves from the space of the mother's care to the space where her activity is controlled by the norms set by her father. It is during this moment that the narrator observes the branding of cattle that takes place during the corrida. In contrast to her recollection of having felt sick when she was forced to help her father remove maggots from a calf, here we find an autobiographical "I" who expresses a different attitude: "I had been longing to take part in this, the last day of *corrida*. Happily I trotted off to take up my post" (222).

At this point in the life story, the autobiographer recounts a moment when her father is in danger of being charged by a cow: "Suddenly the cow lurched to her feet . . . and, finding my father the closest target for her sabers, she charged him. I felt Diamante jump, almost spilling me to the ground. In a split second Diamante had thrown himself between Father and the cow, striking the charging animal's shoulder and shoving her forward. The cow stumbled to her feet again and took off, dragging two ropes, while two horseman went after her" (223). Because this young child was able to remain in her saddle during this difficult moment, she tells us that the "vaqueros gathered around us [and] all at once I was the object of admiration and praise" (223). It is in the time-space of the fall corrida, then, that we find an autobiographical "I" standing in total contrast to the young child who was unable to keep horses from leaving the gap and who, as a result, was punished physically by her father. In this segment the narrator represents herself as having developed into an adultlike child who has mastered the skills necessary for life on the ranch.

Although this is a text in which the narrating "I" focuses on her experiences in the traditional male realm of activities, like the autobiographical subjects evident in the "Early Life" and *Romance* narratives this female child is also exposed to different types of women in her life. Her mother and her maternal grandmother are of Mexican descent and they participate in typical domestic activities such as cooking, cleaning, sewing, and gardening. Doña Tomaza represents a different kind of woman, one who is able to speak at an equal level with men on the ranch and who is capable of riding the range and taking part in ranching activities.

It is the narrator's paternal grandmother, however, who is convinced that her granddaughter is in need of education so that she becomes a proper young lady. In contrast to the autobiographer's mother and maternal grandmother, Grandmother Rafaela is presented as a more refined woman: "Grandmother Wilbur sat very straight with her hands on her lap. Her black hair was done up in a French roll with bangs dropping in curls over her pale, white forehead. Her white blouse had very wide cuffs with white buttons on the side" (232). She is a woman who travels with "a glass bottle full of cotton balls, a pink bottle full of water, and a very small washbasin, like a toy. There were small boxes of powder and some jars of white salve" (243). Grandmother Wilbur is represented as the epitome of female refinement yet is perceived by the narrator as an oddity, as different from her own mother, who is described as "looking like an Indian" (232). From Grandmother Wilbur's point of view, her young granddaughter must be educated to speak properly, to pray properly—from a wild child she needed to be transformed into a young lady fitting her "royal blood" (250).

The autobiographer's response to her grandmother is interesting: "I still felt sorry even then for this bewildered, lonely old woman. Weighed down, as my mother was so often to say later, "with that strange heritage handed down to her from her Castillian ancestors" (251). It is here that we discover a perspective that contrasts significantly with the "Early Life" and *Romance* texts, which idealize the Spanish past as a means of discursively legitimizing a historical tie to the land in Texas and in Mexico. In this narrative we find that Grandmother Wilbur signifies the decline of the Spanish presence in this geographic space of the ranch and the open range. Ultimately the autobiographer presents herself as a child who will develop into a new type of woman. Indeed, in a final segment of the chronotope, when she is situated on a mountaintop, she recalls the first time her father had taken her up the Cerro: "It had been rough and frightening—no trail and the terrain was bad all the way. This time I was going up on the north side. It was much easier climbing and before I knew it I was up on the path. . . . This time I left Diamante near a big cliff and made only the last few yards on my hands and knees. I stood up and again I saw the great blue distance stretching before me" (259). Here the autobiographical "I" finds herself alone on the summit and she recounts, "[M]e and Diamante, we were a team, me and my horse! I walked around the *cima* [summit]. . . I walked on top of my world alone for the first time. I loved the *cima*, and I loved to be alone. This would be my home!" (260). It is through these words that the narrator anticipates the woman she was to become. By the end of the narrative, for example, she digresses temporally to a moment when she was ten years old. Here she narrates the instructions her father had given her about how to handle ranch hands who would work under her: "You hire them and you fire them, but I will hold you responsible for anything that goes wrong. Now when you fire your men, you figure out what they have earned, write them a chit, and let them go. When you hire them, tell them how much you will pay them and what you expect from them. If they agree, put them to work; if they don't agree, send them away. No giggling and no crying!" (270). Thus, within this final segment of the chronotope we see a child who has been encouraged by her father not only to act as an adult, but as an adult male.

This narrative ultimately presents us with a child who prefigures the woman she would become, a woman capable of doing a man's job, of taking over the care of the family ranch.[48] Indeed, the child's story narrated here can be seen as a metaphor, one that anachronously reaches into the future and foreshadows the emergence of a woman whose accomplishments coincide clearly with the successes narrated by the female subjects in both "Early Life" and *Romance*. By narrating life experiences that deal with success outside the domestic sphere, each autobiographical subject is in effect trespassing the constraints of discursive boundaries set for her by tradition, an element that is also clearly evident in *Hoyt Street*.

Mary Helen Ponce's *Hoyt Street*

Through *Hoyt Street*, Mary Helen Ponce presents the story of her early life experiences within the larger context of a Mexican American community in a California barrio. As in the previous three texts, Ponce in *Hoyt Street* presents the reader with her life story by referring to her childhood. As in *A Beautiful, Cruel Country*, the chronotope of this life story focuses on the narrator's childhood years and is composed of three segments that can be seen as specific stages of her development as she emerges into adolescence: "Innocence," "Reason," and "Knowledge." Norma Cantú has classified this text as "strictly autobiographical."[49]

"Innocence" begins by focusing on the autobiographical subject's world and those who live there. Here Ponce recounts what she perceives to be her years of innocence, and like the narrative voices evident in the previously mentioned works, the narrator begins her recollections by detailing her life within a specific place—the barrio in Pacoima, California.[50] Rather than presenting a specific story of the self, the narrator initiates her life story by focusing on a collective "we" of contingent others, the people who inhabited the houses of Pacoima, the "poor folks," "Mejicanos in our town [who] took pride in their homes."[51] Home, then, is situated within the barrio, where "streets were unpaved, full of holes and rocks" (3).

What becomes evident in this early part of the narrative is the way in which it differs from the previous texts I have commented on. Rather than reaching into past history of the land and Spanish ancestors, this text refers to the more recent past of Mexican immigrants who come to work and ultimately settle in California. Indeed, in referring to the "people in Pacoima" the narrator remarks: "I often thought [that they] needed more space than did those in upwardly mobile San Fernando, where homes had sidewalks and paved streets, but sat close together, as if afraid to breathe too much of their neighbor's air. On Hoyt Street most residents had once lived in Mexican ranchitos and had a greater need for land. In the large double lots, they planted fruit trees, vegetable and flower gardens, and assorted hierbas that also grew in Mexico" (7). The residents of Hoyt Street, then, are not introduced as descendants of Spanish conquistadores or as descendants of important landowners. Rather they have lived on *ranchitos*, and like the autobiographical narrator's father, these are people who built modest family homes in the space of the barrio.

The narrative also presents a perspective that emphasizes the economic level of this group of people. For example, the narrator refers to her father as someone who collected and "clung to" junk like the other "folks who were short on money but full of ingenuity" (6). It is through references of this type that the narrator draws a portrait of herself, in relation to those contingent others—her family as well as an entire group of hardworking people of a low socioeconomic status—who, like her father, "hated to be de oquis, with nothing to do" (14). Thus, the primary marker of subjectivity in this narrative is ethnic.

The narrator continues this segment of the chronotope by focusing on a portrait of "La Familia" and other members of the community: "Unlike those of our friends who looked Spanish, with light hair and green eyes, we looked like what we were: Mejicanos, with the coloring found among most people in Mexico" (15). The autobiographical "I" describes herself as the tenth child of eleven children. Interestingly, she refers to the way in which her older sisters, Nora and Elizabeth, introduced her to worlds outside of Hoyt Street. Nora is described as "an intellectual, a seeker of knowledge, a buyer of books. She learned from everyone and passed everything down to us" (19). This was the older sister who had "acquired a taste for good hardwood furniture . . . [and] one piece at a time, paid for in cash, Nora bought most of what sat in our living room." The narrator further points out that "Nora did not spend all her hard-earned money on herself" (19). She is presented as hardworking member of the family. The narrator's sister, Elizabeth, on the other hand, is described as "my mother's right hand, a girl who helped with both the easy and hard chores. She cooked, cleaned, ironed" (21). However, this sister is then described as a "bookworm" who "like me read Nora's Book of the Month Club selection and also checked out books from the library in San Fernando" (21). Thus, like the "Early Life" narrative, which includes references to the "girls" in the family, this text also presents the narrator in relation to her siblings, with special emphasis on two older sisters who will have an influence on the autobiographical subject who is enmeshed in a way of life that emphasizes work. However, it is Nora's subscription to the Book of the Month Club that provides a connection to a hegemonic middle-class literary status.

In terms of her development, this segment of the chronotope ends with a chapter entitled "Kindergarten," in which the narrator explains that "by the time I was four . . . I was tired of playing with my little brother. Chasing after el Duque offered little challenge. Playing in the open field was too safe; I knew every rock and hole by heart. Even our tree house . . . was no longer fun. I wanted to be in kindergarten" (110). Here we perceive the voice of the autobiographical subject who expresses her desire to go to school as her sisters did, and when this moment finally arrives, she tells us that "from the first I loved kindergarten" (111). Indeed, what stands out in this section of the narrative is her excitement over books: "I was in love with words" (112). This love of words is further highlighted as she tells the reader of her thrill at being given three old books at the end of the semester: "I was lucky to get three and thrilled to see that they had been used by third graders. . . . I thought of them as rich treasures. Few parents, mine included, could afford luxuries such as books, crayons, paper, or erasers. These were special; and at home would be put away in a safe place, then periodically be brought out to be looked at, touched, and in time, read" (117). These memories clearly reveal the symbolic importance of school and books with the promise of knowledge they hold for the female subject. The kindergarten experience for this narrator and the world outside of the home that begins at this point are similar to the new vistas that are opened up to the narrator of *A Beautiful, Cruel Country* when she sat on the saddle of Diamante, accompanying her father for her first trip to the mountain where "the whole world lay shimmering at my feet."[52] In the *Hoyt Street* narrative, however, the world cherished by the autobiographer involves the symbolic space of the school, where books, and therefore knowledge, are available.[53]

The *chronos* of the second section of this narrative, "Reason," continues to evoke a collective history as it moves back and forth between two spatial arenas, life in the barrio and the institution of school. The narrator sees herself as Mexican American, and she notes that "I, for one, lived in a loving home, did well in school, played 'kick the can' in the street, enjoyed the church bazaars, and loved catechism; I lived what I felt was a good life." Immediately following this reference to self, however, the narrator mentions that at school "we felt content and could not understand why we had to be singled out as a group when it was suspected that one of us had lice."[54] Once again, the reader perceives an autobiographical "I" who emphasizes her position within a larger group marked as "other." It is important to note, however, that unlike the previous narratives, where there is an emphasis on the narrator's Spanish ancestors, here we find a young girl who acknowledges her position within a group of children with "funny names, customs, and differences," a group that is singled out for its "lack of hygiene and manners" (122). Hence we find an autobiographical "I" unable to grasp her assigned position within an exclusionary discourse that equates poverty with uncleanliness.

This position of poverty is further emphasized in the chapter entitled "Los Calzones de la Piña," where the narrator points out that "my mother worked hard to clothe her large family" (127). She then explains how her mother made underwear for her children out of flour sacks that were decorated with pineapples and wheat stalks. It is within the symbolic space of the school playground where this effort on the part of the mother will result in a sense of shame for her daughter. The narrator recounts a moment when she is invited to play kickball at school; her immediate response is one of excitement as she notes her happiness at being "part of the gang." She then tells the reader: "I played gloriously. I played hard. I played to win. I was so intent on kicking the ball as far as the boys, that it was some time before I heard the giggles and saw fingers pointed in my direction. I realized the pineapple was showing, but I didn't know what to do" (129). What stands out in this narrative episode is an emphasis on a female "I" who played "gloriously," "hard," and "to win." Her intention to compete on the same level with the boys and kick the ball as far as they could demonstrates a desire to go beyond traditional gender boundaries. Limiting this possibility are the homemade bloomers imprinted with a pineapple that could not be washed out. Thus, the bloomers become an object of ridicule, something that marks her as different, as poor, thereby detracting from her skill at playing kickball. The accomplishment that she gloried in is suddenly erased.

The final segment of the story of the life course presents moments that lead up to a discovery of self as a woman. Here the narrating "I" occupies the temporality of eighth grade as she is getting ready to graduate from elementary school into high school. In the chapter entitled "Hide and Seek" she recounts her experience regarding the sexual advances of Peter, and her realization that "[t]his must be how older kids play" (284). This portion of the chronotope continues with another experience in which the world of sexuality is emphasized, as the narrator tells of her discovery that men like Don José, a friend of her father's, were interested in sexually molesting young girls. Her friend Nancy tells her: "If you let him see under your dress, he'll give ya twenty-five cents" (291). Although the narrator recalls that "[w]hat she was saying didn't make sense" (291), the voice of Nancy represents a clear example of a young girl who has appropriated a discourse that assigns meaning to the woman's body as merely an object of male desire.

In contrast to these two previous experiences, it is in "The Movies at Sanfer" where the narrator points out that "by the time I was twelve, my friends and I would make arrangements to sit with someone we liked at the movies" (307). Here Ponce recounts her safe experience of sitting with George, known as "Chochis," who was more interested in eating buttered popcorn than in getting fresh with her: "[W]hile the other girls were kept busy fighting off los frescos, I munched my way contentedly through the movie, mesmerized by the antics of Pauline and Nyoka, secure with an array of my favorite candies" (308). Her contentment at watching movies that presented girls who were continuously "on the brink of death, waiting to be rescued by a handsome hero" (306), is symbolic of a romanticized vision of sexuality, a vision beyond which she was unwilling to venture at this time.

This narrative, then, portrays the emergence of a self-in-process who is positioned at first within the secure space of the home. However, Ponce notes that "the summer I was twelve, I knew it was almost time for me to have my first kiss" (294). She tells of her yearning to practice with someone, and of her decision to ask Nancy, "who knew everything there was to know about kissing" (295). She then recounts her decision of choosing Lupe as the one to give her the romantically envisioned first kiss. Indeed, she recalls how she took the situation into her own hands: "I grabbed him by the shoulders and smacked him on the lips" (295). Here we are reminded that just as the autobiographer represents herself as a child who delves into the world of knowledge found in books, she also presents herself as intent on playing kickball and competing with the boys on the playground. This same energetic persistence is apparent as she reveals her emergence as a young girl who partakes in a situation of role reversal as she takes the initiative to kiss a boy and ask him to be her boyfriend:

Dear Lupe
I think you are cute.
Do you want to be my boyfriend?
Yes [ ] No [ ]
Love and xxxxxx (296)

The reader is told that "Lupe's mother got hold of the letter. She gave it to Doña Luisa who handed me the incriminating paper . . . 'No tiene vergüenza!' Her dark eyes bored into me as she said I had no shame. Chasing after boys was to her a serious matter." The narrator's response: a simple "no fue nada" (296).

I would suggest that this example is written into the narrative as a means of demonstrating the way in which female children are introduced to the confines of a discourse of tradition that assigns them a passive role. Because the female subject presented in this text is a young girl, it becomes evident that the narrator is intent on portraying a childhood that represents the basis of her development, particularly the way in which she tests the limits imposed upon her as a female. On the other hand, she also portrays herself as a teenager content with her own sense of being a woman, as she recounts how she was ready for the physical changes taking place in her life: "And then one day, as if by magic, my arms lost their hairy look. My yellow mustache grew out; the dark veil no longer was visible. My legs grew long and lean, with less and less hair. I threw out the camisetas and was bought a cotton bra. When my mother wasn't looking, I hiked up my skirt hems, then opened up the slits on each side" (337). This passage presents a thirteen-year-old girl aware of her sexuality, who welcomes her first menstrual period as she "snuggled under the covers, sipping té de canela, cinnamon tea, said to be good for It" (338). All of these memories included within the narrative depict the autobiographical "I" as someone immersed in a process of exploration of what it means to be a woman within her life space.

In conclusion, it is important to note that the four texts that make up the corpus of this study provide us with chronotopes that point to the development of the autobiographical subject during different times and spaces. In three of the narratives, "Early Life," *Romance*, and *Hoyt Street*, we find examples of the female and her initial assignment to a domesticating space. *A Beautiful, Cruel Country*, on the other hand, presents a female subject who from the early years of her life is forced to partake in the realm of male activities of the ranch rather than the home space.

However, the first three narrators manipulate the "I" by rewriting their assigned roles within the household as they present their development in other directions. The narrator of "Early Life," for example, presents us with an "I" who as a child seemingly enjoyed listening to stories such as *La Influencia de la Mujer*. Implicit in the autobiographer's mention of these stories is an emphasis on the limits placed on the woman, who is considered inessential and defined as an object. However, in her later life, away from the home, the narrator presents herself as a woman who acts rather than simply listening. That is, she achieves a position as an accomplished researcher and writer, and she also becomes a woman who earns a master's degree during a period when few women entered higher education. The narrator of *Romance* concentrates most of her narrative on her development in the traditional spaces of the father's and then the husband's home. However, within the symbolic space of widowhood she narrates the development of an "I" that moves out of the social roles defined for her as she comes into her own as a writer and founder of the Sociedad Folklórica.

Both *Hoyt Street* and *A Beautiful, Cruel Country* project different perspectives regarding the childhoods of the female subject. Interestingly, although the female subject of the Wilbur-Cruce narrative seems totally content to take part in the ranching activities of the male sphere, she also shows curiosity when she examines Grandmother Wilbur's belongings, especially "a white nightgown with small blue ribbons and a small jacket of white lace." It is at this moment that the narrator tells us "I picked it up and held it against my own body and I looked in the mirror. My heart pounded. Someday! Someday there would come a change."[55] For this one fleeting moment when she is away from her father she is able to experience, albeit tentatively, the mysteries of the female experience, just as she later watches her grandmother brush her hair and put on the lace jacket.

Within *Hoyt Street* the autobiographical "I" situates herself within the space of a Mexican American home where both her mother and father take on traditional roles. The narrator also expresses her desire to imitate both of her older sisters, one of whom works outside the home and one who is her mother's support within the home. More than anything, it is through her sisters that she is exposed to books. She further represents herself as a young girl who is thrilled at the possibility of competing with boys on the playground. Ultimately, however, she narrates her contentment with her passage into womanhood as she learns to hike up her skirt and flaunt her new sense of sexuality. She ends her narrative as she welcomes her menstrual period, a symbol of her female identity. Both narratives, then, point to a female subject who is determined and competitive, yet each is aware of her female identity. However, whereas the narrator of *A Beautiful, Cruel Country* is normally forced to hide her femininity behind "the long overalls she had made me from Father's discarded levis" (49), the *Hoyt Street* narrator embraces her sense of femininity as she tells the reader "I was thrilled to discover I fit into Nora's cornflower-blue formal."[56]

Descriptive Discourse and the Creation of a Cultural Universe

What I have proposed in the previous analysis coincides with Genette's claim that "narrative discourse is produced by the action of telling";[57] it is precisely through the act of telling that the narrator presents her life story, one in which the reader is able to perceive narrative spaces, narrative temporalities, and the presentation of the autobiographical "I." Narrative refers to a succession of events and is the basis for understanding autobiography. However, in this section I address the importance of description as a macro-operation used by the addresser of the border autobiography for the purpose of creating a particular cultural universe to be understood by the reader. My analysis is informed by the theoretical concepts of the School of Neuchâtel, which approaches discourse analysis from the perspective of "natural logic" and its relation to schematization and cultural preconstructs that involve the use of discourse as the means of constructing the cultural nature of the micro-universe.[58] The importance of natural logic, then, is its dialogical nature, which implies an exchange between two or more subjects who take part in a process of communication within a particular social context.

The four descriptive procedures or operations that guide my analysis here are anchoring, aspectualization, thematization, and assimilation.[59] These descriptive networks are derived from a particular name or title that anchors the object being described.[60] The operation of *aspectualization* involves the representation of characteristics or qualities inherent in the discursive object, or fragment of the referential world, being described (130). The addresser is able to further expand the discursive object through the operation of *thematization*, in which one or more aspects or parts are developed in more detail within the text, thereby enriching the descriptive object. Another operation of importance in description is *assimilation*, which is manifested linguistically through simple comparisons and metaphors in which information is presented analogically (128–131).

For the purposes of my discussion in this section, I wish to consider several questions: Which discursive objects has the narrator chosen to describe, and why does she choose these elements? In what way do these discursive objects point to certain cultural preconstructs held by the author?[61] And most importantly, what is the relation between the descriptive elements evident in each text and the way in which the autobiographical "I" has been presented? In the analysis that follows, I argue that those elements of the text related to land and home take on a broader meaning if we carefully examine references to the landscape evident in each text. Therefore, as a means of interpreting those descriptive sections of the text that refer to landscape, I look to the perspectives of Compan and Pieprzak, who theorize "landscape as an imaginary," as a "constructed and negotiated literary space rather than an unproblematic transcription of an external geographic reality."[62]

"Early Life and Education" and *Dew on the Thorn*

"Early Life and Education" is a short text in which the autobiographical narrator presents only brief descriptions, yet most of these inform the more extensive description found in *Dew on the Thorn*. Both texts are related to history of the land, home, ancestors and family members, cultural "others," and Hispanic customs. The present analysis focuses on the operation of thematization and the way it is used to broaden the concepts of land and home. Through an examination of descriptions related to these concepts, I point to the way the authors explore issues concerning those spaces involving historical memory and land rights.

As I have mentioned in the previous section, the narrator in González's works anchors her text through references to her life and education as she situates the autobiographical "I" within the geographic space of Roma, Texas. González initiates her text by focusing on the notion of "land" as a discursive object that involves certain underlying cultural preconstructs, such as territory, home, homeland, and country. I would like to note that the first dictionary definition of "land" is simply "a specific part of the earth's surface." A broader definition makes reference to: "a country, region, etc. . . . one's native land . . . the inhabitants of such an area; nation's people."[63] This definition—"country," "native land," and "nation's people"—points to concepts that are intimately tied to the notion of land as a sociocultural or political space, or both. However, as becomes evident throughout these two texts and those of Jaramillo, Wilbur-Cruce, and Ponce, the concept of land is clearly related to the notion of "home," which is a universal theme that implies a place of one's own, a safe haven.

The descriptive elements evident in both "Early Life and Education" and *Dew on the Thorn* point to the narrator's emphasis on specific aspects of land in relation to a particular geographic space that involves the establishment of settlements in El Nuevo Santander, one of the last provinces of the northern frontier of New Spain and which today includes the area from the Rio Grande to Laredo, Texas. This type of reference to geographic space and the implications of that space correspond to what Susan Friedman defines as "the new geographics," which can be seen as figuring "identity as a historically embedded site, a positionality, a location, a standpoint, a terrain, an intersection, a network, a crossroads of multiply situated knowledges."[64] From this standpoint, it becomes clear that certain descriptive portions of the González autobiography are intended to evoke the history of a family that descended from the first settlers of the area, thereby asserting an ancestral claim to the land. More importantly, we find descriptions of geographic areas such as New Spain, Nuevo León, Tamaulipas, and Texas. The cultural preconstruct that is activated with the mention of these spaces points to the history of conflict regarding national boundaries which were ultimately affected by the Treaty of Guadalupe Hidalgo in 1848, a treaty responsible for affecting the position of Mexican and Tejano population in the region. Thus, this information bears specifically on the identity of inhabitants of the border areas in Texas, and therefore on the identity of the autobiographical "I."

Description in the text also communicates preconstructs concerned with the narrator's knowledge and opinion regarding the land rights of the border people. For example, González describes her mother as the "descendent of a Texas landowner,"[65] and then goes on to narrate events concerned with the movement of "*colonizadores*" from their land in Texas to Mexico after the Treaty of Guadalupe Hidalgo. She then remarks: "After the Civil War my grandfather, with financial aid from his mother, the widowed Ramona Guerra Hinojosa, returned to Texas to regain or buy some of what had been their land. At a place where the Indians had found a dead snake, he purchased land known as Las Víboras. That was the beginning of his ranch in Starr County" (x). In this example a combination of narration and interspersed descriptive phrases such as "their land," "purchased land known as Las Víboras," and "his ranch in Starr County" stand out. This type of description, which employs linguistic markers in the possessive form such as "their" and "his" asserts a history of land ownership. Hence, the narrator clearly argues that because the Guerra family was among the original colonizers of the geographic space once known as El Nuevo Santander, they had land rights that were historically grounded.

It is this sense of belonging to the land that closes the first section of the autobiography: "Texas is ours. Texas is our home. Always remember these words: Texas is ours, Texas is our home." The narrator ultimately indicates, "I have always felt at home in Texas" (xi). Again the use of the possessive form "our" denotes ownership and belonging to the land. The section "Early Life" begins with a description of Texas as the narrator's birthplace, and ends with repetitive mention of Texas as home; thus, the preconstructs regarding home do not simply suggest a physical structure. Rather, land is seen as the homeland.

The second section of the autobiography, "Education," has very little description, yet we do find examples concerned with the importance of the Texas borderlands. The narrator anchors her account of the border area by naming cities such as San Antonio, Rio Grande City, and Austin, as well as Webb, Zapata, and Starr counties. Ultimately this sense of belonging to Texas is accentuated as the narrator notes that "until my retirement I taught Spanish and Texas History" (xi). The point of view evident here is that Texas history cannot be separated from knowledge of the Spanish language, which refers indirectly to those who, like the narrator's family, originally laid claim to land in New Spain or the present-day Texas borderlands.

Dew on the Thorn, as an autobiographically informed text, also presents evidence of the use of thematization to emphasize land: "Rich in the tradition of a proud past, and still rich in worldly goods, the year of Our Lord 1904 found the Olivares on the land which His Excellency Revilla Gigedo, Viceroy of New Spain, had deeded to the head of the family in 1764."[66] This passage presents a restatement of the fact that the Olivares family had "deeded" land rights in the area of Texas previously known as Place Mier, a town in Nuevo Santander where members of the Guerra family were considered established residents.[67] Thus, as suggested by José Limón, the narrative stresses a "sense of place" or home in South Texas.

The description of the process of land exploration and settlement in *Dew on the Thorn* also involves characterization of the early settlers' appreciation of the land: "The commander founded several missions and towns along the coast and hills of what is now Tamaulipas . . . they saw the foundations of the towns along the Río Grande. . . . While exploring the country Don Juan José learned to like the flower-covered prairies along the Nueces and the brush-covered land of the Río Grande. He saw many promises in this land that invited him to remain" (4). Here there is an emphasis on "founding" mission settlements and "exploring the country." There is also further description of the beauty and promise of the landscape, which is "flower-covered" and "brush-covered"; it is this representation of the land as untouched and beautiful that points to its invitation to remain. Historically, however, this is a land fraught with conflict. Indeed, as Limón has argued, the Anglo-Americans who came to South Texas "inundated the area, bringing with them their dominating political, educational and cultural institutions, as well as greatly intensified racism."[68] It is precisely the cultural preconstruct associated with the effects of the Anglo-American intrusion that stands out in the final paragraphs of *Dew on the Thorn* when Don Francisco tells his son, "[I]t will not be long before this land will be invaded by newcomers; it will not be long before you will become an alien in what you once considered the heritage of your ancestors."[69] Once again we find linguistic markers that assert possession as Don Francisco points to the land as a heritage, one that has been handed down from "your ancestors."

It is interesting to note that the narrative also includes descriptive sequences that focus on themes regarding "home" or the family house: "The inside arrangement of the house . . . was typically Mexican. The principal room of the house was a big *sala*, the living room, where the family sat and talked in the evenings. . . . The kitchen and dining room, which formed a separate establishment, were joined to the house by a long rambling portal. . . . Perhaps the most interesting room of all was the kitchen with its enormous fireplace occupying one end of the room. . . . The dining room, inviting and cheerful, with its huge beams across the roof, and its big home-made mesquite table and benches, was always ready to welcome the host of friends, travelers and transients who visited the ranch" (16). These brief quotes taken from several long descriptive passages point first of all to a house that is "Mexican," thus emphasizing cultural preconstructs that refer to an ancestral heritage that informs the style of the house. Furthermore, all of the areas of the house are discursively presented in a positive light as an expression of pride in the Mexican home built on ancestral land.

Ultimately we find further descriptive references within a section of the text in which Don Francisco's wife responds to her husband's fears about being driven from the land: "No, Francisco, we shall stay. . . . This land is ours. It was blessed by the blood of the fathers who made it a Christian land. It was blessed by the blood of our ancestors who fought and suffered for it and conquered it, that we, their children, might have a home. The *Americanos* may come. They may take the land, but our spirit, the spirit of the conquerors, will live forever. Texas is ours. We stay!" (179). Apparent in this final portion of *Dew on the Thorn* is the importance of land as a discursive object, which is carried over from the "Early Life" autobiography to the autobiographically informed text. For example, phrases such as "this land is ours" and "the blood of our ancestors who fought and suffered for it" manifest cultural preconstructs related to issues concerned with a sense of belonging to a place as well as to a cultural group whose blood has marked the land.

Romance of a Little Village Girl

The title *Romance of a Little Village Girl* seemingly refers to the life story of a girl. However, it also presents descriptive sequences concerning the village as the first setting of the narration. Like the "Early Life" narrative, this text also focuses on land and home.

The first two chapters of the text, "The New Spanish Province" and "Government Changes Take Place," present descriptive sequences concerned with the process of settlement in northern New Mexico. Thematization regarding the history of home, a Spanish province, is evident in chapter 1, which begins with an epigraph:

> The first white speck on the Western sea was made by a
> Spanish sail,
> And the first lonely grave on the plains,
> Was dug by a Spanish trail.
>
> They left their loved abodes
> To tempt new seas, and stretched their sails . . .
> To lands unsettled to habitate.[70]

Apparent in these seemingly simple verses is a portrait of those Spaniards, who "left their loved abodes" for "lands unsettled." Like the "Early Life" and *Dew on the Thorn* texts, here we find descriptive elements regarding those of "the Spanish race" who set sail from Spain, "explorers and colonizers" such as Cortez, Coronado, Oñate, and De Vargas, as well as "missionary priests" who venture into a new land. The missionaries are depicted as "toiling and suffering untold hardships"; the colonizers of "stern determination" are known for their "desire to discover and conquer" (2). These people are the initiators of a process of conquest that is meant to "replant the seed of Spanish culture and faith" (2). It is precisely this type of descriptive discourse that presents a point of view regarding Spanish conquest that is clearly adulatory in tone.

Here I would like to point out that in the space of the first two pages of Jaramillo's narrative the words "Spain" or "Spaniards" occurs fifteen times. These repetitive references clearly suggest the narrator's positionality within the geographics of New Spain, especially with regard to her homeland of New Mexico. The use of "Spain" and "Spaniards" functions discursively as a marker of cultural preconstructs, or cultural filters which point to an obvious sense of European self-representation. Indeed, as suggested by Erlinda Gonzales-Berry and David R. Maciel in their introduction to *The Contested Homeland*: "Nuevomexicanos have always been very sure of their identity as a people who for centuries have occupied a particular region which they have come to see as their homeland, albeit a contested one."[71] The authors further note that for close to a century the Nuevomexicanos were known for the "peculiar practice" of "insisting on being called Spanish Americans and reacting adversely to being labeled Mexicans" (5).

The thematic emphasis on European self-representation is also apparent in descriptions concerned with a process in which "the kings of Spain did everything to encourage settlement of the new country."[72] The narrator continues to focus on a European identity as she portrays her ancestors, the Luceros, as "descendents of Pedro de Godoy," who "settled the little valley of Ojo Caliente which had already been discovered by Sosa and Cabeza de Baca" (3). This narrator, like those of "Early Life" and the autobiographically informed characters of *Dew on the Thorn*, considers herself to be a descendant of the first Spanish colonizers, thereby arguing for her family's claim to the land.

This text also highlights a family right to land in northern New Mexico as Jaramillo notes that her great-grandfather, Don Manuel Martinez, made a petition for more land: "[T]he Government heard his petition and gave the Martinez family the Tierra Amarilla grant of over three hundred thousand acres, the richest grant in water, timber and grazing land in the northern part of New Mexico" (4). Pride in the land is also palpable in descriptions where the superlative form is used—for example, "the richest grant." She further highlights the "restless, energetic" spirit of her ancestors who went beyond this land grant to Taos County.

The narrator then points out that her "grandfather Vicente bought lands at Arroyo Hondo" (4) where he built a seventeen-room house, "where afterwards my parents lived and raised their family of five boys and two girls" (4). By focusing on a detailed description of the family house, the autobiographical narrator asserts pride in her home. For example, in referring to the woodwork found in the house, she notes it was "the best woodwork—thick round posts, carved lintels and scroll-cut corbels supported the round beams and the time-stained ceilings. The whole house was built in the best New Mexico architectural style" (11). In much the same way that the house described in *Dew on the Thorn* is said to be Mexican in style, here the narrator is asserting her pride in the New Mexican architecture that is typical of this geographic area. Ultimately it is through descriptive sequences that take the reader from early Spanish settlement to the areas where her ancestors and parents settled that the narrator portrays her family, and others of Spanish descent, as the true heirs to the land of New Mexico.

Further thematic emphasis on the process of settlement is evident as the autobiographer points to this place, this Spanish province, as no longer being occupied by Spaniards but by "adventurers, trappers, wise-eyed gamblers and towering gold seekers [who] discovered even the little hidden valley of the Arroyo Hondo, situated in the northern part of Taos County" (7). The landscape of the valley is described as flowing from a river whose "crystaline [*sic*] waters create green-carpeted meadows and fields. On the west the river surges through the stupendous gate of the Rio Grande and mingles its crystal waters with the musky green ones of the Rio Grande. Three picturesque villages add charm to this small section of the beautiful Taos Valley" (7). The repetitive discursive references to crystalline waters function as markers of cultural preconstructs that suggest the purity of this area, and therefore the purity of the blood of those Spaniards who settled this green, fertile valley that has been invaded by strangers who came in "wagon trains that crossed the plains to New Mexico" (7). The narrator finally notes that the American "men settled in Taos and married into prominent Spanish families" (7). Through this type of description Jaramillo constructs a schematization that represents a perception of her village, her world. This is the world she intends to present to the reader, one that had been settled by her ancestors who are of the Spanish race, men that she characterizes as having a "spirit of adventure." However, the land is ultimately depicted as settled by trespassers, and therefore tainted by their presence.

Like *Dew on the Thorn, Romance of a Little Village Girl* focuses on issues related not only to land settlement but more importantly to the strength of its inhabitants in the face of change. Whereas *Dew on the Thorn* describes this period as a "new age," an "incoming era,"[73] the narrator of *Romance* notes that "times had changed." *Dew on the Thorn* describes "Don Francisco, [who] bowed his head in his hands, said nothing. When hearts weep there is no need for words" (178). In a similar vein, *Romance* depicts the Spanish dons: "Crushed at first with this hard change, but with their spirits still strong, with inherent courage and religious resignation, they bore their trials."[74] Both texts also echo the same decision to remain on the ancestral land. Indeed, the narrator of the *Romance* text points to the determination of the families affected by this change, as she notes, "In an effort to keep satisfied and cheerful, feast days, weddings, and other celebrations were kept up, with feasting, music and dancing." She then mentions that "our families now remained more secluded in our enclosed *placitas* courtyards" (9), and ultimately she explains that "the country had adjusted itself to the new changes" (10). Once again "our" is used as a discursive marker to describe the families of this place who now remain "secluded" in "enclosed *placitas*," thereby pointing to the narrator's perspective—that is, the only way to maintain a "Spanish" heritage is to remain secluded from those who have intruded upon the land.

A Beautiful, Cruel Country

As in the previously mentioned texts, in *A Beautiful, Cruel Country* the autobiographer anchors her narrative in the title theme. The narrator of Wilbur-Cruce's text also depicts the land of Arizona's Arivaca Valley as home. The significance of the concepts of land and home are amplified through thematic references regarding the Lomita de Pesqueira, the Wilbur Ranch, and what the narrator perceives as Indian country.

Unlike "Early Life" and *Romance*, this narrative centers on several notions regarding land. Within the title of this text, for instance, the narrator anchors her perception of the land by using the word "country" to refer to the geographic space taken up in her life writing. Again there are certain cultural preconstructs related to this term. The first dictionary definition of "country" is "an area of land; a region." A more extended definition includes ideas such as "a whole land or territory of a nation or state," and finally "the people of a nation or state."[75] Thus, the narrator's linguistic reference to this country, the Arizona Territory, clearly points to its incorporation into the United States. Of further interest is the use of contradictory terms to refer to this country—both "beautiful" and "cruel."

The first chapter of the narrative begins with a reference to "our house," which is described as positioned "at the foot of Pesqueira Hill . . . the hill was named *Lomita de Pesqueira* for Don Ignacio Pesqueira, the man who had ruled the state of Sonora for twenty years as its governor."[76] It is important to mention that the name of the hill is repeated, appearing first in English and then in Spanish. This repetition points to a cultural preconstruct involving the hybrid history of the land—that is, a history of Spanish and Mexican settlements in northern Sonora and southern Arizona.[77] Interestingly, the name of this area is first expressed in English—Pesqueira Hill. This usage signals an Anglo presence, and the narrator complements this notion as she explains that "it was because of Grandfather Wilbur that we lived here on our land by Arivaca Creek" (3). Again, as we have seen in the previously analyzed texts, "our land" stands as a linguistic marker that indicates possession, an extremely relevant notion given the history of clashes related to national boundaries. These two descriptive references to the land where the family house is located point clearly to the history of "the border country along the creek" (1) that has passed from Mexican to Anglo dominance.

Of further relevance is the description of Pesqueira Hill: "covered with a blanket of blue flax and large clumps of verbena. Above these small plants rose the dainty fairyduster with its orchid and white flowers, delicate little catkins, fresh each morning, or shimmering in the last light of the sunset" (1). Here the narrator communicates her perspective regarding the beauty of this land as she emphasizes flowers that are "small," "dainty," "delicate," and "shimmering." In a later portion of the text, she continues to depict life in this land: "At the turn of the century Arivaca Creek was the life focus for the surrounding country. Thousands of burros grazed in the nearby hills and watered at the creek" (64). In addition to her mention of the animals in this area, she also notes, "The Indians traveled every summer to Tucson to harvest the saguaro fruit and then return to their home—the creek. The enormous cottonwoods and the musical stream were their paradise. And mine too" (64). It is precisely use of the term "paradise" that once again confirms the narrator's positive perspective regarding the beauty of this "land," this "country" that is "home" to Indians, Mexicans, and Anglos.

In addition to descriptions of the land, we find a detailed reference of the family house that is presented through further use of thematization within the narrative: "The *zaguán* (large passageway) divided our house. On the west side were a large storage room, the slaughter house, the dairy house, and the tackroom. Three other rooms in this west part were set apart—detached from the main house. On the east side were our living quarters. There were three bedrooms, but one my father had made into a kind of office. Here he kept Grandfather Wilbur's rolltop desk. Here also were the large picture of Grandfather Wilbur's alma mater, Harvard Medical College, a western saddle, a thirty-thirty rifle, Grandfather Wilbur's portrait, and another picture, a large print labeled 'The Return of the Grand Army 1814'" (13–14). This passage represents the house as a discursive object that is described in a way that draws attention to the lifestyle of those who lived in the Arizona Territory. That is, the "storage room," the "slaughter house," and the "dairy house" present the narrator's construction of a schematization of ranch life.

What stands out in this extensive description, however, is the office kept by the autobiographer's father. This is a space which further accentuates memories regarding Anglo Grandfather Wilbur's role in the family's history. The mix of objects—the picture of Harvard Medical School, the rifle, and the picture of the Grand Army[78]—are referents that point to cultural preconstructs regarding the historical movement west and the use of force in this process. Indeed, the photograph of the Grand Army alludes to cultural preconstructs of imperialist notions regarding the right to land expansion prevalent in the United States during the nineteenth century, especially on the basis of the concept of Manifest Destiny. The fact that the narrator's father keeps these mementos implies his own sense of adherence to the meaning of these objects, which can be seen as vestiges of a system of ideas regarding western expansion. Indeed, these objects underlie his sense of having rightfully inherited the land his father had settled.[79] That is, references to the rifle and the picture of an army can be seen as discursive objects that point to a sense of pride regarding a familial history of homesteading land even though this history involved the forceful displacement of Indians, a major theme that will be discussed in chapter 3 of this book.

Through the use of descriptive elements concerned with land ownership the narrator explains that "by 1865, Grandfather R.A. Wilbur had decided to homestead on squatter's rights, to have a place of his own. You could get about 140 acres by homesteading, but you were required to build a habitable house, and other improvements within a certain amount of time" (4). Unlike "Early Life and Education," *Dew on the Thorn*, and *Romance*, which focus on land that has been conquered by Spaniards, here we find references to the way in which land was acquired by Anglo Americans through homesteading based on squatters' rights. Indeed, the narrator points out that Grandfather Wilbur settled this large area of land for the purpose of acquiring "a place of his own." Again land settlement is represented descriptively in terms of ownership.

After references to Grandfather Wilbur's claim to the land, there is a shift in the descriptive focus, with an emphasis on the mountain: "Many call it El Papago, because our Arivaca Valley teemed with Indians, some who lived there more or less permanently, and hordes of others came and went like ants. We called it El Cerro, as if it were the only mountain in the world" (19).[80] Noteworthy here is the fact that although Indians were the original occupants of this land, they and their name for the mountain are referred to only after Grandfather Wilbur's presence is established. Indeed, the descriptive use of phrases such as "our Arivaca Valley teemed with Indians" and the "hordes" of Indians who "came and went like ants" stand clearly as linguistic markers that articulate a perception of the Indians as trespassers.

Through the operation of assimilation the narrator compares the diasporic movement of the Indians to the movement of ants. Two perspectives come to mind with this analogy: the Indians are industrious like ants, or they are bothersome like ants. The narrator further notes, "El Cerro was the landmark of our Indian country region" (18). Here the use of the word "landmark" denotes land that is marked by an Indian presence. Reference to the Indians is also expressed in possessive form, "our Indian country region," which sets the tone for further description of the natives of this land: "[T]he Indians who moved slowly, almost aimlessly, were our creek-dwellers. Others, large groups, came footing it up the creek in a businesslike manner, and these were only passing through. They were our travelers, or newsbringers" (18). Once again the narrator refers to the Indians in possessive form. This type of linguistic usage demonstrates the existence of cultural preconstructs that acknowledge the Indian presence on land that had been dominated first by Spaniards, then Mexicans, and finally Americans, yet the presentation of the natives of this land in the possessive form points to a sense of ownership in which the Indians are subsumed into the Anglo world.

Although the narrator begins by referring to land that is owned by Anglo Grandfather Wilbur, she also points to the home of her maternal grandfather, Don Francisco Vilducea, and her grandmother Margarita, who also live on the Wilbur Ranch. The narrator further amplifies her memories regarding her "grandparents' house [which] was across the creek, just a stone's throw from ours. Their house consisted of three large rooms, the kitchen, the *sala* (living room), and my grandparents' bedroom" (15). The only allusions to land in relation to the narrator's Mexican maternal grandparents have to do with grandmother Margarita's "*jardín de savila*" and her "garden of medicinal herbs and plants" which "also boasted a big jojoba" (16). The narrator further describes this plant that was tended to carefully by her grandmother: "It spent the winter under a tent of old burlap sacks and old quilts, but during the summer rains, it was always luscious and beautiful. We used the jojoba nuts to make poultices, and many times my mother would also use them to make 'coffee'" (16). In contrast to previous references to land, which emphasized ownership, here the narrator presents the land as a provider of plants such as jojoba, which is described as "luscious and beautiful" (16). These textual details signal a perception of the land, the country, as beautiful, an idea that is initially anchored in the title of the narrative.

In contrast to this sense of connection with the land, the narrator places emphasis on descriptions related to the process of working the land: "Outside the fence at the bottom of the bank, Grandfather had sunk a well. With a windlass he pulled up buckets of water to fill the tank from which he watered the plants. After the rains came, he would hang up the bucket and go to work, hoeing, weeding, and pruning. The long vines of the squash with the large leaves and trumpetlike yellow blossoms covered much of the ground" (111). This segment clearly demonstrates a thematic focus that broadens the meaning of land. Here the autobiographical narrator focuses on the process of working the land as she tells the reader, "Grandfather worked hard for all of us." Anglo Grandfather Wilbur is presented as a homesteader of the land, but it is Mexican Grandfather Vilducea who is presented as one with the land. The narrator has ultimately presented us with a micro-universe that is described as a country where different cultural groups assert their sense of pertaining to the land. Furthermore, it is through different types of descriptive references that she represents the land as beautiful, yet demanding and cruel.

The narrator's perspective regarding the cruel aspect of the land is first evident in the prologue to Wilbur-Cruce's life story. For example, the "hinterlands of the border" are described as a "rugged—a turbulent sea of isolation. There were mole hills, jagged ridges, toothed mountains, buttes, mesas, washes, and gulches" (viii). She also notes the Mexican border region where her father attempts to homestead the Cochis Ranch, a "God-forsaken place," a space known for its "hardships" (61). Another reference of this type is evident in "A Trip to the Mountain" when the narrator depicts the Cerro as "an enormous pile of rocks and boulders. This horrible mound of rocks had no trees, no trails, and no shape" (49).

Her perception of the Cerro as "horrible" certainly has to do with recollections of the first time she went up this mountain as a three-year-old: "We went over the big boulders and I looked down the sharp precipice. The white patch of yuccas was far away. By now I was well convinced that climbing the Cerro was not only serious business, but a pretty risky one" (57). Yet in spite of its barrenness, and the risk of climbing to its peak, the Cerro is also described as a "place [that] was teeming with bird life" and enlivened by "the grayish-green leaves of some of the agave, the glistening green of the bear grass, the tender green of the desert mahogany, and the dark green of the mesquite leaves" (53). Ultimately what becomes evident in the passages I have cited is the narrator's use of thematization to present her view of the land, this country homesteaded by Grandfather Wilbur, as a place of contradictions. That is, various descriptions of the landscape point to a terrain marked by the cultural presence of people of Spanish, Mexican, and Indian origin. This is a land where the cultural structures represented by the figures of Grandfather Wilbur and Grandfather Vilducea come into contact, thereby bringing about new meaning to this hybrid space. Therefore, we cannot help but interpret the writer's reference to the cruelty of the land in terms of its history involving the displacement of the original inhabitants of this space and subsequent struggles regarding land rights and shifting borders.

Hoyt Street

The title theme of *Hoyt Street*, like those of *Romance* and *A Beautiful, Cruel Country*, anchors the text by referring to a place that signals a micro-universe that is presented descriptively by the narrator. This narrative also highlights aspects such as a particular area of land and the idea of home. The first chapter of the text, with its title "13011 Hoyt

Street," is concerned with a particular geographic space, "[t]he town of Pacoima [which] lay to the northeast of Los Angeles, about three miles south of the city of San Fernando. The blue-grey San Gabriel Mountains rose toward the east; toward the west other small towns dotted the area. Farther west lay the blue Pacific and the rest of the world. The barrio, as I knew it, extended from San Fernando Road to Glenoaks Boulevard on the east and from Filmore and Pierce streets on the north. We lived in the shadow of Los Angeles, twenty odd miles to the south."[81] Like the naming of places in *A Beautiful, Cruel Country*, this text also presents the space of Pacoima as a micro-universe with a hybrid history—that is, we find street names in English as well as in Spanish. Of interest, however, is the narrator's portrayal of the town, the barrio, as distant from "the rest of the world" and "in the shadow of Los Angeles." Thus, she presents her perspective regarding the barrio as separate from surrounding areas. However, unlike the previous texts, which present a rural life experience, *Hoyt Street* involves an urban setting.

Once again, through thematization, the narrator continues to expand her perception of this place as she describes the streets of Pacoima as "unpaved, full of holes and rocks. During a rain the rich, brown mud clung to our shoes" (3). There is no reference to ownership of the land as we have seen in the previously analyzed texts. However, it is pertinent to note that the brown mud points to an implicit assertion: that the land in its moist richness clings to, is related to, those who walk the streets of Pacoima, those who live in the barrio.

The narrator broadens her description of the barrio as she explains:

> The barrio was laid out like a huge square. The streets ran up and down with nary a curve or dead end. Streets that ran north and south started at Filmore Street and came to a screeching halt in la Pierce, where the Pacoima airport, known as Whiteman Airport, stood. The airstrip was more like a weed-infested field with cracked pavement. Small shedlike buildings stood at one end. At one time this area was an empty space where students playing hookey from school would hide out. During Easter vacation and in the summer, kids used the unpaved road along the airport as a shortcut to the nearby hills that dipped and rolled toward Hansen Dam. . . . When later a chain link fence with padlocks went up, hiking to the Pacoima hills became less fun. (4)

What stands out here is the airport and its "weed-infested field with cracked pavement." Pacoima is a town large enough to have an airport, yet the airfield is a place that is seemingly abandoned. This sense of abandonment is also apparent in the "unpaved road" which echoes the unpaved streets found in Pacoima. The passage also mentions the Pacoima hills twice. This repetition is relevant because the hills are beyond the confines of the barrio and they implicitly evoke the possibility of exploration outside this space. Ultimately, however, the narrator's reference to the fence with padlocks points to preconstructs in which the barrio is presented in terms of limits, of boundaries.

Further use of thematization is also evident as the narrator continues to amplify the description of her world by focusing on the houses in Pacoima:

> Homes in Pacas, as we called Pacoima, were modest, ranging from a one-room shack where people slept in the "front room," to the more elegant homes such as Rocky's, which boasted an ample living room, a bathroom with tile and chrome faucets, and a separate bedroom for each child. . . .
>
> On Hoyt Street the houses were neither fancy nor ugly, but like the houses of poor folks everywhere. While some were constructed of stucco, the majority were of wood, madera. . . .
>
> Not all homes had electricity or indoor plumbing. Many casitas on Hoyt Street still had an outhouse somewhere in the back, hidden behind a nopalera or standing blatantly in the middle of the yard. (4–5)

Unlike the *Romance* narrative which emphasizes the seventeen-room home where the narrator spent her childhood, and unlike the family house described in *A Beautiful, Cruel Country*, with its different areas assigned for various ranching activities, here we are struck by the simplicity of the homes on Hoyt Street. The description of the houses as "modest" is accentuated through a sequence of descriptive phrases such as "one-room shack," "neither fancy nor ugly," "houses of poor folks," "casitas." All of these evoke a sense of poverty in spite of the few homes like Rocky's that had at least one bathroom and several bedrooms.

Further descriptive sequences draw attention to the larger area of Pacoima. Ponce then mentions the houses found on Hoyt Street, and finally her family's home: "Our house was built by my father when he and my mother and their three older children moved from Ventura to the

San Fernando Valley, sometime in the 1920s "(7). Of particular relevance is the extensive description of the family house, which initially "had three rooms: a kitchen and two bedrooms" (7). The description goes on for more than six pages. Here the autobiographer notes again that "my first memories are of the kitchen with the window, the small room where my parents slept and the large living room with a bed where my sisters slept" (8). The narrator clarifies these repetitive references to the kitchen as she points out that "the kitchen was the heart of our home, the place where my mother cooked, ironed, and bathed her many children. Everyone congregated there to eat, and when relatives visited, they sat there as my mother bustled around the stove. A huge wooden table built by my father dominated the room. Against the wall sat a large bench where we, the youngest children, sat to eat" (10). This space is marked by a familial presence: the mother goes about her tasks, the father participates by providing furniture he builds, children are fed here, and this is also a place where relatives congregate for visits. The result of this description is the construction of a schematization that suggests not simply a house but a home where the kitchen is the "heart" of family activity.

Unlike the previous texts, which make reference to land in terms of conquest or homesteading, the only mention of land and the family home is related to the landscape of the yard: "In our backyard grew an abundance of trees: pepper, eucalyptus, walnut, and a small fig tree, called la higuera, that never gave fruit." The narrator also notes that "in the front yard, to the left of the driveway, grew los pirules. The two pepper trees grew close together and were my favorite trees" (10). Of particular interest is the fig tree that "never gave fruit," a suggestion of barrenness that stands in direct contrast to the "rich" land grant evident in the *Romance* narrative.

Recalling the fenced-in island of land farmed by Grandfather Vilducea in *A Beautiful, Cruel Country*, fences built by the narrator's father are described: "My father had a thing about fences. We had many different ones! One year I counted eight different fences on our property. A picket fence on cement faced Hoyt Street. The wall facing the Montalvos' was made of chicken wire, and cement slabs on a cement foundation. Alongside the men's rooms was a wooden fence that connected with the garage. The back fence next to the alley was made of wood overgrown with cactus. The side fence behind which the goats and chickens were kept was part of the cactus wall. . . . My father's pride and joy was the white picket fence. It faced Hoyt Street and was his original design"

(13). Here Ponce describes in detail the different materials used by her father to build these fences and also reflects on a possible explanation of why fences were so important to him: "While studying the many fences I often thought that perhaps my father's family had not owned property in Mexico. It was important for him to fence, to secure the right of ownership. Or perhaps, unbeknown to us, my father was an artist who liked to express himself in works of cement, wire, and wood" (13–14). Hence, it becomes clear that the narrator is trying to make sense of her father's need to delimit his property, his desire to keep the outside world at a distance. The fences also point to cultural preconstructs concerned with land ownership and the status it bestows. At a more profound level, the fences mentioned in both *A Beautiful, Cruel Country* and *Hoyt Street* would seem to suggest an emphasis on land ownership in geographic areas marked by a history of changing borders, the loss of land, and displacement.

We might recall at this point how the previous narratives refer to the concept of land. The "Early Life" text, for instance, focuses on the narrator's grandfather who bought Las Víboras ranch, land that had been purchased after the Civil War. In the *Romance* text the narrator emphasizes a family land grant in northern New Mexico, whereas *A Beautiful, Cruel Country* refers to the 140 acres homesteaded by Grandfather Wilbur. *Hoyt Street*, on the other hand, speaks of a different type of settlement. Here the narrator constructs a schematization of the family home built on a small piece of property, a home in the barrio, a home settled by immigrants. In this way she emphasizes the boundaries of the barrio, a space that is separated from Los Angeles and San Fernando physically and symbolically. Yet just like the assertion of "Texas is ours" found in "Early Life," the fences described in the *Hoyt Street* text point to the same sense of determination to proclaim ownership of the land where a home has been built.

The point here is that a careful interpretation of narrative and descriptive discourse found in each text allows the reader to gain insight into the development of the autobiographical "I" as well as her perception regarding notions such as "land" and "home." Through the examples presented here, I have examined the internal organization of each text based on the temporal and spatial elements of the narrative. I have also made reference to a set of discursive operations that clearly allow the reader to observe various discursive objects and the way each is developed within the text. Most importantly, by looking at descriptive sequences formulated by the autobiographer, I have highlighted the evident discursive usage of schematizations so as to clarify the narrator's own mental representations and point of view.

Ultimately, by attending to the discursive objects present within the text, we are also able to discern the way in which cultural preconstructs are imbedded within the language of the text. I would like to point out that, although the narrator's knowledge of her micro-universe can be perceived within descriptive schematization, this expression of knowledge is certainly a means of presenting a subjective point of view or argument. Furthermore, the narratives deal with the geographic spaces of Texas, New Mexico, Arizona, and California, and they point to the sociocultural context of these areas, especially in terms of the way they are marked by a history of changing borders and the blending of Spanish, Mexican, and Anglo experience. Indeed, as suggested by Akhil Gupta and James Ferguson, "space itself becomes a kind of neutral grid on which cultural difference, historical memory, and societal organization are inscribed."[82] Thus, the schematizations evident in the discourse of each text reveal not only views on land, landscape, and home, rather they are constructed on the basis of culturally determined phenomena and they respond to certain ideological notions that I will discuss in chapter 4.

Chapter 3

Recovering Cultural and Historical Memory

The Dynamic Quality of Semiotic Structures

In chapter 1, I noted that the border autobiography represents an alternate system of knowledge because it occupies a position outside of the dominant literary repertoire. As such, it represents another type of memory, one that is situated in a semiotic system that involves not only the representation of the autobiographical "I," but also of the collective "we." This type of representation is apparent in the border autobiographies of González, Jaramillo, Wilbur-Cruce, and Ponce where, in addition to references regarding land and home, aspects such as family, "other," education, the influence of religious institutions, and custom also enter into the subject matter of the life narrative that functions as an intellectual depository where cultural memory is maintained. Furthermore, each of the texts in the corpus of this study can be seen as forming a system of texts that point to what may be considered as informal, personal history regarding a particular social group and the cultural "other" within four geographical areas.

My analytic approach in this direction is based on Yuri Lotman's notion of cultural semiotics, particularly his perspective regarding the semiosphere, the text, cultural memory, and cultural explosion. Pertinent to my discussion here are the effects of historical collisions on cultural memory and the way that memory is represented in each narrative. These notions allow me to consider the effects of the intersection of cultures that resulted from historical conquest, land settlement, war, and homesteading, all of which are major themes that I examine in the first portion of this chapter. The focus of the final section of this chapter involves a textual analysis that is oriented toward uncovering information regarding the history of "other" cultural groups and their presence in the geographical area mentioned in each narrative.

The works of Yuri Lotman center on the functioning "of the semiotic space or intellectual world in which humanity and human society are enfolded and which is in constant interaction with the individual intellectual world of human beings."[1] Lotman proposes that culture is governed by a system of rules or a repertoire of texts; that is, culture can be understood as a set of texts and a "non-hereditary collective memory" (xi). Therefore, my intention here is to look at the way this corpus of life stories reveals the autobiographer's project of preserving personal recollections regarding her position within a particular cultural community.

So as to shed light on my perception of the way these border autobiographies can be understood as a meaningful continuum, my discussion in this section refers to Lotman's notion of the *semiosphere*, which he defines as an abstract or "semiotic space which is necessary for the existence and functioning of different languages and the sum total of different languages" or expressions of the life experience (123).[2] For Lotman, the semiosphere is linked to cultural activity, and it is within this space or thinking structure that surrounds us that communicative processes and the production of new information take place. It is precisely the concept of the semiosphere that provides a theoretical framework for examining this corpus of border autobiographies as a multi-vocal continuum of information.

The term "semiosphere" is used in reference to cultural systems that exist as a semiotic *continuum* and present different types and levels of semiosis, and within which communication and dialogue take place. These cultural systems are semiotically heterogeneous; that is, they involve different levels of organization and each functions in what can be seen as a space enclosed in itself yet in constant interaction with other similar structures. The points of contact between different systems represent exchanges that result in new communicative production. These exchanges within semiotic systems have to do with a correlation that exists between the synchronic and diachronic; that is, each of the texts that conforms a particular system involves a dialogue between synchronic or isolated moments and other diachronic aspects that are concerned with the overall evolution of the system. The diachronic character of the semiosphere is of great importance as it is equipped with a complex system of memory without which it would be unable to function.[3]

The semiosphere is further defined as delimited with respect to what surrounds it, or what is considered to be extra-semiotic or outside of this abstract space. For example, the literary texts that exist within the semiosphere of the United States traditionally have been defined in terms of "outstanding" canonical works written by white males; indeed, only two female poets, Emily Dickinson and Elizabeth Bishop, have been included as part of this traditional canon.[4] Anything outside the canon is deemed a lesser or minor work. Lotman has noted the central position of "structurally organized languages," or those canonical texts of a culture that take on a dominant position within the semiosphere, especially in relation to other languages that are considered marginal or peripheral to a particular space.

The determination of what is considered as a canonical/nuclear structure or as a marginal form within the semiosphere has to do with "semiotic irregularity," where the position of the observer is of key importance. Therefore, when a nuclear structure such as a canon of literary texts maintains a dominant position within the semiosphere, this results in the segregation of other systems of metalanguages. For instance, the natural or common language of texts written in the United States is English, and although the texts created by González, Jaramillo, Wilbur-Cruce, and Ponce are written in English, each is interspersed with words and phrases in Spanish, a marginal language in the semiosphere of the United States.[5] The use of Spanish within each of these texts marks them linguistically as "other," as foreign or what Lotman perceives as semiotically "creolized."[6]

Furthermore, because the aspects narrated and described within these texts refer to ethnic and family history, cultural practice, and traditions related to Catholic religious practice, and because they are presented from a marginal Mexican American ethnic perspective, they have been relegated to a marginal space that does not form part of the center or canon of American literary production. However, I venture to say that from the point of view of each autobiographer, the cultural elements presented in her narrative are intended to represent the nucleus of her own semiotic space, one that demonstrates dynamic qualities. Hence, it is the gradual accumulation of diverse types of expressions outside what is considered the canonical system, and their interaction with this system, that results in the dynamic broadening of systemic content.

For example, each text considered here speaks from a different geographical area, and presents its "own" perception regarding history and cultural memory, thus resulting in a heterogeneous set of texts. This semiosphere of texts is the result of a metaphorical intersection between the semiospheres of Mexico, with its memory of the pre-Hispanic and Spanish experience, and that of the United States. Consequently each narrative expresses a distinct Mexican American experience that is derived from the interaction between the systemic and the extra-systemic.

Cultural Space in the Borderlands

Another important aspect of the semiosphere is the concept of boundary or border in relation to the intersection of world spheres.[7] The boundary is the "domain of bilingualism" and it can be defined as "the outer limit of a first-person form." Lotman has suggested that "every culture begins by dividing the world into 'its own' internal space and 'their' external space." Therefore, space can be described as "'ours,' 'my own,' it is 'cultured,' 'safe,' 'harmoniously organized.' . . . By contrast 'their space' is 'other,' 'hostile,' 'dangerous,' 'chaotic.'"[8] The border or boundary is what separates internal space from the external space of the semiosphere, and it operates as a filter or translator of external messages. That is, the semiotic border is the sum of bilingual translators or filters that translate a text from one language or cultural experience to another.[9] Hence, the speaking subject of the border autobiography can be perceived as an interlocutor who is situated in the borderlands created by the intersection of two semiospheres.

Cultural spaces that exist in the borderland, or that symbolic space that forms a border or frontier in a cultural sense, are semiotic realities that unfold in unpredictable and indeterminate ways as a result of historical processes. These borderland realities involve both physical and cultural spaces and they can be seen as "interstices" or in-between places;[10] that is, these are vague, intermediate, and undetermined spaces or conditions.[11] Boundaries, however, also function as semiotic mechanisms that result in individuation; that is, culture in the borderlands "creates its *own* type of internal organization."[12] Essentially, because the borderland is a site of cultural exchange, a space where the coexistence of difference is located, it can be defined as a site of creative ferment characterized by semiotic polyglotism. That is, within each text we find expressions of what Lotman defines as the language of individuals and collective history and culture.[13] Each of the texts referred to in this study can be understood as polyglot because it is created by an autobiographer who is situated symbolically within the semiotic system of the United States, yet her focus is on Hispanic or Mexican American history, culture, and tradition. It is precisely those sectional boundaries that run through the semiosphere that create a multilevel system, one that involves interplay between dominant structures and substructures, thereby resulting in the transmission of information across boundaries.

Due to this interplay of diverse types of information that has been transmitted across the symbolic boundaries of various world spheres, I argue that this corpus of texts can be seen as a semiosphere of border autobiographies. Furthermore, because the life writer of the border autobiography is situated in the space of the borderlands, her function as someone who pertains to two worlds, as someone culturally bilingual, is to translate and transform information, thereby fomenting cultural dialogue. Ultimately, then, the text is not simply a passive carrier of meaning, rather it acts as a dynamic phenomenon that generates meaning.[14]

Cultural Memory and the Effect of Cultural Explosion

From a semiotic perspective, culture can be understood as "collective intelligence and collective memory, that is, a supraindividual mechanism for the conservation and transmission of certain communications (texts) and the elaboration of new ones."[15] On the basis of this definition, cultural space can be defined as a space where memory is shared and where certain texts that deal with that memory are conserved. Lotman has also suggested that cultural memory varies internally; that is, there are different "dialects of memory" that correspond to a cultural collectivity. Another key aspect of cultural memory involves its informative as well as its creative function, especially in texts that have been forgotten and then recovered. It is precisely this process of recovering the past that demonstrates the dynamic or diachronic aspect of culture, specifically its creative memory. For example, the texts that I center on in the present study at one time may have been considered simply as registers of memories concerned with the woman's private life. However, as noted by Tey Diana Rebolledo, early Mexican American women authors can be considered as "foremothers" of modern Chicana literature, and, as such, their writing merits examination of the "female experience usually left out of history."[16] This commentary by Rebolledo coincides with Lotman's assertion that those texts that form a common collective cultural memory are useful because they provide the basis for understanding texts from similar historical periods as well as for generating new texts.

In chapter 2 I examined the symbolic meanings of "land" and "home," and as we will continue to see in the analysis that follows, each of these texts uses cultural and historical language to recount memories concerned with the autobiographer's life as well as a collective way of life that she wishes to preserve. For example, in "Early Life and Education" the autobiographer, as a researcher, writer, and educator, expresses interest in preserving the cultural memory of the people of the Texas borderlands, whereas the narrator of *Romance* points to an invisible current of New Mexican village life that she wishes to revive in her autobiography. In *A Beautiful, Cruel Country* the autobiographical narrator states her desire to share memories about "country life" in the "hinterlands of the border."[17] Through her recollections about life in the barrio, the *Hoyt Street* narrator presents her perspective regarding "Mexican-American culture in general . . . , a social history."[18] As Lotman has suggested, culture is a mechanism that is capable of creating a set of texts, and it is clearly a desire to communicate cultural memory that underlies the creation of the autobiographies I consider here.

A major question arises: how are we to understand the dimension of cultural memory evident in this semiosphere of border autobiographies? As I have mentioned previously, the autobiography presents the life story of the autobiographical "I" who formulates the question "who am I, and where do I belong?" However, because the depth of the human experience must always be presented in terms of past history and the relationship of self with others within a specific culture, I believe that the autobiographical "I" must also ask "where do *we* belong?" True knowledge of self involves a dialectic between self and the world that conforms the life; therefore, the dimension of cultural memory that involves the "I" as well as the collective "we" also involves a process of cultural collisions.

I have pointed out that one of the fundamental aspects of the semiosphere is its heterogeneity; that is, semiotic space contains numerous fragments of various structures or subsystems that coexist within the semiosphere and whose cyclical movements involve different speeds. At particular moments in history a semiotic space may undergo an increase in activity that results in what Lotman refers to as dynamic explosive processes, or collisions between systems that bring about a dramatic change in the makeup of a particular sphere.[19] In spite of these clashes, however, the different semiotic systems that exist within a sphere demonstrate an interesting capacity for survival and a capacity for conserving cultural memory. Thus, it is important to understand the way in which information in a system is affected and ultimately recorded within different "texts" that have been generated as the result of these collisions. Lotman has suggested that "the 'facts of an epoch' form a complex and heterogeneous picture. Each genre, each culturally significant kind of text, makes its own selection of facts . . . from the point of view of the addresser, a fact is always the result of selecting out of the mass of surrounding events an event which according to his or her ideas is significant."[20]

This "heterogeneous picture" can certainly be perceived in relation to the way in which historical events are selected and recounted and made evident in the set of texts presented in this study. Since three of the texts present traces of information regarding a Spanish heritage, I will begin my discussion with a brief introduction regarding an example of a historical clash that took place between the United States and Spain. So as to underscore the way cultural memory is recorded by observers from different semiotic spheres, I will then present a brief synthesis of several perspectives and the selection of events presented by historians regarding the War of US Intervention (the Mexican War) and the Treaty of Guadalupe Hidalgo. Finally, I will analyze the way in which each addresser presents a selection of her "own" memories regarding specific historical moments that inform the life story.

Exploring Historical Ruptures

Chicano scholar Ramón Saldívar points out that "for Chicano narrative, *history* is the subtext that we must recover because history itself is the subject of its discourse.[21] History cannot be conceived as the mere "background" or "context" for this literature; rather, history turns out to be the decisive determinant of the form and content of the literature."[22] As I argue here, this is particularly true for literature that focuses on the life course prior to the Chicano movement, where we find a female voice intent on constructing a woman's own view of the world as she "negotiates spaces between worlds and sensibilities in order to record the 'significant.'"[23] Therefore, as a means of exploring history as a "discursive determinant" evident in the content of the texts authored by González, Jaramillo, Wilbur-Cruce, and Ponce, it is important, first of all, to understand the different cycles of historical ruptures that took place in the semiotic space of North America between Spain and the United States, and then later between independent Mexico and the United States.

Early clashes between Spain and the United States began soon after the American Revolution when the United States acquired the Ohio Valley as part of the Treaty of Paris of 1783. This land bordered the Louisiana Territory, which had originally been acquired by France in the seventeenth century and which then came under Spanish dominion in 1769. As the Ohio Valley was settled by US pioneers, the Mississippi River and the seaport of New Orleans were crucial—goods were sent down the Ohio and Mississippi rivers for trading purposes. Both the Mississippi and New Orleans were within Spanish territory, yet a history of early incursions by US settlers into the territorial domain of Spain and violation of navigation regulations was common. These incursions resulted in disputes that were ultimately settled in the Treaty of San Lorenzo, which provided for free access to the Mississippi River by both Spaniards and Americans. It was during the Kentucky Convention of 1788, however, that the United States declared its natural right to navigate the Mississippi, yet in 1798 Spain decided to close the port of New Orleans and was determined to stop US navigation of the Mississippi.[24]

Evident in this historical moment are the various cycles of history regarding clashes over navigation rights and land appropriation in North America. If we recall Lotman's view that subsystems that coexist within the semiosphere demonstrate cyclical movements that involve different speeds or velocities,[25] it becomes clear that the United States demonstrated a rapid acceleration of expansionist tendencies as well as a desire to increase her economy through trade with Spain's colonies. However, a treaty sponsored by John Jay, US secretary for foreign affairs, and Spain's representative Diego de Gardoqui in 1786 allowed Americans to trade with Spain, but not with her colonies.[26] This example points to Spain's interest in maintaining her historically dominant presence in North America, but her decision to limit trade between her colonies and the United States demonstrates a slower velocity in terms of Spanish colonial development at a time when the United States was determined to increase trade.

This historical reference demonstrates one of the effects of an "explosion," the American Revolution, which resulted in a change in the balance of power in North America where the Spanish, British, and French had initially vied for power. Ultimately one of the consequences of cultural explosion is the formation of a new cultural situation, one that results in a new system of self-description that reorganizes preceding states, thereby creating a new concept of history. From a US standpoint, for example, cultural memory regarding the Kentucky Convention emphasizes the importance of the convention as a moment in the history of contact with Spain when the declaration of natural navigation rights before this European power were seen as crucial for continued expansion. However, a different perception of this historical juncture is noted by Moyano, who asserts that the United States looked for the necessary justification to maintain its stance with regard to incursions into Spanish territory: "[the American decision] was above all based on the natural right to security. . . . They decided very early in their history that, what they called a natural right to future security, was superior to the legal rights of another nation."[27] These two perspectives involving cultural memory that surrounds the history of struggle between the United States and Spain suggest the way in which each area of the semiotic structure preserves its own memory of an event.

The nineteenth century was marked by further clashes between semiotic systems. In 1810 the *criollos* supported by the Indians and *mestizos* began a revolution for independence from Spain, similar to that of the United States a few decades earlier. This revolution was fought until its successful conclusion in 1821, when Spain lost control of the nation. For the United States, on the other hand, the beginning of the nineteenth century was marked by resurgence of nationalism and economic expansion, and in President Monroe's seventh annual address to Congress in December of 1823, the Monroe Doctrine was proclaimed: "The American continents are henceforth not to be considered as subjects for future colonization by any European powers. . . . We should consider any attempt on their part to extend their system to any portion of this hemisphere as dangerous to our peace and safety."[28] Monroe further stated that any "interposition" against the sovereignty of existing American nations would be interpreted as an unfriendly act. In referring to "American continents" Monroe was obviously demonstrating his concern regarding the possibility of further European intervention in the continent with regard to both Mexico and the United States. Essentially he was proclaiming that a particular system was closed to outside interference, and at the same time he was validating the existence of Mexico as an independent nation, one that would eventually suffer intervention not on the part of Europe but by the United States.

The speed with which the United States moved forward was clearly evident by the 1840s, a decade that marked a period of American territorial expansion that brought more than a million square miles of land under US domain. This expansion was fueled by the idea of Manifest Destiny, which asserted the American right "to overspread and to possess the whole of the continent which Providence has given us for the development of the great experiment of liberty and federative self government entrusted to us."[29] This perspective presents territorial expansion as a "right," whereas Mexican American historian Manuel Gonzales terms this so-called experiment "land hunger."[30]

Mexican historians have recorded their views regarding the position of the Republic of Mexico before the United States as follows: "so naturally privileged, full of those elements that form a great and happy nation, [Mexico] had among other misfortunes . . . that of being situated in proximity to a strong and enterprising nation." This enterprising nation would ultimately be described in terms of "insatiable ambition" and a desire to be "absolute lords of almost the entire continent."[31] In references to the war between the United States and Mexico, Alcaraz and the other contributors to *Apuntes para la historia de la guerra entre México y los Estados Unidos* note that the "true origin of the war" was the fact that the United States was able to take advantage of Mexico's weakness. Thus, ambition and a Mexico in the midst of difficulties related to building an independent nation and consequently unable to confront the United States set the stage for territorial expansion.

This desire for more land would eventually result in a disruption of the settlements in Mexico's northern frontier, which ranged from Texas to California. Manuel Gonzales notes that US expansion into Mexican territory had its beginnings as far back as the 1820s. In its interest to populate the expansive area of Texas, Mexico encouraged Americans to settle there as a means of buoying the frontier economy. Many of these settlers were awarded land grants of about five thousand acres. They were to abide by Mexican law, speak Spanish, and accept Catholicism; however, by 1830 in Texas "Anglos outnumbered Mexicans 25,000 to 4,000."[32] This was a gradual process, but it nonetheless resulted in clashes between two spheres.

By 1835 another explosive process took place as Texas began its rebellion to separate from Mexico and become independent. This area became incorporated into the United States in 1845, just prior to war between the United States and Mexico. One of the major issues regarding the annexation of Texas had to do with the boundaries between Mexico and Texas. The Texans claimed that the Rio Grande was to be considered as its southern and western border. Mexico claimed the Nueces River as the border, but the United States refused to accept this view. From a Mexican perspective, the annexation of Texas by the United States was interpreted as a declaration of war. Indeed, the Mexican press emphasized the importance of defending national territory, and, according to Moyano, the US proposition to buy California and New Mexico was considered an insult to national integrity.[33] On the other hand, newspaper articles such as "Annexation" by John O'Sullivan suggested that Mexico was unable to govern her outlying districts and that the lands of California would eventually come under the dominion of the United States.

Once again, what becomes apparent are the divergent perspectives registered in cultural memory regarding those situations that led to war between Mexico and the United States. What the United States perceived as its "right" to rapid territorial expansion and the promotion of a particular way of life was perceived as "the aggression that the United States of America [has] initiated and sustain[ed] against the Republic of Mexico."[34] It was precisely during this historical juncture that Mexico was focused inwardly as it continued to consolidate a newly formed independent nation, whereas the United States was involved in a "grand venture" of expansionism, which, according to historian Patricia Nelson Limerick, looked to Mexico to be a "shameless land grab and an aggressive attack on Mexican sovereignty."[35] In addition to the US expansionist tendencies during this period, Nicolás Kanellos argues, a major focus of Manifest Destiny was the notion of the superiority of the Anglo-Saxon race as well as the necessity of supplanting races considered inferior. Indeed, a major intention on the part of Americans was the population of "the American continent with their own race,"[36] a tendency Kanellos has defined as "racial expansionist destiny" (1-5).

The aggression or renewed clash between two cultural systems ultimately involved a major collision—the US invasion of Mexican territory or what would be called in Mexico the War of US Intervention (and, in the United States, the Mexican War). President James Polk, an avowed expansionist who was determined to turn the United States into a continental nation, ordered General Zachary Taylor to invade northeastern Mexico and occupy the land between the Nueces and the Rio Grande. Two other offensives, against New Mexico and California, took place, starting when Colonel Stephen W. Kearny moved across the Santa Fe Trail to seize New Mexico in 1846.[37] He was then ordered to enter California, which was also conquered that year. In addition to these incursions, General John Wool moved toward Nuevo León, Coahuila, and Chihuahua as General Winfield Scott traveled a route from Veracruz to Mexico City.

History recorded from a US perspective notes that "American forces were generally successful in their campaigns against Mexicans, [yet] final victory did not come nearly as quickly as Polk had hoped."[38] In referring to Polk's attitude, another text points out that "a short and decisive war" was expected to "force the cession of California and New Mexico to the United States."[39] Mexican historians such as Moyano, on the other hand, suggest that victory for the US Army was not quick, precisely because of resistance on the part of Mexicans to these incursions. She further asserts that "North American historians decided to omit the rebellion of thousands of armed Mexicans against the invading army."[40]

David Weber also points to New Mexican hostility when "disaffected Mexicans joined with Pueblo Indians at Taos to rise up against their conquerors. This Taos Rebellion ended only when the United States Army besieged the Pueblo of Taos and killed many of the rebels." This historian further states, "Like the New Mexicans, Californians also revolted against the Americans after an apparently peaceful conquest."[41] Mexican American historian Manuel Gonzalez mentions an effort on the part of "Californios" under the leadership of Capt. José María Flores to "reverse the momentum" of the war as they attacked Kearny's troops in the Battle of San Pascual. However, under the 1847 Treaty of Cahuenga, Californios were forced to recognize that California had been lost to the United States (78–79).

From an American standpoint, with the signing of the Treaty of Guadalupe Hidalgo in 1848, the United States acquired "500,000 square miles of territory. The treaty enlarged the size of the nation by about 20 percent, adding to its domain the present states of California, Utah, New Mexico, Nevada and Arizona and parts of Colorado and Wyoming."[42] Indeed, Mexican American historians David R. Maciel and Erlinda Gonzales-Berry interpret the result of the Treaty of Guadalupe Hidalgo as a cession of "51.2 percent of Mexico's territory to the United States," an agreement that "not only 'incorporated' the desired territory, but it also gained a Mexican-origin population of more than 100,000, 60 percent of whom resided in New Mexico."[43]

Ultimately a desire to find a southern route for the transcontinental railroad resulted in the Gadsden Purchase, "through which the United States acquired the southernmost parts of present-day Arizona and New Mexico."[44] Mexican historian Moyano has also suggested that "technical advances, especially the railroads, stimulated economic expansion. . . . The North American industrial revolution was ready for a second phase of development. For this reason, it was necessary to expand its population into the new territories and acquire more [land] if this were possible."[45]

Moyano further notes that the land acquired by the United States as a result of this war "changed its history with the incorporation of immense territory" (103). However, she also argues that the Treaty of Guadalupe Hidalgo "was not simply an agreement to end the war. The intent of its twenty-three articles was to modify subsequent relations between the two countries even though it contained a number of inaccuracies. [Due to] a lack of advice regarding geographic problems, complaints over the border would not end for more than a century afterward" (117–18).

From a US historical perspective, on the other hand, the Treaty of Guadalupe Hidalgo involved Mexico's agreement "to cede California and New Mexico to the United States and acknowledge the Rio Grande as the boundary of Texas. In return, the United States promised to assume the claims of its citizens against Mexico and pay the Mexicans $15 million."[46] In the American version of this history, the dominant narrative emphasizes the right to land acquisition, whereas the Moyano account focuses on "inaccuracies" and "complaints" regarding the results of the treaty and the boundaries it set. Chicano intellectual Alfred Arteaga carries this criticism of the results of the treaty even further as he suggests that "in order to project a narrative of the apex of democracy, the history of the U.S. military conquest of northern Mexico is written as a simply financial transaction . . . the conquest of Northern Mexico was not imperialism, it was a bloodless transfer of an unpopulated territory."[47]

Genaro M. Padilla presents another view of this same historical event:

> "When Mexicans were colonized by the United States, when, as David Weber writes, they were 'quickly conquered, subjected to an alien political system in an alien culture,'[48] they immediately gave utterance to the threat of social erasure. The rupture of everyday life experienced by some 75,000 people who inhabited the far northern provinces of Mexico in 1846 opened a terrain of discursive necessity in which fear and resentment found language in speeches and official documents that warned fellow citizens to accommodate themselves to the new regime or at least to remain quiet lest they be hurt or killed outright."[49]

From Padilla's standpoint this collision between Mexico and the United States most significantly had to do with its effects on thousands of people. This was a conflict concerning land, but it was a conflict that "colonized" and "conquered" the people of this land.

For example, as we have seen in "Early Life," the narrator recounts her great-grandmother's response to colonization and conquest: "Texas is ours. Texas is our home."[50] This history of conquest was to become a "nightmare" for those Mexicans who lived in the far northern provinces, where the "ever-invasive North Americans . . . wanted not to share the map but to redraw it entirely."[51] What ultimately becomes evident from these different perspectives on history are the complex and contradictory memories of different semiotic worlds that are present in the retelling or translation of history. Indeed, as a result of cultural collisions such as the war between Mexico and the United States, concepts of history are reformulated as new systems of self-description reorganize previous perceptions regarding stages of history.

History and Memory: Cultural Collisions and Social Transformations

As we have seen in chapter 2, the works of González, Jaramillo, Wilbur-Cruce, and Ponce involve the narration of the life story and the description of geographical spaces and the home and homeland in areas of Texas, New Mexico, Arizona, and California from an "other" point of view. Therefore, these works represent a type of textual expression that functions not only as a registry of information, but also as a generator of meaning. This meaning, as we will see in the following sections, is presented by narrators who take on the role of interlocutors who attempt to communicate their "own" point of view regarding history, life, and traditions of Texas, New Mexico, Arizona, and California Hispanic communities, as well as those of "other" cultural groups within these geographical areas. In addition they provide information about the role of the church and religious practice, as well as the process of education. Thus, the four narratives under consideration here can be interpreted as literary texts that involve a multi-structured message.

This message is not simply the history of self, but rather the response of the individual and collective "we" to social transformations brought about by cultural collisions between two related systems. Although all of the above-mentioned elements make up the various layers of the text, in this chapter I will focus only on history and the life and traditions of "other" cultural groups evident in each of the narratives. My intention in the present section, therefore, is to examine certain historical fragments that are recounted in each narrative as a means of understanding a particular semiotic space that involves the intersection of various strata of experience.

"Early Life and Education" and *Dew on the Thorn*

Because cultural space is organized in an unequal matter—that is, with a nucleus of information that represents the dominant perspective and the periphery representing marginal points of view—it is pertinent to examine González's "Early Life" and *Dew on the Thorn* and the way they use literary language as a means of describing a particular social reality. The autobiographer of "Early Life and Education" initiates the communicative process by focusing on her perspective regarding the effects of the Treaty of Guadalupe Hidalgo and the US Civil War. That is, she refers to key moments in a family history that involved land claims in the border region of southern Texas, a history that is echoed in the fictional narrative *Dew on the Thorn*.

In reference to her mother's ancestors, who were originally Texas landowners, the autobiographical narrator stresses the following: "After the Treaty of Guadalupe Hidalgo, fearing the reprisals of the new conquerors, most of the *colonizadores* on the Texas side crossed the Rio Grande to live among their kinsmen in Mexico."[52] The *colonizadores* she refers to are those families, like hers, who had either Spanish or Mexican land grants that were acquired during a period of Texas history that was marked by a "Hispanic historical context and responded to Spanish-Mexican social, economic, political, and religious norms."[53] Ultimately these land grants were challenged as a result of the Mexican War.

Article 8 of the Treaty of Guadalupe Hidalgo, for example, determined that Mexicans who had been established in territories that were now part of the United States "shall be free to continue where they now reside, or to remove at any time to the Mexican Republic, retaining the property which they possess in the said territories, or disposing thereof, and removing the proceeds wherever they please, without their being subjected, on this account, to any contribution, tax, or charge whatever."[54] This article further stipulated the obligation of those who remained in the dominated territory to declare their decision to "either retain the title and rights of Mexican citizens, or acquire those of citizens of the United States." Those who did not declare their decision within the one-year time limit would automatically be considered US citizens, a situation that is further clarified in Article 9: "The Mexicans who, in the territories aforesaid, shall not preserve the character of citizens of the Mexican Republic, conformably with what is stipulated in the preceding article, shall be incorporated into the Union of the United States." This same article also provided for "the free exercise of their religion without restriction." These articles can be seen as historical texts that emanate from the semiotic space of the United States, and, as such, they generate two types of meaning. They proclaimed that Mexicans who chose to remain on their land were faced not only with annexation into another world sphere, but also with forced assimilation into another culture. It is precisely this threat of American incursions into Texas that informs both "Early Life" and *Dew on the Thorn*, which are marked repeatedly with the cry of "Texas is ours."

Both of these treaty articles would seem to guarantee property and civil rights of Mexicans who chose to remain in those territories that came under US control. However, as suggested by Armando Alonzo in his article "Mexican-American Land Grant Adjudication," many of the land grants held by Mexicans were long-standing and "the treaty provided no standard for validation of land grants."[55] Ultimately the state of Texas rather than the federal government decided the way land titles should be settled. Therefore, the narrator's reference to "fear of reprisals" as the reason for abandoning family land that had been conquered by the United States involves a memory that points to the limits of the Treaty of Guadalupe Hidalgo. Thus, although the treaty is a text that communicates a message declaring rights and guarantees for Mexicans, "Early Life" generates a different meaning, one that contests those very guarantees.

Although the information registered in "Early Life" does not present a detailed account of the autobiographer's ancestors and their return to Mexico, *Dew on the Thorn* is more clearly marked with historical references that are intended to restore memory of a cultural past. It is worth noting that in his introduction to *Dew on the Thorn*, editor José Limón points out that a letter written by González to an editor in Pennsylvania states her intention to initiate her narrative by focusing on 1906, a date at the beginning of the century when "Americans from the middle west came in great numbers to develop what is now the Rio Grande Valley." She further notes that "they found these ranchmen, impregnable in their ranches, holding tenaciously to the traditions of their forbears. What I have tried to do is to show life as it existed then."[56] However, rather than initiating the text with a reference to 1906, the autobiographer chooses to refer to 1904, the year she was born, and a description of the Olivares family, which remained in possession of "the land which His Excellency Revilla Gigedo, Viceroy of New Spain, had deeded to the head of the family in 1764.[57] The grant which extended into territory destined later to become Texas, was located thirty miles east of the Rio Grande, and ambled leisurely along through fertile plains and grass-covered prairies within five miles of the Nueces River."[58] There are also references to the Mexican Revolution and "the newly created Mexican republic" and the "astonishing news" regarding Americanos who were colonizing "country north of the Nueces" (6). Thus, from the beginning of the narrative, the reader is presented with the intersection of the three semiotic worlds of Spain, Mexico, and the United States, and the text presents characters who divide their world into "our own" space and "other" space.

The fictional Olivares family is depicted as living in "peace and contentment," and even the Mexican War of Independence did not seem to interrupt a life that is described as one of "easy-going placidity" (6). This cultural space seems to be harmoniously organized, yet the Olivares family can be seen as representing the fate of those who chose to remain on "their" land. For example, Cesareo expresses his surprise at the incursions of the Americanos, the "blue-eyed strangers," into "land that was not theirs." The narrative then points out that "the foreigners had openly declared their wish to take the country for themselves and many battles had been fought between them and the Mexicans" (6). Here we see a clear sense of division between the semiotic world of the Texas Mexicans and those outside that space; that is, this place is described as a harmonious sphere being invaded by cultural others who are perceived as "strangers." Because these outsiders desired "land that was not theirs," they were perceived as hostile and dangerous by the Texas Mexicans, "who resented the conquest of their territory" (8). This negative perception of the Americanos is further registered within the text as cultural collisions between members of the Olivares family and Americans who had taken over land in the Texas borderlands. In addition the reader is also told of the "constant warfare waged along the frontier" that resulted in Don Cesareo's action to "abandon the land won by the sweat and blood of his ancestors" (9), a reference that coincides with family history evident in the "Early Life" text.

"Early Life" presents only a brief historical reference to the autobiographer's grandfather, who "at the close of the Civil War returned to Texas to regain or buy some of what had been their land."[59] This emphasis concerning the recuperation of land is also evident in *Dew on the Thorn*, which narrates that with the close of the American Civil War, "the State of Texas had recognized Doña Ramona's rights to the land where the Olivareño was located, sixty thousand acres in all; but the land on the Nueces was gone. . . . It had been appropriated by a powerful man, a cattle baron of the state."[60] Here the fictional text points to the return of Texas Mexicans to the "land of their fathers," a land that eventually was inhabited by people from "Virginia, Alabama, Kentucky, and the Carolinas, people of culture who had been impoverished by the Civil War" (10). Of particular importance here is the mention of the borderland areas of the Rio Grande and Nueces River, which is the area where the histories of the semiotic systems of Mexico and the United States come into contact.

Further mention of the intersection of cultural spaces within the borderland is also evident later in the text. Chapter 13 of *Dew on the Thorn*, for example, points to a school that had been set up at the Olivareño ranch. Although the ranch is described as situated in Texas, the school day began with the singing of the Mexican national anthem. Indeed, the narrative recounts that once these students reached the age of twenty-one, "of their own accord they crossed the Río Grande into Mexico; those born in Texas to naturalize themselves as Mexican citizens; the others to pay allegiance to the land of their birth and reinforce their citizenship" (144). This passage alludes to the realities of historical processes that have resulted in changing borders and, therefore, a cultural memory that emanates from the space of the borderlands where there is an emphasis on Texas as an area hostile to Mexican identity. The Olivareño ranch, then, is presented as a "cultured" space of individuation based on a Mexican sense of identity, yet once the land is invaded by the "newcomers" it is considered tainted by a foreign presence. It is pertinent to note, then, that the history evident in this text represents the "newcomers" as the invading "other," whereas it is the Tejanos (Texas Mexicans) who are marginalized in their own territory, which is eventually dominated by an Anglo presence.

The narrative concludes with a final reference that laments the intrusion of the Americans into what had been a Mexican sphere: "These people, who were coming in crowds, were not helping the situation with their attitude towards the Mexican population. Perhaps they resented the air of reserve and arrogance with which the Texas-Mexicans received them. . . . But trouble there was to be. . . . It would be not only an economic and social strife, but a racial struggle as well. It would be a contest between an aggressive, conquering, material people, and a passive, proud, volatile race. It would be a struggle between the new world and the old, for the Texas-Mexican had retained more than any other people, old world traditions, customs, and ideals" (175). This textual registry of a social reality presents discursive markers such as "trouble," "strife," and "struggle," which point to the history of a semiotic sphere that is marked by a cultural memory of collision. But it is the description of the Americans as "aggressive" and "conquering" in contrast to the Texas Mexicans as "passive" that demonstrates historical interplay between two cultural spheres in which the Americans are signaled as guilty intruders who force a way of life on the Texas Mexican people. Indeed, as Don Francisco tells his son, "The *Americanos* bring a new age . . . it will not be long now before this land will be invaded by the newcomers; it will not be long before you will become an alien in what you once considered the heritage of your ancestors" (178). It is through information of this sort that we can perceive the type of meaning generated by the text, a meaning based on cultural memory that communicates a different version of reality and therefore contests history established by the dominant sphere. Thus, the text functions as a different type of observer. Indeed, by focusing on violations and anomalies that have taken place as part of the historical process, the text intervenes as a mediator as it attempts to restructure the American reader's historical perspective.

Romance of a Little Village Girl

A focus on the historical junctures and the results of the Treaty of Guadalupe Hidalgo and ultimate US dominance of Mexico's northern frontier is also evident in the historical memory recounted in Jaramillo's *Romance* text. Like "Early Life" and *Dew on the Thorn*, the autobiographical narrator as observer presents clear references to the intersection of three semiotic worlds—Spain, Mexico, and the United States. As a result of these intersections the cultural space of New Mexico referred to in the narrative involves different types of identities: Spanish, New Mexican Hispano, Mexican, and Anglo.[61]

As I have mentioned previously, the historical references that initiate the text point to early Spanish exploration of the area as the narrator communicates a tone that exalts "Queen Isabel of Spain" and the "brave," "intrepid" explorers such as Cortez, Coronado, Oñate, and De Vargas. The purpose of these references has to do with the autobiographer's insistence on a Spanish rather than a Mexican heritage, in spite of the fact that she was born fifty-seven years after Mexico's independence from Spain. As suggested by Gonzales-Berry and Maciel, this tendency to emphasize a Spanish heritage is an attempt to exalt European lineage rather than Mexican and therefore indigenous roots.[62] I would further suggest that because the period between Mexican independence from Spain in 1821 and the signing of the Treaty of Guadalupe Hidalgo in 1848 represents a lapse of only twenty-seven years, the cultural memory of this region regarding its sense of identity is one that is more closely tied to Spain than to Mexico.

Within the preface to her text, the autobiographer directs the reader's attention to her home, the valley of the Arroyo Hondo River, as "situated to the northern part of the state of New Mexico, hemmed in by high mountains and hills, sheltered from the contamination of the outside world, [where] the inhabitants lived peacefully, preserving the customs and traditions of their ancestors."[63] Implicit in this passage, which emphasizes New Mexico's separation from the "outside world," is a desire on the narrator's part to communicate information regarding a particular historical and cultural context—that is, this area's remote position in New Spain, which resulted in "a unique pattern of social, cultural, and political traditions that would condition and shape its history and society."[64] The narrator is certainly emphasizing New Mexico's history, which included 300 years of Spanish dominance, but also a pride in her knowledge with respect to its relatively autonomous development, which resulted in "cultural maintenance . . . of traditions, language, land holdings, political participation, ethnic identity, and individual way of life" of the Hispanic people.[65]

In contrast to the positive tone used to describe Spanish explorers, and the autobiographer's privileging of her Hispano identity, she communicates a different perspective about Mexico as she complains that once "Mexico had won its independence from Spain under the leadership of Gen. Iturbides [*sic*], the Mexican government concerned itself but little about this northern province, except in collecting heavy taxes from its inhabitants" (6). She continues this historical reference by noting that "the United States government, learning of its rich resources, cast a covetous eye westward." She then points to the year 1846, when the United States "sent Gen. Kearney [*sic*] with his army to capture the capital, Santa Fe. This was easily accomplished. Gov. Armijo with his soldiers had already abandoned the capital to its fate and left for El Paso" (6).

Ultimately, in recounting past history, the autobiographer presents her own observations to the reader: "The people had no means to resist the intruders. . . . Cannons boomed announcing the conquest of New Mexico by Gen. Kearney [*sic*]" (6). Her description of this conquest contrasts with General Kearny's proclamation as leader of the "conquering" US Army: "I have come amongst you by the orders of my government, to take possession of your country, and extend over it the laws of the

United States. We consider it, and have done so for some time, a part of the territory of the United States. We come amongst you as friends—not as enemies; as protectors—not as conquerers. . . . Henceforth I absolve you from all allegiance to the Mexican government, and from all obedience to General Armijo."[66] As we can see, the narrator of *Romance* intervenes with her own contesting view, which enters into dialogue with the reader regarding this historical juncture that she perceives as a situation of intrusion and conquest. Kearny's text, on the other hand, demonstrates different discursive markers; that is, he uses words such as "friends" and "protectors" to describe his invading army. Kearny also states: "We come as friends, to better your condition and make you a part of the Republic of the United States. We mean not to murder you or rob you of your property. Your families shall be free of molestation; your women secure from violence. . . . I advise you to attend to your domestic pursuits, cultivate industry, be peaceable and obedient to the laws. . . . I hereby proclaim that, being in possession of Santa Fe, I am therefore in possession of all New Mexico."[67] He once again states "We come as friends," but the real intention of this interlocutor is to instill fear into the listener. Although he claims that families "shall be free of molestation; your women secure from violence," the fact that these actions are even mentioned is intended to communicate a sense of threat to the dominated, who are expected to "be peaceable and obedient," or, in other words, to accept a subaltern position in their own land.

This proclamation determined that the people of New Mexico were "granted" US citizenship. However, this type of discourse also signifies that the Nuevomexicanos, who now became part of the United States, would be expected to adopt traditions, governmental policies, and the language of the colonizer. The narrator of *Romance* initially communicates a position regarding the helplessness of the Nuevomexicanos before the Anglo conqueror who would attempt to force a different way of life on a people. It is interesting to note as well the way in which Kearny's invading army is presented in a negative light, whereas her description of prior Spanish conquest of the area of New Mexico is perceived as an "exciting adventure" of brave conquerors who would "replant the seed of Spanish culture and faith."[68]

This point of view communicated by the autobiographer is further visible as she consistently chooses to privilege her Spanish heritage instead of a Mexican one. Indeed, the memories recorded in her text regarding Mexico are generally negative. To her Mexico is a "languid, exotic land of leisure that lies drowsing under scorching suns, . . . [a] paradise of souls, where the sole ambition of most is to obtain just enough for their daily needs" (106). Characterization of Mexico as a "languid" and "drowsing" land contrasts with her idealized references to that "land across the Western sea" that was home to the Spanish race. Thus, home is New Mexico and, in spite of the cannons that announced the victory of the American invaders, it is only the cultural memory derived from the semiosphere of Spain that she considers as positive and worth being preserved within her life story.[69] As we have seen in a previous passage, the autobiographical narrator critiques the "covetous eye" with which the United States viewed New Mexico. This perception indicates a different sort of collision within the sphere of New Mexico—the discovery of gold and all the effects brought about by this: "A boom struck the canyon. Two log cabins, those of Twining and Amizett, sprang up among majestic pine and aspen groves. Miners lured by the glamour of gold ore filled the canyon. William-Fraser's Company was formed and put up a mill, bringing the ore down the mountain in buckets by cables. Riot and speed increased as years went by, drowning the quiet that had surrounded the villages before" (8). Once again the narrator laments the intrusion of outsiders into what had been a secluded space. This historical reference, and the meaning it generates regarding the narrator's position, stands in clear contrast to the traditional US perspective that notes that once gold was discovered in places like California and New Mexico, "a flood of emigrants from the East and several foreign nations arrived by ship or wagon train. . . . The gold they unearthed spurred the national economy."[70] American historical observations represent expansion as positive since it was tied to an increase in economic development. The text of the *Romance* narrator, on the other hand, emphasizes another result. Incursion of mining prospectors into the "picturesque villages" of the Taos valley is perceived as a collision between the riotous life practiced by "gold seekers" who introduced "Anglo liquor" and the Hispanos of New Mexico who were accustomed to drinking "the soft grape wine of the Rio Abajo."

The narrator continues to delineate a symbolic border that separates these Anglo "gold seekers" from the Hispanos, who from her standpoint represent the nucleus of life in New Mexico. Indeed, from the outset of her text she explains that "our families now remained more secluded in our enclosed *placitas* courtyards,"[71] thus suggesting the way in which they separated their own space, "our" space, from that of Anglo settlers who began to move into this area after 1848. We might ask whether this seclusion and enclosure was self-imposed. Maciel and Gonzales-Berry have suggested that "eager to consolidate its power, the recently arrived Euro-American population engaged in classic patterns of colonial domination, relegating the native Nuevomexicano population to second-class status."[72] Thus, we can assume that the area of the *placita* represents a cultural site where members of the Hispano community congregated. However, after New Mexico became part of the United States, these spaces would be marked as "other" or as non-semiotic by the dominant Euro-American invaders.

Ultimately the type of textual commentary that I have highlighted points to a new type of reality that defines what Arteaga has termed "the plot for the future."[73] That is, the Hispanos of New Mexico would necessarily have to accommodate their lifestyle to the effects of Anglo incursions and the resulting dominant narrative, which emphasizes US expansion and progress. However, as a response to this narrative, not only does the *Romance* narrator present her own textual perspective on history, she resists this incursion, as I will discuss later, by creating a text that focuses on the cultural memory of New Mexico.[74] Once again we see evidence of the narrator as a mediator who enters into dialogue with the reader by inserting those aspects of Nuevomexicano cultural memory that generate new meaning, meaning that counterbalances history that occupies the center of a dominant sphere.

A Beautiful, Cruel Country

In my previous observations I have argued that "Early Life," *Dew on the Thorn*, and *Romance of a Little Village Girl* are texts that reveal the perspective of an autobiographer and observer who critiques Anglo migration into Texas and New Mexico. Wilbur-Cruce's *A Beautiful, Cruel Country*, on the other hand, communicates reminiscences of a way of life that initially seems to privilege a history of Anglo domination in the Arizona Territory. The narrator chooses to begin her text with a chapter entitled "Grandfather Wilbur and His Friends," which focuses on Anglo incursions into the Arizona Territory prior to the US Civil War. However, we also find numerous references throughout the text that mark this space as a multilevel system that involves dominant structures such as those of Spain and the United States as well as substructures that refer to the Indians and Mexican laborers.

The text created by Wilbur-Cruce begins by recalling Ignacio Pesqueira, who had been governor of Sonora for twenty years. The narrator offers little detail about Pesqueira other than commenting on his reputation as the "Tigre de Mejico" who "was widely feared as a merciless man, little better than a barbarian."[75] This particular reference to a Mexican governing official and the discursive use of the term "barbarian" to describe him echoes the *Romance* text in which the narrator refers to Mexico as "languid" and "drowsing." In both texts we perceive a message that communicates negative undertones with regard to Mexico.

After this commentary about Pesqueira, the autobiographical narrator of *A Beautiful, Cruel Country* then notes that in 1865, territorial governor A. P. K. Safford and her grandfather Wilbur "traveled to Sonora to look at some mining properties" (4). Thus, from the beginning of her text, she communicates a cultural memory that is based on the relation between Sonora and the Arizona Territory, but also the fact that she is a descendant of a man who was involved with political leaders of this period. Unlike "Early Life," *Dew on the Thorn*, and *Romance*, which emphasize the semiotic world of Spain and those who came to the new world as conquerors, here the narrator initiates her reminiscences by focusing on the intersection of the world of Sonora and that of Arizona.

The first chapter of this narrative continues to convey additional historical information regarding personalities such as Charles Poston and Gen. Samuel P. Heintzelman, who were shareholders in the Sonora Exploring and Mining Company and friends of the narrator's grandfather: "Grandfather Wilbur was a physician, a graduate of Harvard Medical College. He came to Arizona Territory sometime in the early 1860's with Charles Poston, who was a good friend of his. Within a year or two, Poston had become manager of the Cerro Colorado Mining Company, and Grandfather Wilbur had become the company physician" (3). The autobiographer then goes on to explain the history of the mine; that is, after this first mention of the Cerro Colorado Mining Company, she points out that its original name had been Sonora Exploring Company only later to be renamed the Arizona Mining Company. Thus, the references to Pesqueira, Poston, and Heintzelman, as well as the change in the name of the mine, are relevant discursive markers that generate meaning with regard to the historical collisions between the spheres of Mexico and the United States.

So as to illustrate the layers of history and those historical figures evident in the semiotic space represented in the text, it is interesting to note Miguel Tinker Salas's view that by the 1850s, "small numbers of Anglo-Americans [would] trickle into the Arizona-Sonora border region in search of mining opportunities. Border interaction reflected politics and power relations."[76] These power relations are observable within this text as the narrator specifically points to history regarding economic expansion during the 1860s and those men such as Poston who took on positions of power. Furthermore, one of the ultimate effects of this incursion into the area is the displacement of Amerindians.

Further examples of these power positions can be found within the text as the narrator recounts that for a time Poston managed the Cerro Colorado Mining Company, and Heintzelman, who was an investor, also became the superintendent of the mine. It is relevant to note that from an Anglo perspective, Charles D. Poston has been considered the "Father of Arizona."[77] Historically he is known for the expeditions he made into Sonora in search of mines that had been abandoned by the Spanish due to numerous Indian raids. As suggested in *The Mission, Means and Memories of Arizona Miners*, those traveling with Poston "sailed up the Gulf of California and traveled overland to the Tubac area where they located previously worked mines. Returning to San Francisco, Poston was able to get enough financial backing to form the Sonora Exploring and Mining Company and open several mines in the Tubac area. By 1858 Poston employed more than a thousand Mexican miners."[78] Thus, Poston can be seen as a figure that represents an Anglo presence as the nucleus of economic power within the semiotic space of Arizona during the territorial period from 1848 to 1912.

This reference to the Mexican miners employed by Poston also coincides with the autobiographer's recollections regarding Mexican Grandfather Vilducea who "used to haul freight for the mine." Indeed she mentions her grandfather's memories about this area: "There were pieces of machinery scattered like rosary beads, all the way between the mine and the Rio Grande."[79] Once again we find a discursive reference that signals the historical process of Anglo settlement that involved territorial dominance of this area as well as economic expansion in the field of mining. It is important to point out, however, that many of the Mexicans, like Grandfather Vilducea, came from Sonora into the Arizona Territory due to political unrest in Mexico. As the autobiographer explains: "Grandfather was a victim of the Mexican Revolution at that time. He was an officer in the former government and now the ones in power were hunting him" (40). Thus, as Grandfather Vilducea recalls, "I decided to go north to the Territorio. And that's what I call a sharp and painful ending" (40). This type of reference touches on a history of the intersection of life experiences from two semiotic spheres, which also include historical memories about leaving Sonora to make a new life in the Arizona Territory, a life which, as Grandfather Vilducea notes, involved "a rough painful beginning" (40).

The narrator continues to emphasize the border as she describes ranching activities: "The rest of the afternoon was spent clipping the manes and the tails of horses that Roberto and Damián had brought in from the range that morning. The horses belonged to other ranches; some were from Mexico. The Mexican boundary was not fenced at that time and stock went back and forth at will" (186). Here the boundary is presented as open, "not fenced," thus presenting a point of view that minimizes the effect of the border on the ranching communities of the area.[80] Indeed, this discursive reference to movement between the spaces of the Arizona Territory and Mexico "at will" stands in stark contrast to the sphere of the mining industry, which is marked by Anglo administrative control in an industry that made use of Mexican laborers.

These allusions to the border suggest its functions as a semiotic mechanism that is responsible for contact between dominant spheres and those that are considered non-semiotic. It is also important to note that these passages are registries of information that coincide with the history of this area, specifically with regard to Sonora prior to the Mexican-American War and the Gadsden Purchase, which resulted in the demarcation of new borders.[81] For example, as suggested by Tinker Salas, "Separated from southern Mexico by distance and geography, Sonora interacted with areas later annexed by the United States. Long before the border with the United States materialized, exchanges with the north proved critical to the economic survival of the state."[82] Hence, this history of "exchanges" and interaction evident within *A Beautiful, Cruel Country* point to the dynamism of the semiosphere in which cultural memory records the effects and adjustments that resulted from historical collisions and changing borders.

In addition to those parts of the text concerned with an Anglo and Mexican presence in this area, the autobiographer also points to her Spanish ancestors, especially in the final chapter of the narrative. Here she recounts her memory of a moment when as a young child she expressed distaste for her relative Ruta Moraga's heavy beard and pleaded with her father not to "tell anybody that Ruta Moraga is your relative."[83] In this final moment in her life story the narrator notes her father's response: "'Eva!' said Father, laughing. 'And why not? We *are* related. Lieutenant Moraga was the very last conquistador to come to Arizona and he is one ancestor I'm very proud of'" (301). He continues to explain that Alférez José Joaquín Moraga was a blood relative who "traveled with Juán [*sic*] Bautista de Anza and they had beautiful horses and good saddles and dressed according to their rank" (301). He then points out that it was their relative Moraga who "had left San Miguel together with their families, horses, cattle, chickens and masses of equipment to go and explore the north" (302). This passage, which includes discursive references to *conquistadores* who were noted for their "beautiful horses," "good saddles," and a way of dressing that was in accord with their rank, is clearly reminiscent of the *Romance* text that refers to a cultural memory of Spanish conquerors in a positive light.

Of relevance in this text is the way in which the various semiotic spheres are represented. First of all, mention of Grandfather Wilbur, Poston, and Heintzelman in the beginning of the narrative and later references to de Anza and Moraga as *conquistadores* point a space marked by conquest first by Spain and then by the United States. This history of conquest and invasion resulted in cultural contact and it is precisely the way in which the autobiographical narrator presents family members—her Spanish, Anglo, and Mexican grandparents, her Anglo-Spanish father, and her Mexican mother, whom she often describes as having "indio" ways—that the reader is able to observe the consequences of a violent historical process.

Hoyt Street

My previous discussion highlights a semiosphere of texts that are heterogeneous in their attempt to take the reader on a journey through history in different areas of the Southwest and West. In a somewhat different format, the introductory "Note from the Author" in *Hoyt Street* mentions that the narrative deals with "a social history of sorts";[84] that is, she recalls history that deals with life in the barrio during the 1940s. So as to clarify the historical dimensions presented in this text, I would like to refer to time periods that have been classified. For example, Manuel G. Gonzales's text *Mexicanos: A History of Mexicans in the United States* points out that the period from 1900 to 1940 has been referred to as "the Great Migration" and the period between 1940 and 1963 has been classified as "the Rise of the Middle Class."[85] I would suggest that the period of the Great Migration is of particular importance in understanding the life of those Mexican immigrants who lived in the barrio referred to in *Hoyt Street*.[86]

The social history apparent in *Hoyt Street*, then, is different from the previously mentioned texts as it clearly points to this history of migration during the first thirty years of the twentieth century. For example, the autobiographer tells the reader that "most of the townspeople were Mexican immigrants, as were my parents, who had moved to Pacoima in the 1920s."[87] This date points to the end of the revolution in Mexico, which resulted in peasant discontent regarding "difficulty in acquiring land in an area where the hacienda system was so firmly entrenched" and where agrarian reform did not keep pace with demands of the landless.[88]

This historical process of immigration demonstrates the penetration of a foreign cultural system into the dominant system of the United States, where the Mexican immigrant was forced to look for economic opportunities and to elaborate a new way of life as a means of adapting to a different cultural system. One of the ways in which the dominant system dealt with this foreign presence was through the "politics of spatial segregation [that] led to the creation of the barrio where a vibrant community life developed in the spaces of the neighborhood."[89] Indeed, the social communicative focus of the autobiographical narrator of *Hoyt Street* is to present her text as meaning generator with regard to the barrio and its border position outside of mainstream American life: "The barrio, as I knew it, extended from San Fernando Road to Glenoaks Boulevard on the east and from Filmore and Pierce streets on the north."[90] Mention of the four streets that set the outer limits or borders of the barrio points precisely to the delimited character of a semiosphere of experience that the autobiographer intends to translate for the reader.

One of the major aspects she chooses to highlight about life in the barrio has to do with her extended family. She describes a separate part of the family home, "the men's rooms," where her brothers slept. She also mentions that her uncles "who emigrated as braceros, also slept in the men's rooms. As was the custom, they first stayed with a close relative, in this case my father. Much later their sons laid claim to the beds used earlier by their fathers" (8). The narrator also explains that "Mexicans were known to be hard workers, muy trabajadores. At that time few braceros, workers imported from Mexico, lived in the north, although many lived in Pacoima. I had heard that Mexicans were a cheap source of labor. Mostly we were poor folks who welcomed the extra money earned in summer" (170). The barrio is discursively represented as a space where many of the Mexican laborers lived and the autobiographer creates a text that enters into dialogue with the reader as she clarifies that because these immigrants were poor, they were used by farm owners who benefited from this "cheap" labor source. She also communicates her pride in the fact that these people from Mexico formed a community and, like her father, were "muy trabajadores."[91]

Emphasis on the Mexican laborers and the effect of this lifestyle on their families is evident in the chapter entitled "Walnuts." Here the narrator explains that "in the summer many Mexican families in Pacoima harvested crops. Picking fruit entre familia was what folks did come June, July, and August" (169). The autobiographer further describes what she considers "one long adventure" when "one year in late September, my father, coaxed by his compadre Rocky, arranged for us to pick walnuts for Mister Berenson, a walnut grower from Camarillo, who was kind and considerate of his workers. He paid well, and at the end of the season gave each family a sack of walnuts in addition to a well-earned cash bonus" (170). Although she describes Mister Berenson as "kind" and "considerate," it is relevant to point out that the laborers and their families were segregated: "the workers' camp was next to the main house, beneath a walnut grove. It consisted of corrugated tin buildings separated into units of two rooms each: a kitchen and a large bathroom" (173). Thus, the confines of the worker's camp imply another delimited space with a border standing between the worker and the space of the Anglo farmer Mr. Berenson.

The narrator clarifies that her father did not allow his wife or daughters to work, and she also notes that one year, "as part of a program to provide education to migrant kids (as we were identified), we were enrolled in a school in Camarillo . . . [where] students were all blond Anglo's [*sic*], the children of growers and other local people." She further explains that "our stained hands betrayed us as migratory workers; our imperfect English told of a lack of education" (180). These textual references point to the autobiographer's intention to emphasize the metaphorical intersection between the semiotic and the extra-semiotic—that is, between the Anglo sphere and that of the Mexican immigrant. Allusions to the world of the migrant worker in the barrio and the workers' camps demonstrate an intention to convey a particular family history as a means of representing a larger social history and collective memory. *Hoyt Street* clearly emphasizes the immigrant experience in California and therefore greatly contrasts with *Dew on the Thorn* and *Romance*, which present a history of people whose way of life changed as a result of American invasion and settlements in the area of Texas and New Mexico. Instead this text presents the life of those who formed part of the semiotic space of Mexico but who ultimately emigrated north into the area of California. Therefore, although this narrative represents the voice of the autobiographical "I," as a border autobiography its message is multi-vocal in that it presents the voice of a cultural collectivity, one that is considered as a peripheral semiotic formation in the space of California.

Representation of the Cultural "Other"

My claim thus far is that the border autobiography is not simply a text that deals with the individual life story, rather it can be seen as a multi-layered text that generates different types of meanings. Indeed, semiotic space, as noted by Lotman, "is full of conglomerates of elements, that can be found in the most diverse relations with each other."[92] These elements have to do with the different dialectics of memory apparent in the semiotic space that is symbolically presented in the border autobiography. The texts created by González, Jaramillo, Wilbur-Cruce, and Ponce focus on numerous aspects related to the history of a cultural collectivity that exists as a substructure in relation to the dominant sphere of American experience. Further analysis of the cultural memory evident in these texts, however, reveals evidence of another type of history, one that involves "other" cultural groups that also form part of the complex and heterogeneous picture of life alluded to in the border autobiography.

"Early Life" and *Dew on the Thorn,* for example, transmit information regarding "peasants," "ranch hands," and "*peones*." *Romance* makes specific references to Indians and Mexicans as "other" cultural groups, and important passages of *A Beautiful, Cruel Country* point to "Indian humanity." *Hoyt Street* is similar to both "Early Life" and *Dew on the Thorn* where the autobiographer communicates her perceptions regarding Anglo as "other." In *Hoyt Street*, the cultural "other" is situated outside of the Mexican community of the barrio, which functions as an enclosed space similar to that of the family ranch evident in "Early Life," *Dew on the Thorn*, and *A Beautiful, Cruel Country*.

In the analysis that follows I spotlight those segments of each text where the narrator describes certain cultural groups as outside the boundary of her "own" semiotic sphere. However, it is also possible to observe a relation between these distinct groups that corresponds to what Alfred Schütz has referred to as "multiple realities."[93] That is, everyday life involves intersubjective, shared, and common experiences that have to do with our surroundings, our ancestors, and our cultural origins, all of which constitute reality. Like Lotman, Schütz also suggests that the "world within our actual and potential reach" (245) is one that is recalled, hence meaning is conferred upon a world that also includes interactions with those outside the common cultural sphere. Therefore, my intention in the present section is to point out the way in which each autobiographer presents herself in relation to "other" realities or those who are considered members of a peripheral semiotic space.

"Early Life and Education" and *Dew on the Thorn*

For the most part, "Early Life" details those moments in the autobiographer's life that are concerned with a family history of settlement in Texas and González's own process of educational development. Because the text is only five pages in length, very little information regarding those outside of the family household is mentioned. However, there is a brief passage that presents the reader with the narrator's memory regarding "long walks with father" to the "homes of the cowboys and the ranch hands" who worked at Las Víboras: "There was Tío Patricio, the mystic; Chon, who was so ugly, poor fellow, he reminded us of a toad; Old Remigio who wielded the *metate* with dexterity of peasant women and made wonderful *tortillas*. Tía Chita whose stories about ghosts and witches made our hair stand on end, Pedro, the hunter and traveler, who had been as far as Sugar Land and had seen black people with black wool for hair, one-eyed Manuelito, the ballad singer, Tío Camilo; all furnished ranch lore in our young lives."[94] All of the individuals mentioned in this passage form part of a semiotic sphere where Texas Mexican landowners and their families formed the nucleus of ranch life, whereas those who worked on Las Víboras ranch, the cowboys and ranch hands, were those who occupied a peripheral position within this space. It is interesting to note that the autobiographer communicates a romantic view of those who make up this life space. For example, the text introduces the reader to a "mystic," the maker of tortillas, a storyteller, a "hunter and traveler," and a "ballad singer." Each is singled out because they contribute to "ranch lore" that formed part of the autobiographer's early life memories. These songs and stories contribute to the cultural memory of a unique border community that is portrayed in *Dew on the Thorn* and other texts authored by Jovita González, which, as suggested by Gloria Louise Velasquez, portray a world that is "a closed and cohesive social unit isolated from American culture."[95]

Like "Early Life," *Dew on the Thorn* refers to "the founders of these border towns and ranches. . . . They were *gente de razón*," or those of Spanish descent.[96] The use of this term to refer to the rancheros, who are also described as having a "desirable character . . . of good family and well to do" (5), functions semiotically and discursively as a means of determining the symbolic border that exists between "the culture and civilization of the Spanish race" and the "*peones* and *vaqueros*" (5). Indeed, as suggested by Montejano, the *patrones* "maintained paternalistic relations with permanent *vaquero* workers. It was commonplace to find ranches with generations of workers on the ranch. Here the class distinctions between ranch owner and worker were clearly drawn, but these actors were bound to each other in a manner that tended to produce a sentiment of kinship. Such a bond tied the fate of the two classes and races together, making the ranch a self-sufficient and insular social world."[97] This "bond" or social relation between the ranch owner and those who worked for him is evident in the second chapter of the text, where the reader is told that Don Francisco de los Olivares intended "to make his ranch a miniature Mexico. His family was encouraged and expected to keep intact the customs and traditions of the mother country; the servants and *peones* were commanded to follow in the footsteps of their equals in Mexico."[98] This passage points directly to the intersection of two different spaces—that is, the Olivareño, which is situated in Texas and representative of a semiotic system that draws on the cultural memory of Mexico, and the enclosed system of the hacienda, where the *peon* led a life of submission to the landowner. This is further evident within the text as the reader is told that "the Olivares had brought them to Texas to work. They had been with the family for generations, obeyed the master's orders blindly and had no will of their own" (14). Here we find that in stark contrast to previous references regarding the founders of the border towns as "*gente de razón*," the *peones* are represented as capable only of blindly obeying their masters because they lacked a "will of their own." These discursive representations demonstrate what Montejano describes as the "*patrón-peón* relations characteristic of this region";[99] that is, this type of social relation mirrors Mexico's colonial past, one entailing the relative enslavement of indigenous groups by the conquering Spaniards.

In contrast to the subjugated position of the *peones*, the *vaqueros* were more independent of the landowner. Indeed, we find that "the landowner was merely the owner of the cattle he [the *vaquero*] punched. A social, racial, and economic gulf separated the *peones* from the landowner, but the *vaquero* might some day rise to the level of his more fortunate associate" (75). Velasquez has noted that the Texas Mexican *vaquero* can be seen as a positive symbol of border culture because he represents the "dual cultural heritage [of] a unique social reality," one that is registered in the text as part of a cultural memory that emphasizes the "social, racial and economic gulf" between different cultural groups.[100] In spite of the fact that the *vaquero* is represented positively in the text, the word "gulf" points clearly to a symbolic border that separates the aristocratic owner from the *peones*, and to some extent the *vaqueros* who worked on the ranch but did not own land.

Whereas the *peones* and *vaqueros* pertained to the closed space of the ranch owner and his family, they were also considered as part of the "Mexican race." On the other hand, the "war-like Indian tribes" in this "Indian infested region," this "wild Indian country," are situated outside the semiotic space of life on the Olivareño ranch. At the beginning of the text there is mention of early Spanish settlers such as José Escandón, who intended to "subdue the war-like Indian tribes."[101] There is no mention of the names of the Indian tribes that are encountered by the invading Spaniards. They are simply portrayed as standing in the way of Spanish settlement; therefore, the Indians can be understood as non-semiotic entities or realities that are external to the culture of the conqueror.

Later in the text, however, a different point of view is highlighted through allusions to the "past greatness of the indigenous races," especially the Aztecs and "the valiant prince Cuauhtemoc." In this case the text points not only to "Morelos, a man with Indian blood" but also to Benito Juárez, who is described as "a pure-blooded Indian." Ultimately we find references to Porfirio Diáz, a mestizo, and the "race of bronze, the race of strong heroic men" (145–46). Thus, although the Indians initially encountered by the Spaniards in their early explorations are considered as "war-like" and "wild," later in the text, the Indian is characterized as "strong" and "heroic." This change in perspective points to a new cultural reality, one that involves a history of racial mixing.

Those considered as the cultural "other" in the world sphere of the Olivareño ranch were the "*Americanos*, men from the north, who came seeking homes in a land that was not theirs" (6). Descriptions of the Americans as "blue-eyed barbarians who were the born enemies of anything Mexican or Spanish" (144) suggest that they are foreign elements and situated totally outside the semiotic spheres of Spanish and Texas Mexican settlements where a heritage of "old world traditions, customs, and ideals" (175) had been maintained. Ultimately, then, the semiotic space presented in this text is one that involves a plurality of cultural groups and different layers of cultural experience.

Romance of a Little Village Girl

Like "Early Life" and *Dew on the Thorn*, the *Romance* text presents a picture of a semiotic space marked by the presence of "other" cultural groups. In the very first chapter of the text, "The New Spanish Province," the autobiographer refers to the year 1680, when "the Indians rebelled against Spanish rule . . . and massacred the soldiers and missionaries."[102] Although this passage casts the Indians in a negative light, it is important to recall that the revolt of the Pueblo Indians, as suggested by Vélez-Ibañez, was the result of "the restrictions of a caste-ridden colonial regime" in which Indians were abused and exploited in a situation of forced labor by "upper-caste settlers."[103]

Romance continues with an account of the reconquest of New Mexico by the Spaniards, who are presented as heroes who fight against "hostile Indian tribes." The reconquered land is described as "a wilderness inhabited only by Indians," who are further referred to as "savages."[104] Although the text initially communicates a perspective of the Indians as rebellious "savages," Vélez-Ibáñez has also noted that "what developed between the segundos pobladores and native peoples was a common purpose: their defense against Utes, Apaches, and Navajos."[105] This is clearly reflected in the *Romance* text as the narrator recounts memories concerned with various Indian groups: "For two weeks before the San Geronimo feast day, fierce-looking, filthy Utes trekked slowly over rocky mountain trails from southern Colorado. From the Navajo country in north-western New Mexico came the aristocratic Navajos, riding better steeds. And the tamed Apaches arrived, seemingly peaceful but with their wild spirit still smouldering. . . . The friendly Picuris, Santa Claras, San Juans, Tesuques and other tribes arrived at Taos from the south."[106] This passage presents the reader with a view of a semiotic space where the relationship between Hispanos and Indians has evolved; that is, rather than the use of linguistic markers that label the Indians as "savages," we find references to the "fierce-looking" Utes, the "tamed" and wild-spirited Apaches, and the friendly tribes celebrating an occasion together with non-Indian members of society who participated in "the Spanish part of the fiesta" (21–22). The text presents the Feast of San Geronimo as an Indian feast, and, in contrast to previous negative characterization of the Indians, here they are described as "original Americans" who had built "four-story pueblos" that were known for their "architectural grandeur" (18). In spite of this seemingly positive view, however, the Indian is still considered as being outside the Spanish cultural sphere. Indeed, as the autobiographer notes, it was "at the plaza of Don Fernando de Taos where the Spanish part of the fiesta was in full swing" (21–22). Thus, although the Indian feast is presented as a colorful one that is "unrivaled in New Mexico" (20), it is separate from "the round of fiestas throughout the valley" (22).

Of further importance in this section is the narrator's commentary on the Taos Rebellion of 1847. Again, rather than presenting the Indian in a negative light, she recalls the "Indian and Spanish uprising against the American occupation . . . while the United States soldiers were bombarding the old pueblo church where the natives had fixed their stronghold" (18–19).[107] Here the text provides evidence of the plural dimension of life within a semiotic space that focuses on a "whole way of life" during a historical juncture in which Indian and Spanish cultural groups come together to fight a common enemy. What becomes evident, then, is the way in which the voice of the autobiographer functions as a source of information concerning racial strata in New Mexican society.

Mexicans are also presented as a cultural "other" situated outside of the autobiographer's sphere of experience. For example, in the chapter entitled "An Enchanting Trip," she describes her trip to Mexico and the "ancient city" of Chihuahua where her parents had been married. She then mentions visits to Aguas Calientes, Guadalajara, Queretaro, Zacatecas, Mexico City, and finally Cuernavaca, which she singles out as a city that "dates back to the time of Cortez, 1529" (102). Although she comments that the driver of the cart that transported them to their hotel was "a true Aztec type," she emphasizes her visit to the Palace of Cortés and a "grey monument to the memory of the intrepid Cortez." In addition, she emphasizes that inside the monument were "large pictures of Iturbides [*sic*], Hidalgo and other famous generals in their gorgeous uniforms, showing their proud Spanish heritage" (103).

Repetitive mention of Cortés and a "proud Spanish heritage" marks the collective cultural memory of a Spanish legacy functioning within the text. It is interesting, however, that Genaro Padilla has termed Jaramillo's focus on a Spanish heritage as "illusory given our understanding of the mestizo heritage of almost all New Mexicans." He suggests that the portrayal of self and the collectivity can be seen as providing a "symbolic identity" that was a way of speaking "resistance through the master romance of the colorful Spanish past."[108]

Indeed, the narrator's consistent concentration on a Spanish past stands in stark contrast to her description of a visit to a public market, where "one learned to know Mexico and its native people."[109] This portion of the text ends with Jaramillo's narration of a visit to the "*Arbol de la Noche Triste*, the tree of great antiquity under which Cortés shed tears that eventful, sad night when the Aztecs rose in arms and massacred his brave soldiers" (106). This clearly demonstrates a master romance that exalts Cortés and his "brave soldiers" in contrast to the Aztecs who are represented in a negative light, as those who interfere in the process of Spanish conquest. Noteworthy is how this negative representation of the Aztecs contrasts with positive references to "past greatness of the indigenous races" evident in *Dew on the Thorn*. The *Romance* autobiographer instead associates herself with the remains of a Spanish historical past that is present in Mexico, whereas the "Aztec" types who populate this "languid, exotic land of leisure" form an "other" reality that is extra-semiotic or outside the symbolic boundary of what she considers as a superior cultural reality.

Like "Early Life" and *Dew on the Thorn*, *Romance* presents the Anglos as intruders in a semiotic space that is identified as a place where "our interesting old customs" were celebrated. The autobiographer expresses her concern about preserving customs and stories as she tells the reader that she remembered over twenty-five of the stories told to her by her mother, which she "translated into English and published in book form under the title *Spanish Fairy Tales*" (167). Here the narrator can be seen as situated on the border of two worlds—the sphere of New Mexico, which has been populated by the cultural "other" or "these smart Americans" who thought they knew about Hispanic folklore, and the sphere of those, who like herself, truly knew about "our Spanish traditions" (170). Jaramillo's text stands as a message that she chooses to translate into the language of the dominant culture, thereby bringing about contact between those who form part of a Hispanic cultural collectivity and the Anglo "other," or those truly unable to appreciate "that richer era when our ancestors reigned supreme in this land, when the dress, manners and customs of Old Spain were echoed here in New Spain" (190).

A Beautiful, Cruel Country

Of the four texts considered in the present study, *A Beautiful, Cruel Country* stands out because of its detailed treatment of the various cultures that make up this area. As Vélez-Ibáñez has remarked: "Of all the regions of the Northern Greater Southwest, Sonora/Arizona's culture was shaped by its reliance on force of arms for basic survival, its continuous relations with the south, its very late disengagement from the Republic of Mexico, and the ease with which populations moved north to south and back again."[110] As I have mentioned, Wilbur-Cruce initiates her life story by referring to her Anglo grandfather and the important role he played in the settlement of Arizona's Arivaca Valley. However, this text also transmits information regarding various Indian tribes, their role within this area, and their cultural traditions. Of particular importance are those references that have to do with Indians who were constantly "coming and going in search of mere existence."[111]

To begin, the chapter entitled "Indian Country" points out that "El Cerro was the landmark of our Indian country region" (19). However, although this is a region marked by the presence of the Papagos, now called Tohono O'odham, this text, like "Early Life" and *Dew on the Thorn*, situates the rancheros as the nucleus of this semiotic space, whereas the Indians are presented as a cultural group that was "constantly on the move." Unlike the ranchers, who "stayed home," it was the Indians who "milled in and out of our valley occupied in traveling and newsbringing, in their 'industrial' or 'factory' activities, and in other, impenetrable 'Indian,' contemplative things." The narrator further notes that "Papagos" was "a name that had been foisted on them by the 'Europeans' (Americans, Mexicans and others who had trickled into Indian country), and therefore they never used the name, calling themselves and all other Indians, instead, Parientes, a word which meant 'kinsmen'" (19).

As these examples illustrate, two major perspectives permeate the narrative. First of all, the activities of this cultural group are described as "impenetrable 'Indian' things," representing a way of life that could not be understood by the Europeans, Americans, or Mexicans. Indeed, as the narrator suggests: "the Parientes, or most of them, were not 'settled.' Their centuries-old way of life had been disrupted gradually as European descendants settled the Southwest; most of them owned no land and had no 'trades' or ways of making a living that were recognized by the newcomers to the region" (19–20). This portion of the text, then, highlights a version concerned with Indian life in this area, one that the autobiographer claims to understand, but which is incomprehensible to the "newcomers," who are not familiar with this world sphere.

The narrator's empathy toward the plight of the Indians is also evident as she portrays her interactions with them. For example, she explains that she interacted often with Indian children "who came to play with me [and] taught me which branches made the best prayer sticks." Indeed, as she recalls, it was the Indian child Wahyanita who "taught me most of what I know about Indian beliefs." Of particular importance in this section of the text is the commentary regarding the Papagos, most of whom had been converted to Catholicism, and although "they spoke reverently of the God at the Mission and of the miraculous Saint Francis Xavier . . . they clung to their own religion as well, simply adding the Christian theology" (22).[112] This portrayal of a process of assimilating imposed religious practice clearly communicates a history of semiotic contact between two different cultural spheres, contact that has resulted in a mixture of beliefs on the part of the Indians, who represent a semiotically creolized structure within this space. Ultimately the narrator describes herself as living in close contact with the Indians, whereas it is the "stranger" who situates Indian beliefs as "senseless" and outside the Anglo-European cultural sphere. This type of commentary within the text functions as a register of information regarding the historical process of colonialism also evident in the previously analyzed narratives.

The text presents another perspective with regard to the reality of the Indian cultural group, or those "nameless Indians": "they came in large groups and sat along the wall or on the corral fences to watch the ranch activities. Occasionally, some of them worked or helped a little, but mostly they just got in the way" (31). Here the Indian is viewed as an intruder who does not contribute to ranch life in a way that is acceptable to the ranchers. Indeed, people like Grandmother Rafaela, who considered herself to be a descendant of the original Spanish *conquistadores*, refer to Indians as "savages" and "pagans."

The movement back and forth, north and south, mentioned by Vélez-Ibáñez results in another type of cultural reality that is evident in the text as well. For example, we find a description of the Indians who sat patiently "along the wall or on the corral fence and looked toward the kitchen for hours at a time, signaling their hunger silently, as always" (98). According to the autobiographical narrator, one of the men of this group, Mateo, "didn't look like any Indian to me. His skin was dark but he looked Castilian, dressed in fine clothes, unlike the other Indians" (98). Mateo is a man of Papago origin who traveled to Acaponera, Mexico, where he explains that he was raised by a white man he calls "Pa White." It is from this man that Mateo "learned a lot," and as a result "had earned quite a lot of money" (99).

Although Mateo has traveled both south to Mexico and north to New Mexico, he tells the autobiographer's father, "I don't wear these clothes at home. . . . I go half-naked like the other Parientes . . . I was born in the village because that is where God wanted me to be" (100). Mateo, an Indian who wears white man's clothing—"a jacket and trousers, a cowboy hat and good boots"—but was born a Papago is a figure who generates meaning with regard to a space that is the result of the collision of the reality of the white man's world and that of the Indian. Mateo clearly has adopted an ambivalent mode of self-representation that is mimetic.[113] As an Indian dressed like a white man, he would seem to represent the hybrid or creolized identity of those who are situated between two worlds, two cultures. To the Papagos, Mateo's clothes mark him as an outsider. However, it is important to note that Mateo's mimetic action of dressing like a white man is "almost the same, but not quite."[114] His dress is only an outward sign of his decision to conform to the white man's world, for at "home" in the village he remains "stark naked" like other "Parientes" of the Papago community. As the autobiographer recalls this moment, she tells the reader that "everything I thought I knew seemed to shift."[115] That is, here was an Indian dressed as a white man, yet he called himself a Papago.[116]

Though the text often presents the Indian in a positive light, it also registers information regarding the way those of a more moneyed class, or what Wilbur-Cruce called "catrines," perceived the Indian.[117] A case in point is Wilbur-Cruce's rendition of her family's preparation of a farewell dinner for the Indians who are leaving this land. She points out that her father prepared the barbecue for this occasion, a "civilized dinner" that would take place for those invited by the family and especially those invited by Grandmother Rafaela. However, the Indians were taken care of "out here"—that is, outside the house. Again the text communicates the way in which a symbolic border separates the Indians from those who considered themselves as "civilized." Indeed, the reader is told that these "guests stood on the slope above admiring the country and expressing their disgust with the milling hordes of Indians who were cluttering up that scenery" (287).

What I want to emphasize through references of this sort is the manner in which the text generates meaning regarding those historical changes that resulted from a collision of cultures, which finally resulted in the Indian's exodus from the territory. As the narrator recalls, "for the first time, I think I realized that the Indians were leaving the country *forever*." Her father also comments that this was "Indian country. And now it would no longer be that." (304). As the autobiographer notes at the end of her text, this was a place historically marked by an Anglo, Hispanic, and Indian cultural presence. However, in spite of a dynamic interaction among three semiotic realities, the Indians would finally be forced to leave their ancestral home. This area, the open range, that at one time was known for its freedom of movement between Mexico and the United States, would ultimately be marked by fences that limited that movement.

Hoyt Street

As part of my discussion of the texts created by Gonzalez, Jaramillo, and Wilbur-Cruce I have pointed out that the cultural "other" is presented in a number of different ways: in terms of those who work on the family ranch—the ranch hands, the *vaqueros*, the *peones*—and those, such as the Indians and Anglos, who are considered to be outside the experience of the familial and cultural space. Each text is written from the perspective of an autobiographer who presents herself and her family within the nucleus of a particular semiotic space where either a Spanish ancestry or—as in the case of *A Beautiful, Cruel Country*—an Anglo heritage is emphasized initially. *Hoyt Street*, on the other hand, introduces the reader to the cultural space of the immigrant, one that is situated in the margins of US culture. Although this text presents the Anglo as the cultural "other," the autobiographer also presents herself and her family as "other" in relation to the Anglo experience.

In her description of the barrio the narrator designates "the people in Pacoima" as "poor folks," "Mejicanos" who "lived in the shadow of Los Angeles."[118] She clearly situates herself and other poor Mejicanos outside of the urban center of Los Angeles, and therefore, as suggested by Gayatri Chakravorty Spivak, we find the "Other as the Self's shadow."[119] In other words, the self or the dominant cultural identity of this semiotic space is represented through those such as the doctors and nurses who visited the barrio. The autobiographer points out that the "public nurses, most of whom were dedicated to improving our lives, were often critical of how we lived, what we ate. They made Mexican women feel uncomfortable."[120]

Here the text emphasizes the difference between the Anglo women, who would consult a doctor very early in their pregnancy, and "the expectant mothers of our town [who] did not consult la Doctora Barr until the pregnancy was well into its final months" (56). The Anglo women and those of "*our* town" clearly point to different cultural spaces. Although the autobiographer suggests that Dr. Barr was different from the public nurses because she "understood the problems faced by poor women," she is also presented as the cultural "other" who "did suggest that women lay aside old Mexican customs and do things the 'American way'" (57). This part of the life story clearly communicates the way in which Mexican customs were considered foreign, extra-semiotic, and therefore to be eliminated from the dominant American sphere of reality.

Although I intend to discuss education as a cultural aspect in more detail in chapter 4, it is important to note here that the school is a place in which the self/"other" dichotomy is evident as well. The autobiographer recalls her marginal position with regard to a dominant culture as she notes that "our generation of Mexican-Americans was intimidated by the Anglo world, especially at school where at times we felt like second-class citizens with our funny customs, hard-to-pronounce names, and bad English" (121). The text clearly focuses on the immigrant as someone who "lived in two worlds: the secure barrio that comforted and accepted us, and the Other, the institutions such as school that were out to sanitize, Americanize, and delice us" (121). This allusion to "two worlds" demonstrates the way in which the autobiographer perceives herself and other Mexican Americans within the borderlands of a semiosphere in which semiotic irregularity is evident. That is, the Anglos form the nucleus or organized and "cultured" part of this space, whereas those outside the center are considered marginal and therefore "non-semiotic" or "non-structures" who speak Spanish, a non-language.[121]

In addition to the teachers, who pertained to the dominant Anglo sphere, the school nurse is described as having "eyes that missed nothing," and were constantly "inspecting our ears, mouths and hair." We are told that she used purple iodine to disinfect those parts of the children's bodies that might be infested with lice, and the autobiographer declares that it is precisely this "purple medicine" that "marked me as 'diseased.'"[122] Those children who were found to have lice were given a message on a yellow slip of paper that was to be taken home to inform parents that their child was infested. Ultimately the narrator explains that "this experience was part of our culture, of being Mexican-American—like having black hair and brown eyes. The inspections went with our identity, as did the yellow slips we wore home as badges of honor" (125). It is through this type of commentary that the text enters into a dialogue with the reader, who cannot help but compare the yellow slips of paper, these "badge[s] of honor" with the two superimposed yellow triangles used in Nazi concentration camps to denote those who were of Jewish descent and thus considered impure.

Further evidence of contact between two semiotic spaces, that of the Anglo and that which corresponds to the Mexican American, is evident in the chapter entitled "Funeral of Daniel Torres." The reader is told that "during World War II many young men from the barrio of Pacoima joined the armed forces. . . . In time many of them came home in a coffin or as a memory, as did Daniel Torres, posthumously awarded the nation's highest award for valor while under enemy fire: the Congressional Medal of Honor." The autobiographer also notes that Father Mueller, the pastor of Guardian Angel Church, announced that government officials would attend the mass and ceremonies to celebrate "the war hero of our town (whom few could remember)" (213). She further emphasizes that Daniel was remembered by few because he had only lived a short time in Pacoima, but the fact that he was Mexican American was emphasized in local newspapers. She describes the military and civil representatives who attended the funeral as follows: "There were from thirty to forty men in navy dress uniforms with gold braid on their shoulders, snow-white hats on their heads and spotless white gloves on their hands. In addition to the military, various community members (none of whom we knew) sat in the places of honor in the front pews. There were few occasions for Anglos to venture into the barrio (aside from the cops who now and then chased a stray pachuco), let alone attend our church. However, Father Mueller had stressed the importance of the funeral to the community; we welcomed the white strangers, those in uniform and those in civilian dress" (217). Of particular relevance in this passage is the autobiographer's use of linguistic markers that highlight the color of the military uniforms of those present at the funeral, the "gold braid" and the "snow-white hats" as well as the "spotless white gloves" worn by "white strangers." Her focus on the color white, together with the description of "the officials and dignitaries [who] were ensconced in the shiny black cars," stands in stark contrast to the description of the barrio and "the small clapboard house in a weed-covered lot" where the war hero had once lived. The autobiographer tells the reader, "I slumped down in my seat, mortified to know that these fine gentlemen in military hats and white gloves would be subjected to our poverty" (218).

As an observer of the semiotic space she occupies, the narrator points to the white Anglo as the cultural "other" "ensconced in shiny black cars." Her use of the word "esconced," which signifies hidden, concealed, or sheltered,[123] demonstrates her perception of the distance between those who were white and those who lived in the barrio. She explains, for example, that the barrio is "our town," where homes are "not pretty, nor modern, but like those in most local barrios: of wood, with odd-shaped windows, the yards full of fruit trees and assorted pieces of junk" (218). Here she presents another example of her recognition of the difference of those like herself who were children of Mexican immigrants. The barrio is presented once again as separate from the Anglo world, as the autobiographer ultimately communicates her sense of shame to the reader: "My face flushed with shame at what these men had seen. I was just a kid and wanted people to know only the good things about us" (218–19). Thus, within this text Ponce represents herself as a member of a community situated in the marginal or border space of a semiosphere that is dominated by those who are white and who consider those who live in the barrio as "other."

The crucial point of my discussion in this chapter has been to suggest the way in which the present corpus can be seen as a system of texts that present a cultural memory concerned with a collective history as well as a perception of "other" cultural groups. These narratives can also be defined as meaning generators that pertain to an extra-semiotic reality; that is, each text can be seen as a closed structure with its own sense of meaning with regard to different areas of the Southwest and California. Most importantly, however, each narrative registers information concerned with different points of view regarding historical collisions and cultural memory. Through the autobiographer's account of those memories, the reader comes into contact with a broader vision regarding the essential characteristics of a cultural collectivity that has traditionally occupied a marginal position within the semiosphere of the United States. Finally, by giving voice to this cultural reality through the written word, each text communicates information that contributes to the formation of a continuum of perspectives that interact dynamically and complement each other.

Chapter 4

The Female Subject and Expressions of Life Experiences

Social Practice and Imaginary Formations

The border autobiographies created by González, Jaramillo, Wilbur-Cruce, and Ponce can be understood as a system of texts that interact dynamically. Each of these narratives provides the reader with information regarding a cultural explosion that affected various semiotic spaces. Therefore, each life story includes certain memories about the historical process, especially those events concerned with the changes brought about by this explosion. Ultimately, then, these texts function as a reserve of cultural memory that points to the autobiographer's attitudes regarding land rights, home, history, and the cultural "other."

Of further relevance is the way in which discursive production and mechanisms of power and ideology are represented in the narratives of the four female writers considered here. As I suggested in chapter 2, each text provides the reader with a narration of the life course of an autobiographical subject. The life story presented in "Early Life and Education" involves the autobiographer's development first of all in the space of the father's home, then within the public space of school and the university, and finally in the space dominated by her husband's endeavors. Similarly, the autobiographical "I" of *Romance of a Little Village Girl* charts the early phase of her development within the space of her father's home and boarding school. Jaramillo then points to her transition into married life and the space of her husband's home, and finally into the symbolic space of widowhood, where she lived first with her daughter and then alone. It is in this final space that the reader contemplates a woman who is capable of managing her "own" life.

In *A Beautiful, Cruel Country* the autobiographical narrator also presents life experiences in terms of her position within her father's home, especially his ranch. As I have explained, those spaces such as "the Cerro" and "the gap" involve the autobiographer's initiation into the father's realm. Activities involving a female space are also presented. That is, Wilbur-Cruce recalls her mother's activities within the home, a place of comfort and nurturing for a young girl. Ponce's *Hoyt Street* also emphasizes the development of the autobiographical "I" within the space of her parents' Mexican American home in the barrio. Ponce further focuses on her development at school and ultimately within a private space where she discovers her own sense of sexuality.

In this chapter I examine the social world mapped out by each autobiographer and the manner in which she articulates her subjugated position within certain cultural and religious systems. As part of her life story each writer focuses on certain practices within a cultural space. Indeed, as suggested by Edward Said, "Culture is a sort of theater where various political and ideological causes engage one another. . . . Culture can even be a battleground on which causes expose themselves to the light of day." Said also notes that "stories . . . become the method colonized people use to assert their own identity and the existence of their own history."[1] I would argue, therefore, that because each life story examined here presents the reader with a social world and various types of cultural practice, the autobiographer is clearly exposing "to the light of day" the Mexican American experience within the United States. However, each of these life narratives also presents the story of a female subject who asserts her own sense of identity in a sphere marked by a patriarchal system of authority. Thus, I continue my reading of these four authors by examining the discursive practices evident within their narratives, particularly in terms of the way each text presents a vision of a world that is affected by ideological constructs and struggles that are reflected in the realm of family life where discourse circulates. Here I am interested in how the power structures of religious and cultural institutions and doctrines affect the way the female subject represents herself within the life story. Indeed, as Foucault has argued, "in every society the production of discourse is at once controlled, selected, organized and redistributed according to a certain number of procedures whose role it is to ward off its powers and dangers."[2] To initiate my discussion, then, I present a brief overview of the prohibitory aspects of discourse and procedures of control that serve as the basis for analyzing those sociocultural aspects that have been chosen by the autobiographer to present in her text.

As a means of highlighting the way social structures and cultural practice are represented in each text, and especially in terms of their connection to certain ideologies, this chapter is further informed by Pierre Bourdieu's notion of *habitus* and the "cultural field." Here my focus involves an exploration of the female autobiographer as a speaking subject and what she says about her position within a particular social reality, especially in terms of how that reality affects her sense of self-identity. My analytic approach in this direction is based on Michel Pêcheux's definition of "imaginary formations" that are produced within discourse. Of special interest, then, are those references within each text that allow us to uncover the meaning behind certain discursive formations, especially in terms of the power-resistance dynamic.

Discourse Production and Mechanisms of Power and Ideology

In his study *Chicano Narrative: The Dialectics of Difference*, Ramón Saldívar argues that "Mexican American communities of the American Southwest in the nineteenth and twentieth centuries have produced a significant body of texts." He further argues that "this literature presents a serious challenge to the established ways of defining canons of both the theory and the practice of literature and its criticism as these have developed in the Anglo-American world."[3] He also points out that these works are "literary products of a segment of contemporary American society that in many respects continues to define itself in opposition and resistance to mainstream social, historical, economic, and cultural modalities" (3). I agree with Saldívar's assertion that the Mexican American narratives written by both "men and women are predominantly critical and ideological" (6). However, his analysis privileges those texts written by Américo Paredes, Tomás Rivera, Oscar Zeta Acosta, Rudolfo A. Anaya, Ron Arias, Rolando Hinojosa, as well as the autobiographies of Ernesto Galarza and Richard Rodríguez. Although he suggests that this and other Mexican American literary production intends "to produce creative structures of knowledge to allow its readers to see, to feel, and to understand their social reality" (7), he in fact relegates a discussion of the works of Isabella Ríos, Sandra Cisneros and Cherríe Moraga to the last chapter of his text. Here Saldívar points to "the emergence of a significant body of works by women authors in the 1970s and 1980s" as representing "an alternative to the writers with whom we have dealt" (171). With this perspective in mind I argue the importance of the works of González, Jaramillo, Wilbur-

Cruce, and Ponce precisely because this segment of autobiographical literature brings the reader into contact with discursive strategies that demonstrate a desire on the part of the writer to represent her "own" cultural group, and at the same time to present a female perspective that contests the confines of social configurations such as patriarchy that involve relationships between men and women that are "power-asymmetrical."[4] Therefore, the speaking subject, and her discursive representation of these relations, is also of key importance here.

Of major relevance, then, is the way discourse production is evident within each text and what it reveals about individual female identity and the woman's position within a Mexican American collectivity. Again I refer to Foucault's project concerning the politics of discourse production, which he defines as those "practices obeying certain rules."[5] In his inaugural address presented at the Collège de France in 1970 he critiques societal control of discourse production: "we do not have the right to say everything, . . . we cannot speak of just anything in any circumstances whatever, and . . . not everyone has the right to speak of anything whatever."[6]

Foucault sees Western society as one based on procedures of exclusion, such as "prohibition." His discussion begins with a definition of the first of three procedures of exclusion: "taboo on the object of speech, and the ritual of the circumstances of speech, and the privileged or exclusive right of the speaking subject" (26). These limits are of particular interest as we try to understand what each autobiographer chooses to say and what she only alludes to in her narrative. The second principle of exclusion involves "a division and a rejection . . . opposition between reason and madness." Here Foucault uses the example of the Middle Ages and the discourse of the insane, whose words were considered as outside "the common discourse of men" and as "null and void, having neither truth nor importance, worthless as evidence in law, inadmissible in the authentification of deeds or contracts" (53).[7] I would suggest that at a macro level the border autobiography fits this principle of division and rejection as a text that presents information that has been separated from the canon of mainstream American literature. That is, it recounts a way of life that focuses on the cultural practices of a Mexican American collectivity, which to a certain extent has been treated as though it were "null" and "void" of meaning. This is certainly true in the case of the present corpus of border autobiographies created by women. The third type of exclusion mentioned by Foucault involves the opposition between what is true and what is false. Here truth is considered "arbitrary" and is sustained by an entire system of institutions that are consistently imposing and manipulating, and that "act in a constraining and sometimes violent way" (54). Consequently, "true discourse" is that which is pronounced by those who have the right to do so. For example, as I noted in chapter 1, "true" autobiographies were traditionally seen as those that dealt with self-assertion in terms of a cultural elite and the representative male life. However, the border autobiographies considered here present a discourse of self-representation that focuses on the female life and a woman's position within a cultural collectivity. I would argue, then, that the female writer of Mexican descent uses her text as a means of responding to the discursive aspects of power that are embedded within the practices of everyday life.

In addition Foucault asserts that discourse can never be transparent or neutral, rather it "translates struggles or systems of domination" (53). This perspective is clearly related to the female subject who has chosen to work out her own conflict with systems of domination by writing her life story. The autobiographers of the narratives considered here stand as translators of a way of life that they present to the reading public as part of their struggle to make themselves heard. Furthermore, each writer also struggles to translate her life experience, one that has been controlled by a system of patriarchal domination. Thus, each text speaks to other women as well.

Foucault also points to other procedures of control and limitation. Those that I have mentioned previously correspond to external systems of control. However, there are also those internal procedures of control in which discourse exercises its own control. The first of these internal procedures is commentary that has to do with "major narratives, which are recounted, repeated, and varied; formulae, texts, and ritualized sets of discourses which are recited in well-defined circumstances; things said once, and preserved because it is suspected that behind them there is a secret or a treasure" (56). Of interest in this direction are those portions of the border autobiography that refer to major narratives concerned with ritualistic aspects of social practice and the meaning they represent, especially in terms of the woman's role in the perpetuation of culture. One of the methods of continuation of culture that will be examined in the discussion that follows are certain "discursive ensembles" or doctrines that are represented by the speaking subject within the text. For instance, I am interested in the way the female subject presents a perspective regarding her allegiance (or non-allegiance) to the discourse of religious doctrines or practice and the system of patriarchy.

A second internal procedure that is pertinent to my discussion concerns the author who is often falsely considered as the unifying principle behind the origin and significance of certain groups of discourse. Here the emphasis is not necessarily on the existence of individuals who write but rather on the author function assumed by the autobiographer and the symbolic power of her writing as she chooses to speak about certain topics related to her world and her response to the historic structures and *habitus* in which she is immersed.

In chapter 1 I pointed out that autobiographies written by women did not take on a preponderant position in theoretical considerations concerning the genre until the 1980s. Hence, we can say that this marginalization of autobiographies written by women, and particularly Mexican American women, corresponds to "limits on the right to pronounce" or the exclusion of those texts that focus on matters such as everyday practice in the domestic sphere, religious practice, and cultural traditions and festivities, which are normally relegated to the woman's realm. As suggested by Foucault, the subject cannot speak from a position of truth, and because each of the autobiographers analyzed here is a female subject within a patriarchal society, her text is marginalized or outside the discourse that has been pronounced by men. Therefore, as I point out in the analysis that follows, she speaks within those limits that have been imposed upon her. It is important to note, however, that we must read the discourse of her text for clues that lead us to understanding the way in which she circumvents those limits through her autobiography, which is situated on the border between self- and collective revelation.

On the basis of these considerations, I would argue that these texts involve various purposes which contribute to their multi-structurality. First, as noted in chapter 3, the writer stands as a witness to the historical process. Second, by writing about her experiences in the domestic and cultural spheres, the autobiographer is enunciating her desire to assure the continuance of a particular way of life. Third, she is breaking through boundaries and, as noted by Rebolledo, she becomes a creative, speaking subject through the power of the written word.[8] Indeed, Edward Said has suggested that the power to narrate is important for the continuance of culture,[9] and it is precisely the speaking female subject who breaks through boundaries or limits by means of the narrative process. Here it is worth mentioning Foucault's perspective on the concept of subject:

"There are two meanings of the word subject: subject to someone else by control and dependence, and tied to his own identity by a conscience or self-knowledge. Both meanings suggest a form of power which subjugates and makes subject to."[10] As we shall see, both meanings are relevant to the present discussion.

Why does each female subject choose to break through the barriers of oppression and speak through the autobiographical narrative? An answer to this may be found in John B. Thompson's perspective concerning culture as a "meaningful doma" in which "social life is not merely a matter of objects and events which occur like happenings in the natural world: it is also a matter of meaningful actions and expressions, of utterances, symbols, texts and artefacts of various kinds, and of subjects who express themselves through these artefacts and who seek to understand themselves and others by interpreting the expressions they produce and receive."[11]

Therefore, the cultural practices and ideological systems that are presented within these texts involve a process through which the autobiographer is trying to make sense of and respond to the ideology present in certain cultural artifacts. Ideology in its broadest sense is a system of ideas. Thompson, for example, mentions several modes of operation of ideology—legitimation, dissimulation, unification, fragmentation and reification.[12] My discussion here refers to the ideological operation of legitimation, or the way relations of domination are sanctioned through various strategies and often expressed through the strategy of narrativization or "claims [that] are embedded in stories which recount the past and treat the present as part of a timeless and cherished tradition" (61).

In an attempt to broaden Thompson's perspective, I find it useful to refer to several concepts based on Olivier Reboul's definition of ideology, which involves five distinct features: 1) it is partial in the sense that it pertains to a limited community, and it stands in conflict with respect to other ideologies; it is not only imposed through reasoning and proof, but also by means of different degrees of pressure that can range from simple seduction to violence; 2) ideology is anonymous as it has no specific author and is situated as that which has already been thought of; thus, because ideology does not originate at an individual level, it is always collective; 3) ideology is essentially concealed as it attempts to pass itself off as something else—for example, as scientific or moral thought; 4) ideology is seemingly critical and appears to be based on rational, authoritative arguments; 5) ideology is a way of thought that is connected to a particular power structure that consistently attempts to justify and legitimize its existence. The use of power is collective—that is, a particular social group exercises power over another.[13]

Reboul also mentions three types of ideology. The first type, "diffuse" ideologies, are constituted by means of a complex of widely extended beliefs that serve as the basis for justifying prevailing power structures. A second type, "sectarian" ideologies, involve minority groups that aspire to power takeovers based on change. This type of ideology is explicit and often comes under the banner of "doctrines," "systems," or "thought." A third type can be defined as "segmentarian"—that is, a complex of beliefs, such as clericalism, nationalism, or sexism that may form part of other types of ideologies (22–25). Reboul's approach provides a framework for understanding the collective aspect of ideology, as well as the diffuse nature of patriarchy and the way it permeates the social world of the Mexican American community as presented in each of these border autobiographies.

Habitus as Social Practice

In previous chapters I have focused on key aspects such as "land" and "home," perspectives on personal and public history, and the position of the cultural "other" within the semiosphere. In addition to these elements, which contribute to the multivocality and complementary unity of the narratives, I would like to suggest the relevance of the way the autobiographer has chosen to present her social world through an emphasis on certain cultural practices, such as Hispanic, Mexican, Indian, and American traditions,[14] as well as on familial customs and religious and educational practice within the home and school. Therefore, some major questions at this point are: In what way are these practices to be seen as a social legacy that the autobiographer intends to preserve through the written word? Furthermore, how are these practices and the autobiographer's response to them articulated within discourse, and how does this contribute to the way meaning is produced within the text, especially in terms of the identity of the female subject who is immersed within ideological systems?

Informing the present chapter's focus on those cultural practices emphasized in each narrative is Bourdieu's notion of the "cultural field," or those "series of institutions, rules, rituals, conventions, categories, designations, appointments and titles which constitute an objective hierarchy, and which produce and authorise certain discourses and activities."[15] Of further importance is the concept of "linguistic field," which is generally associated with the dominant or "legitimate language" or, as Lotman has suggested, natural language, which functions as the primary modeling system of a particular semiotic sphere.[16]

In the United States, the linguistic field is marked by the use of English and those topics that have to do with the concept of nation building. Indeed, as Sarah M. Corse asserts, "national literatures have traditionally been understood as reflections of the unique character and experiences of the nation." Corse further emphasizes "the unique experience of national life [that] generates a national, collective consciousness, or in some formulations a 'collective unconscious' marked by a distinctive set of values, tensions, myths, and psychological foci, that produces in turn a certain readily identifiable national character."[17] The texts under consideration here, for example, run counter to the national collective conscious of the United States. That is, they do not focus on elements such as "self-reliant individualism" or traditional notions of Americanness. However, because they focus on a "different" type of experience related to a sense of identity that is derived from "other" national and cultural spheres, I would argue that they interact dynamically with the dominant linguistic field and function as a source of information regarding a distinct area of literary production that complements the dominant literary sphere. As I have mentioned, each of the autobiographers has written her text with a particular audience in mind. Thus, she intends "to speak and to say determinate things" that are intended for the "awakening" of the "singularity of individual experiences [that are] socially characterized."[18]

One of the ways this individual experience is awakened within the text is through an emphasis on ethnic identity. "Early Life" and *Dew on the Thorn*, for example, focus on Spanish ancestry as well as a Texas and Mexican identity that stands in clear contrast to those identified linguistically as the Americanos, or the cultural "other." *Romance* points clearly to an identity connected to the "white men" of the "Spanish race," who are presented in contrast to the "Americans," who are seen as outsiders. The autobiographer of *A Beautiful, Cruel Country* emphasizes her father's "Americano" and Castilian roots and her mother's Mexican and "india" roots. The *Hoyt Street* autobiographer, on the other hand, focuses on the identity of the "Mejicanos" in Pacoima as well as her own Mexican American identity. By emphasizing ethnic identity, then, these border autobiographies involve linguistic production that has to do with, as Bourdieu puts it, "the structure of the space of expressive styles [that] reproduces in its own terms the structure of the differences which objectively separate conditions of existence."[19]

The linguistic production observable in this set of works, and the separate conditions of existence the works present to the reader, point to a *habitus*.[20] That is, each of the texts of the corpus can be seen as an object of knowledge that refers to specific cultural practices associated with Spanish, Mexican, Indian, and Mexican American identity within a particular semiotic space. The knowledge about the life practices of these different ethnic groups is one that is reconstructed by the autobiographer within the literary text, and this reconstruction involves what Bourdieu defines as "a *field of struggle*" in which the literary text struggles to "defend" the social agent's position regarding her "own" perspective about cultural practice and identity. Ultimately, because the *habitus* involves individual sets of expectations and understandings encountered within a specific social atmosphere, my discussion here examines examples of how the writer perceives and takes in those rules, values, and dispositions that constitute systems of structures within a particular cultural field.

"Early Life and Education" and *Dew on the Thorn*

In "Early Life" the autobiographer explains that her master's thesis, "Social Life in Cameron, Starr, and Zapata Counties," was written with the intention of focusing on the history of border life. Although this brief text makes no further comment on the content of the thesis, José Limón suggests that *Dew on the Thorn* incorporates "some of the folklore in her earlier work and some new material based on the field research she carried out from 1934–35."[21] Limón further notes, however, that the narrative includes commentary that is imbedded within the text as a critique of class hierarchy. I would argue, therefore, that this narrative presents evidence of a cultural field that involves male dominance, with Don Francisco as head of a Spanish social hierarchy: "the government of the ranch, as understood by Don Francisco, was a paternal hierarchy with himself as absolute ruler."[22] Thus, from the beginning of the text, the narrator comments on the practice of patriarchy as a type of collective ideology that functions as a "structuring structure" that affects all aspects of life within the Olivareño.

This hierarchical structure is further emphasized in the role of Father José María as a member of a religious institution and head of a congregation that was spread out among various ranches: "Father José María, as Father Closs was lovingly called by his parishioners, was expected at the Olivareño. . . . His coming always created a stir. Among other things it meant that people would come to the ranch and Doña Margarita, who prided herself in her hospitality as a hostess, had been busy for many days making preparations. . . . The women laughed and gossiped as they baked bread and cakes, and roasted cocoa beans that soon would be converted into foaming cups of spiced chocolate. . . . Rosita and the grown girls of the ranch made the altar. . . . Pictures of saints and angels formed a celestial host, and holy statues, some of wood and some of marble, were placed on the altar table" (41). The social conditions of the Olivareño emphasize the priest's role in a social hierarchy. Although described as a "quaint figure," as the "black-robed Oblate," he is nonetheless presented as a symbol of the religious institution of the Catholic Church. For example, his arrival "created a stir" as the women of the congregation went about those activities deemed necessary in preparing for the priest's arrival, and he is greeted as a man of authority as people "crowded around him kissing his hand and asking for his blessing" (38).

Not only do people kiss his hand, they also bestow gifts upon him as the leader of this religious community. At one point they give him a horse, a "*potro*, [that was] pawing and foaming at the mouth" (40). This is not a horse for a simple, "quaint" man, but rather a man of strength: "And without another word, not even taking off his cassock, the priest mounted the *potro*. He took firm hold of the reins, lashed the horse with his quirt, punished him with the sharp spiked spurs and sat as firmly as though he were sitting on a chair" (40).

This "cowboy priest," this man who "lashed the horse" and "punished him," is not simply portrayed as a benign presence; rather he is represented discursively, as a strong leader, the implicit educator of his flock as he "prayed his beads" and expected others to follow his example. Indeed, we find that "guests joined the priest at the improvised altar to recite the rosary and hear a sermon. After each decade of the rosary the hoarse voices of the *vaqueros* and *peones* mingled with the tenor of Capul and the voices of the women and children in praises to the Mother of God" (41). As the spiritual head of this community the priest represents a cultural field involving a religious institution in which certain rituals form part of what Bourdieu defines as "doxa," or the core values of the community. One of these values has to do with continuing to be faithful to the leaders of the Catholic Church. We can assume, therefore, that the act of joining the priest to pray the rosary is not a voluntary one, but rather an act that demonstrated obedience to an authority figure who represents a system of restriction.

The constraints of this system are evident in religious rituals that stipulate the roles of members of a Catholic community. For example, as the reader discovers at the beginning of this text, the land inhabited by those of Spanish descent is described as "Christian territory" (7); that is, the Texas Mexican landowners were obedient to Rome, whereas the English, who were enemies of Spain, "had even dared to oppose the Pope" (7). The Americans who were closely tied to English identity were thus perceived as heathen, "enemies of everything Spanish" (7), especially those such as the Texas Mexicans who descended from the Spaniards. Thus, Father José María is responsible for the continued faithfulness of his flock to the doctrine and practice of the Catholic Church.

Further emphasis on Catholic religious practice as the center of life on the Olivareño is evident in traditional celebrations such as the Good Eve. Nochebuena is mentioned as a time when people of the ranch would "watch and wait for the coming of the Little Jesus." However, this celebration is also described as a "patriarchal feast . . . when all the friends and relatives gathered there for the annual Posadas and Tamalada" (92). Once again we find an accent on a religious ritual which is historically situated as "patriarchal"; that is, its origins are derived from the father as head of the family, which in this case refers to a familial history that begins with Don Juan José as the "first of the Olivares," who came to New Spain "as Surveyor to the Spanish Crown" (3). However, this ritual is not simply a "Spanish" one, but one that represents the *mestizaje* of the borderlands, where the Mexican piñata also forms part of cultural practice.

As for the use of the adjective "patriarchal" to refer to these rituals, I would argue that the narrator once again intends to portray this history of rituals as being imposed from a hierarchy of power—the Spanish Crown, the Catholic Church, and then Don Juan José. Early in the text Spaniards such as Don Juan José, who was one of the original founders of the border towns, are described as "*gente de razón*" with a "desirable character." Indeed, these founders "were of good family and well to do" (5). Ultimately the reader is told that Don Juan José was "a man of great physical strength, he spent most of his time going through his possessions; he loved the sense of ownership. He liked to feel that he had brought to this out-of-the-way corner of the Spanish Empire, the culture and civilization of the Spanish race." He is also described as having "died in the bosom of our Mother, the Holy Roman Catholic and Apostolic Church" (5).

These discursive references to "good family" lines clearly point to a cultural field that is marked by adherence to the institutions of the Spanish Empire, its "culture and civilization," as well as the "Holy Roman Catholic and Apostolic Church." Both institutions represent a hierarchy that imposes a certain way of life, yet it is interesting to note that this world is described as an "out-of-the-way corner of the Spanish Empire," one that takes its identity from Spain and is situated in the outer reaches of the Spanish Empire, the home of Texas Mexicans. The text particularly emphasizes how a way of life is handed down from father to son—that is, from Don José to his son José Alejandro, to José Alejandro's son Cesario, and then to Cesario's eldest son Francisco. Therefore, it is through the ideology of "paternal hierarchy" (13), one that also included the paternal role of the priest, that certain activities were authorized.

The reader continues to find evidence of a *habitus* dominated by Catholic cultural practice in rituals such as the setting up of "*El Nacimiento*," where "Mary and Joseph stood in the Manger before the Holy Child and shepherds were kneeling in adoration" (93). Another aspect of this feast was that of the piñata, "an earthen pot filled with candy and nuts" (93). Finally, the reader is also introduced to the singing of Las Posadas, which were "introduced from Mexico by Don Francisco, [and] had become very popular on the border" (94). This practice is ultimately described as "a service which those who are still Christians and speak God's language hold every year in remembrance of the wanderings of the Holy Family in Bethlehem, that cold night so many years ago" (94). The narrative also demonstrates an exaltation of the moral superiority of those of a "conquered race," who "were forced to abandon their land," as a people who "are still Christians and speak God's language" (7). Indeed, this ritual of recalling the "wanderings of the Holy Family in Bethlehem" stands as a type of discursive commentary regarding the way in which the Texas Mexicans who had suffered at the hands of the Americanos, and "who had come to take possession of their land," find comfort in knowing that they were not the only ones who ever were forced to leave their home.

Another festivity presented in this text is St. John's Day, a practice that begins with a blessing: "Blessed be this day and its holy patron Saint. Blessed it be forever" (99). It also involves rising early to wash one's face. As Doña Margarita suggests, this is a feast day in which "vain little creatures . . . want to make [themselves] pretty so [they] can get a sweetheart"

(99). The feast, with its emphasis on covering one's face in the dew of the *albahaca* plant and bathing in a tank of water, has its beginnings in Spain and can be considered as a constitutive practice. That is, it focuses on the accepted practice of female coquetry, the act of "making" oneself pretty for men as well as being cleansed of sin; hence, this Spanish tradition is one that is reproduced and continues to circulate in the Texas borderlands.

Interestingly, the description of this ritual is interrupted by Doña Margarita's reference to the field of *albahaca* (basil), which was brought to America as a "seed from Spain."[23] She recalls how an early ancestor, Don José, brought this herb, which ultimately took root in New Spain: "This made him feel as though a little corner of his home had been transplanted to the New World" (99). Once again we find a discursive reference to the Olivareño as "a little corner" of the Spanish world that is replicated in the New World. Within the Olivareño, this cultural space that reproduces customs from Spain, Doña Margarita is described as the female authority, and it is she who controlled the actions of the girls: "'Stop your talking,' commanded the mistress of the Olivareño, 'and do as I say. . . . After breakfast we trim the hair on the block, don't forget!'" The response by the young girls is simply, "*Sí, sí señora*, we'll come" (100–101). Thus, we find that Doña Margarita is responsible for educating young girls in the cultural traditions of the Olivareño.

The narrative presents the reader with the following commentary as well: "Whether transplanted from Spain or whether it originated in the new world, this custom was no doubt reminiscent of the decapitation of Saint John for the tresses were laid on a mesquite block and chopped off with a sharp ax or hatchet. It was believed that if the hair was trimmed on this day, it would grow four times as long by the next anniversary. If Doña Margarita wielded the ax, the effect was more efficacious; in fact this custom had become a ceremonial rite in which the mistress of the Olivareño acted as priestess" (101). This passage presents discursive references regarding a "custom" that is related to religious practice that ultimately becomes a "ceremonial rite," one that is handed down by Doña Margarita, who functions as a "priestess" and authority figure. Indeed, "one girl after another laid her hair on the block" (101). The narrator, therefore, is suggesting the key role of the female in the control and reproduction of cultural practice that is historically constituted as a ritual that is acceptable and "true," in spite of the fact that each young woman must lay her head on a chopping block, an action that can be considered somewhat "mad." This custom is accepted because girls were taught to be "proud of their long hair" and the treasure behind an action that emphasizes hair as part of woman's beauty is the hope of having hair "four times as long by the next anniversary."

All of these narrative references function discursively as a means of distinguishing the people of this place, their specific social reality and regional identity. That is, they are situated in the Olivareño, which can be seen as a semiosphere where we find evidence of the intersection of various spheres. Indeed, we find repetition of a social practice that is said to be derived from the religious memory of Saint John's decapitation. Furthermore, it represents the intersection of the cultural spheres of Spain and the New World, where we find that the discourse of Catholic religious practice continues to circulate. The "border people" and their way of life are therefore restored through the written word. Essentially, it is through repetitive references to specific cultural practices that the narrative structures describe the space of a particular collectivity as a means of explaining their "conditions of existence," one that is based on a patriarchal system that also includes the authoritative elder female who reproduces folkloric practice with its hidden truth.

As we have seen, this is a world closely tied to the Catholic Church, an institution traditionally situated outside the dominant sphere of Protestantism. Here it is important to mention that throughout US history few Protestants have bothered to understand the Catholic way of life, and many have seen Catholicism through the lens of the Reformation and Puritanism, which involved a cultural memory of anti-Catholicism. Furthermore, it is significant to recall that Protestants came to America with the intention of "purifying" Anglicanism of its Catholic tendencies. Protestants were distrustful of what they perceived as the subservience of Catholics to their priests and particularly to the pope. As suggested by Leonard Woolsey Bacon in *History of American Christianity*: "No sincerely earnest and religious Protestant, nor even any well-informed patriotic citizen, with the example of French and Spanish America before his eyes, could look with tolerance upon the prospect of a possible Catholicizing of the new States at the West; and the sight of the incessant tide of immigration setting westward, the reports of large funds sent hither from abroad to aid the propagation of the Roman Church, and the accounts of costly and imposing ecclesiastical buildings rising at the most important centers of population, roused the Christian patriotism of the older States to the noblest enterprises of evangelization."[24] This passage points clearly to the animosity toward the Catholic Church, which was seen as a threat to Protestantism, especially during the last half of the nineteenth century.

Through this type of perspective we are able to perceive a collective ideology that points to the superiority of white, Anglo-Saxon, Protestant ethnicity, one that permeated nineteenth-century thought within the United States. Therefore, those portions of *Dew on the Thorn* that draw attention to a Catholic way of life can be seen as a type of imbedded commentary with respect to an ethnic identity that stands in opposition to a dominant American religious form or practice. Indeed, these references can be seen as contestatory discourse that alludes to the struggle between Mexican Americans and the invading Americanos, especially in terms of the taboo of Catholic practice within a Protestant United States.

Romance of a Little Village Girl

Like *Dew on the Thorn*, the *Romance* text presents the reader with a cultural reality based on religious practices that are generated by a *habitus* that is the product of a history based on Spanish experiences. Life in this New Mexican social world is also described as revolving around religious feasts: "The first celebration was the parish patron saint's feast day. It opened with the accustomed vespers on the eve before, and high mass next morning."[25] We are further told that "the priest brought with him from Taos the French singer, and Miguel accompanied the singing with his fiddle" (24). Although there is no description of the priest, his role as the leader of the feast is implicit.

In addition to prayers and the mass that opened the festivities, the autobiographer notes rigid social roles that have been learned and followed by members of the society. Descriptions of women readying themselves for the "dance, the closing event of the fiesta" provide the reader with a clear example of the division between men and women in this social reality: "The women used the high window sills as dressing tables, resting their mirrors against their oil lamps while they applied the red carmine to their cheeks and the white *albayalde* to their faces and necks with their fingertips. With hair dressed up high and a few flat ringlets pasted with sugar on their foreheads and the high-bustled dresses donned, the *doñas* and *señoritas* were ready to be escorted to the dance" (25). This passage and its emphasis on the pains taken by women to beautify themselves for a dance coincides clearly with *Dew on the Thorn* and descriptions of a female practice of washing the face with early morning dew as a means of catching a "sweetheart." In both instances we are able to see how cultural practices promote a view of the woman as an object to be beautified and readied for the male.

Within the text we also find discourse that continues to emphasize the woman's subjugated role in the male-female relation: "The niceties of courtesy were still observed. In inviting a lady to a dance, the man bowed before her. Offering his arm, he escorted her to the center of the hall to stand in line with the other ladies. The men stood also in line before their partners until the music started" (25). This passage clearly demonstrates the women's conformity with a discourse that marks her as feminine; that is, she coquettishly prepares her appearance for the festivity and assumes a passive role as she waits to be escorted by the male.

The discursive reference to "the niceties of courtesy" responds to what Sandra Gilbert and Susan Gubar have noted as conduct that points to a cultural field of conventions that are rooted in eighteenth-century thought that dictated that young women be encouraged to take on an attitude of "submissiveness, modesty, selflessness [thus] reminding all women that they should be angelic."[26] This sense of "all women" and the importance of conforming to the societal convention of submissiveness is evident as the autobiographer tells her reading audience that her mother was often invited to stand as an attendant at weddings: "My mother dressed the bride so tastily, and she herself looked so lovely in her fine silk or velvet gowns and fine jewels, I was always at her side silently admiring and learning, happy to go when she chose to take me and contented to stay if she chose to leave me at home."[27] Here the autobiographer explains how she dutifully learned from her mother the path she was to follow. Her submission to a tradition that continues to circulate as a type of diffuse ideology reveals a female who is subject to a major narrative that is passed down from mother to daughter. This is similar to the myth that is taught to the young women of the Olivareño in *Dew on the Thorn*, who compliantly placed their hair on the "mesquite block" to be chopped off with an ax by Doña Margarita.

This type of cultural practice points to what Gilbert and Gubar have called the "eternal feminine" or "virtues of modesty, gracefulness, purity, delicacy, civility, compliancy, reticence, chastity, affability, politeness," which are passed down from one generation of women to the next.[28] These references regarding submission to men and matriarchal authority are clearly related to the notion that discourse can never be transparent or neutral. Indeed, although the autobiographer describes herself as "admiring," "happy," and "contented," these passages instead reveal the female as subject to major narratives that are recounted and continue to circulate through the mother's example.

The repetition of a master narrative regarding proper obedience to authority figures is further evident in the discourse of the text in the chapter entitled "Penitente Ceremonies of Holy Week." Here the autobiographer notes, "For the four days of Easter vacation, my father again took me home to Arroyo Hondo." She then points out that to the people of that "hidden isolated" area: "Religion was the most important thing. . . Still holding to ceremonies carried on from the medieval age of faith and religious traditions, during Lent every year they reenacted with sincere religious fervor the sorrows of the Passion Play. The *penitente* brotherhood took charge of the religious ceremonies, inasmuch as there was no resident priest in the town in my time."[29] The type of discourse evident here reveals what Foucault has termed as the "will of knowledge that prescribes." The autobiographer's father as the patriarch of the family "takes" his daughter home to partake in religious traditions that had been handed down from "the medieval age." We hear, then, the voice of a female subject in dutiful compliance with her father's will regarding her presence for the religious activities of a Catholic community. The fact that religion is described as "the most important thing" further accents a cultural struggle to express an identity that stands as different from that of a Protestant America.

The practice of religious ceremonies organized by the "*penitente* brotherhood" is clearly linked to the exercise of power invested in the institution of the church in spite of the absence of a priest. Instead of the priest as head of this type of practice, we find a brotherhood of men—that is, "half the male population," which "took charge" and participated in what can be considered as a tradition that focused on the reenactment of physical suffering that is imposed by tradition: "With a field glass my family had a very good view of the *penitentes* as they came out of the *morada*. . . . The *penitentes* took up their crosses, and a blanket was thrown over them, leaving only their heads and feet exposed. Followed by the *hermanos de deciplina* [*sic*] (flagellants), they dragged their heavy crosses around to the back of the *morada* and proceeded on their painful way up the rocky trail to *El Calvario* (Calvary Cross on the hill)" (36). This passage points to a custom that directs attention to a historical past and the ritual of penance that reveals discourse that is deemed valid and therefore reproduced yearly within the community.

An emphasis on physical suffering and penance is further stressed as the autobiographer tells of her own curiosity as she followed the wife of a *penitente* "who was going to pay a votive promise to the *santos* at the *morada*. . . On the wall of the hall dividing the chapel from the secret room hung a row of palm whips. The woman crawled on her knees from one statue to another, placing lighted candles before each. I was left kneeling before the statue of the Crucifixion. Paralyzed with fear, I could not move, for there before me on the mud altar table stood the statue of Death staring at me with one glass eye, the other eye shut, aiming at me with her drawn bow and arrow" (37). Interestingly, the autobiographer does not question religious tradition that includes crawling on one's knees and palm whips hung in a secret room; she instead presents herself as subject to tradition. However, the fact that she expresses her sense of fear and inability to act points to what Foucault has defined as the imposing and manipulating aspects of institutions where questioning is prohibited. The writer further describes the visit of a *penitente* to her family's private chapel. Here she notes that "the brother lay prostrated with arms extended on the floor before the altar. He got up and stood by the door while flogging himself" (37). All of these examples can be seen as constitutive practices in which the construction of certain roles carried out by male members of the community are not questioned, rather they are preserved as part of the hierarchical structure of society.

The fact that the autobiographer presents a social world and various cultural conventions that are not questioned has to do with what Bourdieu has defined as knowledge or the way people understand their world in terms of certain beliefs and values.[30] Both of the examples cited here—the young women who learn to follow certain rituals before and during the festivity of the dance, and the customary observation of *penitente* rituals—are not simply beliefs and values that are passively recorded. Instead they are constructed through *habitus* that is a product of history. In this case, as mentioned by the autobiographer, these religious practices go back to the medieval period, thereby presenting a past that is perpetuated through rituals that are communicated to members of the community through the strategy of narrativization, in which a way of life is recounted verbally, or taught through example. What is recounted concerns a past of cherished traditions that point to a collective ideology or "shared system of beliefs" that form part of a common cultural heritage.

The autobiographer also recounts her knowledge of this system of beliefs as she describes a trip with her father to Loretto Academy. She recalls that after a day of travel they arrived at Los Luceros, the home of her father's uncles. Once again she refers to history of the region: "This was the region of the explorer Oñate. Here with his courageous colonizers and pious friars, Oñate founded the first Spanish settlement and built the first church near San Juan de Los Caballeros, and started a culture of religion, arts, and science in the New Spain even before the Atlantic seaboard was settled."[31] This reference to early Spanish settlement and the initiation of "a culture of religion, arts, and science" involves discourse that has been appropriated by the autobiographer, who has excluded any mention of the fact that her heritage is also tied to Mexico. This is further evident as she emphasizes her beliefs regarding the courage and piety of those who brought their way of life to New Spain. For example, she comments on "this city of the Holy Faith rich in its three centuries of glamorous early history and still holding to many of the old Spanish customs which injected that ancient flavor found so interesting by the newcomers" (49). Phrases such as "glamorous early history" and "old Spanish customs" suggest the autobiographer's keen awareness that one of the historical taboos of American culture was and continues to be the assimilation of different races, particularly those of a mestizo cultural identity. Emphasis on her Spanish roots, then, is a way of presenting herself and her community as European rather than Mexican and of mixed blood.

In these references we find evidence of what Bourdieu defines as "the space of literary or artistic position-takings."[32] That is, the autobiographer as a social agent involved in the field of literary production uses the discourse of her text to make pronouncements intended to defend her point of view regarding a way of life or social practice that has been passed down from courageous men such as Oñate and the pious friars to the community. Her discourse, which focuses on "three centuries of glamorous early history," demonstrates a sense of knowledge and "truth" regarding the dominance of Spanish explorers and leaders of the Catholic Church, who are considered superior to British settlers who would much later settle "the Atlantic seaboard." Thus, it is through the narrativization of her life story and that of the larger community that the autobiographer reproduces discourse that asserts an identity within a cultural field that involves a hierarchy of power based on male and Catholic dominance. Her text, therefore, can be seen as a struggle to present what she considers as the "true" history of her people, one set before an Anglo audience.

A Beautiful, Cruel Country

As we have seen, "Early Life and Education," *Dew on the Thorn*, and *Romance of a Little Village Girl* initially highlight the autobiographer and her family's Spanish roots. *A Beautiful, Cruel Country*, on the other hand, focuses on a *habitus* that is the product of a hybrid history based on Anglo-American, Mexican, Indian, and Spanish experiences. In addition, this text presents the reader with a cultural field marked by rules and conventions that constitute a patriarchal hierarchy within the world of the Arivaca Valley. The first two chapters of this autobiography, for example, present Grandfather Wilbur and Grandfather Vilducea as heads of the family. Grandfather Wilbur, as I have mentioned, is described as an educated man—"a physician, a graduate of Harvard Medical College."[33] He is noted for homesteading the family land and for his close friendship with people such as Charles Poston, Don Ignacio Pesqueira, and the Arizona territorial governor, A. P. K. Safford.

Although Mexican Grandfather Vilducea is described as simply "a God-fearing man," he is clearly presented as the patriarch of his family: "He had snatched my mother, his daughter, back from my father after he had married her in 1901. They had been married at the Wilbur Ranch by Charles Poston, *El Cadi*, which meant one with the authority of a priest to perform the rites of marriage and other sacraments. But my Grandfather Vilducea soon found that, when the Jesuits had been run out of Tubac, Poston's authority had been lifted—before the marriage. He came and took his daughter and told my father that if he wanted her back, he must arrange to do it properly" (10). The reader is then told that the following spring her parents were married again at the Dolores Mission. Grandfather Vilducea is obviously interested in conforming to approved ritual; that is, his daughter must be "properly" married on the basis of the "rites of marriage," and any other type of ceremony is unthinkable. The priest or *El Cadi* are the only authorized representatives within this cultural field who have the power to utter proper discourse, and because Poston's authority had been lifted, and the marriage was not legal, Grandfather Vilducea "snatched" and "took his daughter."

These references correspond to a discourse that invests the father with a sense of ownership and power over his daughter as well as his daughter's spouse, particularly in the absence of official authority. Thus, we see a struggle between two authority figures—the father as guardian of his daughter and Poston as a government representative. Indeed, according to Bourdieu, "the success of these operations of social magic—

comprised by acts of authority, or, . . . authorized acts—is dependent on the combination of a systematic set of interdependent conditions which constitute social rituals."[34] Grandfather Vilducea is intent on complying with the social ritual of marriage based on proper authority. What stands out in this example, however, is the power of authorizing discourse that stipulates the dominant roles of the male speaking subject, whereas the daughter is without a voice in the matter; she is simply subject to her father's will.

In addition to the power and constraints exercised by the elder male, the narrative also includes discourse that points to a space marked by a history of religious institutions. Although the autobiographer only briefly notes a Jesuit or Catholic presence, it is important to mention that Catholic missionary activity had a long history in the territory of northern Sonora and southern Arizona. One of the outstanding figures in this history is Father Francisco Eusebio Kino, who in 1691 entered the Santa Cruz Valley where he undertook the work of evangelizing Indians, building missions, ranches and farms. As suggested by the autobiographer, "the Jesuits had been run out of Tubac." That is, their missionary efforts were only partially successful and after a half-century of Spanish domination the Pima Revolt took place in 1751. However, by 1752, Spanish troops defeated over 2,000 Piman warriors and the Presidio of San Ignacio de Tubac was garrisoned and came under the command of Capt. Juan Thomas de Belderrain. In 1767 the Jesuits were expelled from Spanish possessions by Carlos III and replaced by the Franciscans.[35] This history of proselytizing, of imposition of Catholic rituals and beliefs, clearly contributes to the cultural field of this area.

An example of the role of religion is evident early in the narrative as the autobiographer introduces Grandfather Francisco Vilducea as "the man with the Bible." She further notes, however, that "no one could understand why he had a Bible—a Protestant Bible, the forbidden book of scriptures. Neither did any of them know why it was forbidden, or by whom, but it was forbidden, and Don Francisco Vilducea had that forbidden book."[36] This passage points to the Bible as taboo because it represents a Protestant presence in what is considered Catholic territory. Interestingly, the taboo continues to circulate although no one is quite sure why the Protestant Bible is forbidden. This belief is based on a diffuse ideology that forms part of the prevailing power of the teachings of the Catholic Church that permeated this space. Thus we are introduced to a cultural field that is similar to the one represented in *Dew on the*

Thorn and *Romance*; that is, life is dominated by the institution of the Catholic Church, where the "devoutly Catholic Don Francisco Vilducea, with his practically memorized Protestant Bible" (317) took a prominent role in the continuance of certain ritualized practices.[37]

One of the major traditions mentioned in the narrative is the Feast of the Holy Cross. As suggested by Bourdieu, *habitus* drives practice, and like the previous narratives we find that practice limits and fixes gender roles. For example, the autobiographer emphasizes the traditional role of cooking that is assigned to women: "My grandmother filled three ten-gallon crocks with corn mash and other ingredients. This was the ninth day of fermentation and it was time to strain the product, *tesguin* which was a delicious but mild intoxicant—a lady's drink, but enjoyed by men as well[38] . . . as large kettles of frijoles simmered behind them on the stove, my grandmother and mother tested the *tesguin* that would be served this evening on the *vispera* of the Holy Cross" (134). A drink assigned to the woman's sphere because it was only mildly intoxicating—here again we find evidence of discourse that points to the limits placed on women's actions.

The occasion of the feast also involves a feminine ritual that demands that girls wear dresses in preparation for this fiesta: "Aunt Juanita took Ruby and me to her tent to give us two pretty dresses she had made for us to wear to the Velorio. She also gave us pictures of the Virgin Mary and rosaries—pink beads for Ruby, blue ones for me" (137). The autobiographer then explains that her aunt had asked, "Who is your patron saint, Vita? . . . What saint do you pray to when you ask for help?" The narrator then recounts her response: "I don't ask for no help." The aunt's reaction is a vehement one: "¡Ay! Jesús libranos de todo mal . . . Jesus deliver us from all evil." Juanita expresses her shock as she exclaims, "The nieces of Father Suastigui do not pray. . . . One of our uncles was a priest" (137). This passage clearly demonstrates the way in which religious ideology permeates this cultural field. For example, the fact that the autobiographer and her sister do not comply with the ritual of praying to saints and asking them for their help is perceived as evil, and therefore in conflict with Catholic practice. Aunt Juanita responds to her nieces' deviation with an argument that is based on seemingly rational and authoritative grounds; that is, because the girls are nieces of a priest, she insists they should be educated in and expected to follow certain religious practices.

In addition to roles assigned to women, the text presents information regarding an Indian response to the feast. For example, they are conscious of the importance of the festivity: "Perhaps in honor of the occasion, José-José had substituted a pair of tattered coveralls for his loin cloth" (133). Aware of what is expected of him, José-José complies with the stipulated role of covering his Indian nakedness and appearing more civilized for a Catholic, non-native custom. Of further interest is the way Indians take part in the feast. For example, the ritual included a "prayer room [that] would be tended and vigil kept all during the night. Anyone who wished might come to pray and light candles" (139). The autobiographer also recalls that "Grandfather soon left the room and when I followed him outside I saw the three Indians—Pete, José-José, and Carmelo—taking the cross up Pesqueira Hill with Grandfather leading them" (139). Noteworthy here is the role Grandfather takes in leading the Indians in this ritual. Thus we find a world marked by diffuse ideology based on beliefs derived from a history of conquest and an evangelization process that was imposed upon native people by a Catholic European power structure.

The autobiographer then notes that the rest of "the Indians who had gathered in the yard were becoming quite restless. Mateo spoke to them, asking them to wait until Grandfather and his close friends—'the people of Pa'—had started up the hill before they moved. Then, he explained, my father would give them the signal to follow by shooting a rifle" (140). The reader cannot help but perceive the subjugated position of the Indians. Although they participated in the feast, the autobiographer tells us that for the most part they were waiting for food. Indeed, Indians such as Carmelo, who "came without shoes, without shirt, and without a hat [and whose] baggy, ankle-length pants were held up with baling wire . . . said they hadn't had anything to eat since the last Feast of the Holy Cross a year ago" (133). Thus, the participation of the Indians in the ritual of the Feast of the Holy Cross can be seen as an appropriation of form, or what Foucault has termed "ritual recitation." They are excluded from the group known as "the people of Pa," and they are required to go through the motions of this religious ritual in order to enjoy "[a] generous serving of lentils, a tortilla, a slice of the beef" (142).

The submission of the Indians and their condition of existence within the *habitus* is further accentuated in the chapter entitled "The Desert Harvest." Here Wilbur-Cruce recalls that when she woke up after the feast, a family friend, Phoebe Bogan, was speaking to her father about the way he treated the Indians: "I think it is outrageous for you to hit a poor Indian like that, Agustín." However, Phoebe's husband responds harshly to her comment: "[T]his is Agustín's property. When the Indians are told to go they had better go" (148–49). This passage points to a history of education of the Indian that is based on procedures of subjection, involving a collective ideology that is expressed by John Bogan: "But did you ever think about this? If they were left to do as they please you'd sink to your ankles in human feces" (149). Thus the Indian, deemed an uncivilized being, is subject to certain religious practices and the authority figures of a patriarchal hierarchy that originated during the early centuries of Spanish conquest and missionary activity and that is reproduced by those, like the narrator's father, who freely exercised their role of power. The life of the Indians, then, can be summed up in the way they perceive their fate: "'First go Tucson, pick fruit,' said José-José. 'Then walk, walk, to Magdalena for St. Francis Day. Then go reservation." The autobiographer points out that "it was an annual custom of the tribe after spending much of the summer in Tucson harvesting cactus fruit, to make the pilgrimage to Magdalena in Mexico. Many, many weary miles, all on foot" (133–34).[39]

These references within the life story are not simply memories presented casually. I would argue that this autobiographer, like the narrator of *Dew on the Thorn*, is presenting the reader with a critique of what she considers to be the cruel aspect of the social world of the Arivaca Valley, especially the imposed exodus of the Indians to reservations by the US government. Narrativization of the uncivilized way of life of Indians is part of an ideology that permeates both Spanish and American history and ultimately legitimizes the displacement of the Native people of this area. However, the narrator chooses to include a brief dialogue that stands as a commentary within her life story. This moment involves a final visit by one of the Indian women, who tells Grandmother: "All broken-hearted . . . going don't know where. No need to stay. Gup'ment men will come and drive us away. They drive Pariente away before, many people died. People could not walk fast like horses and they hit people. Run down people. This our beautiful home. Now we leave before they come" (307). Hence, the Indians, perceived as uncivilized beings, are subject to a discourse of power that excludes them from their "beautiful home." It is through references of this sort that the autobiographer explains the title theme of her life story concerned with a social legacy that marks this beautiful country with cruelty.

Hoyt Street

Each of the previously mentioned texts presents a type of regionalist discourse that allows the reader to understand a space that is delimited and in opposition to the dominant culture of the United States. *Hoyt Street* presents Pacoima as a region of California that has its own set of what Thompson has called "artefacts" or the assemblage of those distinctive aspects that constitute the whole of the autobiographer's experience. This experience focuses on a heritage based on a system of domination that also has to do with patriarchy and the role of the Catholic Church as an institution of control within a community of Mexican American immigrants.

The autobiographer begins her life story by focusing first on Pacoima, then on the houses within the town, and ultimately her family and their home. She tells the reader, "Our house was built by my father when he and my mother and their three older children moved from Ventura to the San Fernando Valley, sometime in the 1920s."[40] As I mentioned in chapter 2, the narrative emphasizes "the large kitchen [that] extended the length of the house." The room is described as the "heart of our home, the place where my mother cooked, ironed, and bathed her many children" (9–10). This is obviously a space dominated by the female presence. However, the autobiographer then notes that "as we grew older my father built los cuartitos. The men's rooms as we called them, were separate from the main house" (9). This was the area where the male children and eventually the autobiographer's father slept, since "after my mother gave birth to my younger brother, Josey (at age forty or so), she decided that in order not to have more children, she and my father should sleep apart." She further notes: "I often think my father agreed to sleep in the men's rooms because by the time my mother was forty, she had already given birth to eleven children and was often sick. . . . Still my father, a healthy man in his forties, often sneaked into my mother's bedroom. I once saw him near her bed. I heard him say the word 'tetas,' but did not understand this Spanish word. When I lingered to talk with my mother, he quickly left the room. My mother who was taking her afternoon nap, appeared relieved" (8–9).

This narrative moment suggests the stipulated role of the female subject. Although the autobiographer's mother "decided" she and her husband "should sleep apart," and although the husband "agreed to sleep in the men's rooms," he enters his wife's room to impose his sexual needs upon her. In this scene recounted by the autobiographer, she notes that her mother "appeared relieved" when her husband left. Thus, we can assume that had the young child not entered her mother's bedroom, her mother would have submitted to her husband's demands since to say no to him and deny his "right" to her body was considered taboo.

This scene clearly corresponds to Foucault's perspective found in *The Use of Pleasure* where he refers to Xenophon's *Economics* as an important work regarding the relationship between husband and wife. From this perspective the wife is the owner of the home and essential for governing the *oikos*.[41] The relation between man and woman is a political one according to Foucault—that is, between government and one who is governed. Order would be achieved in a male-female relationship in which the male would possess a bounty of virtues that would be the basis for the exercise of his position of command. The woman, on the other hand, with the man as a model, would exercise her virtue of subordination.[42] This perspective is relevant since throughout *Hoyt Street* the narrator's father is represented as the head of the household, as the one who builds the home, whereas the mother's role is to cook, iron, and care for the children. This stipulation of roles involves a discourse produced within the home, where we find a struggle between husband and wife as she attempts to exclude him from the marital space. However, he intrudes and attempts to trespass the limits set by his wife, thereby demonstrating an intention to subordinate her decision and limit her power over her own body.

We find further references to the mother's and father's roles within the home, where "it was the custom to wait until everyone finished eating before leaving the table. Josey and I were forced to sit while our elders finished supper. Often we tired of the wait" (10). As a means of circumventing this "custom" the autobiographer notes that the children would often fight, and then, "[i]n her moderate voice my mother would caution us not to fight. My father would say nothing, merely fixing us with a stare that ended all arguments" (10). This set of rules, or objects of knowledge, are constructed within the home and constitute a *habitus* in which women are separated from men and where the father controls the actions of his children "with a stare."

Like "Early Life," *Dew on the Thorn*, *Romance*, and *A Beautiful, Cruel Country*, this text also presents a cultural field marked by patriarchy that has its roots in historical practice that stipulates the roles of both male and female subjects. Indeed, as I commented in my discussion of *Dew on the Thorn*, this system of patriarchy is handed down from father to son. In *Hoyt Street* we also find that the eldest son holds a special place in the family: "Berney . . . readily assumed the authoritarian role and privileges of el hijo mayor . . . a typical brother who liked to give orders. Being the responsible, older male in the family made Berney serious"

(23). This seriousness on the part of the eldest son is further noted by the autobiographer as she points out that Berney imitated his father in a number of ways: "Berney liked to throw his weight around at home. He felt responsible for my sisters' reputations. He disapproved of the tight skirts then in vogue, and although Elizabet was older, she was too short to have much authority. Even Norbert rarely argued with the brother who had a car and could outshout him. Berney was not mean, nor did he hit us (in our house, no one was allowed to hit), but in our mother's eyes he could do no wrong" (23). Thus, although the role of the male in this home does not include hitting, the son is nonetheless assigned a position of authority similar to that of the father, a status that is further authorized by the mother. Once again, the narrative clearly points to an ideology of power that underlies cultural practice within the home. Indeed, although we have witnessed the struggle of a wife attempting to deny her body to her husband, we also find she is unable or has no desire to limit her son's power over his siblings. It is important to note here as well the narrator's commentary regarding Elizabet, who, although older than Berney, is unable to exercise any authority because of sexual difference. Described as "short," Elizabet's body signals her lack of power within a system that "requires that women be excluded from the single true and legislating principle" of male authority that marginalizes the woman within the home, a space that is marked by a patriarchal symbolic order.[43]

An example of compliance with rules and the way discourse circulates and is reproduced within the family structure is evident in the chapter entitled "Las Camisas Blancas." Here the autobiographer devotes an entire chapter to explaining the importance of ironing Berney's shirts, since "Mexican mothers in the barrio took pride in how they clothed la familia, especially the eldest, and often the favorite, son."[44] This chapter includes an extensive description of how Berney's shirts are washed separately and the fact that "mother took pride in how she cooked the blue starch for Berney's dress shirts." Ironing Berney's shirts is the "obligation" of the older sisters; however, the autobiographer points out, "From the age of twelve or so, of the five girls in our family, I alone ironed best the white dress shirts worn by my older brother Berney" (276). Once again, the narrator emphasizes the barrio, which stands out as a semiotic space marked by the actions and attitudes of "Mexican mothers" who insert a practice that is connected to the cultural space of the home country and also, most importantly, to a specific attitude of subservience to male family members such as the eldest son. Thus, as we have seen in the previously analyzed narratives, this text also presents the wife and mother as a figure who accepts the validated discourse of male dominance within the family, and this practice is handed down to and appropriated by other females within the family.

The text also presents the reader with discourse that focuses on the institution of the Catholic Church as a major factor within this cultural field. The chapter entitled "El Padre Mickey" emphasizes the role of "the Reverend Richard S. Mueller, O.M.I. [who] was assigned to Guardian Angel Church" (253). Father Mueller is described as settling into the parish "with ease" as he organized the church choir, renovated the rectory, and reorganized church clubs such as the Holy Name Society and the Altar Society: "The Holy Name Society continued as before; once a month the body of elderly men marched into church behind a white banner to receive holy communion. The women of the Altar Society remained in charge of church altars, all of which were periodically dusted and polished to a bright sheen" (257). References to the elderly men who "march" into church and the women who were "in charge" of altars suggest a doctrinal allegiance on the part of those who were members of these religious societies that project an essence of exclusivity.

In addition to these adult societies we find that "older boys, even rowdies like Mundo, who hated going to church but feared being left out of things, volunteered as altar boys." The autobiographer notes that she and her friends joined the Stella Maris Club, "an offshoot of an older organization, the JCFM (Juventud Católica Femenina Mexicana), affiliated with chapter groups throughout Southern California. This organization that has its roots in Mexico, but is situated in the parish of the barrio, once again demonstrates the intersection of two semiotic spaces. Indeed, as noted in the text, the purpose of the organization is to bring together 'nice' Mexican girls under the auspices of la santa madre iglesia" (258).

Just as we have seen in *Dew on the Thorn* and *Romance*, this text also presents the reader with a cultural field that refers to the role of the institution of the Catholic Church as a system representing what Foucault has termed as "discursive ensemble" or set of truths that are held in common by members of a particular group. It is precisely through the various societies within the church that members conform their beliefs to the validated discourse of "la santa madre iglesia." Indeed, as mentioned in this chapter, the young girls who were members of the Stella Maris Club participated in "numerous events and many boring jobs." Father Mueller, who is situated in a position of authority within the *habitus*, reinforces the participation of the girls by telling them that "our Blessed Mother appreciates any and all efforts . . . nothing is too small when done for Our Lady" (260). Interestingly, both Father José María in *Dew on the Thorn* and Padre Mickey in *Hoyt Street* are described as benign, yet their authority holds the religious community together through a validated discourse based on religious ritual and practice.

What becomes apparent from this type of analysis, then, are the many discursive references within the texts created by González, Jaramillo, Wilbur-Cruce, and Ponce that point to a practice of patriarchy that is manifested within the family as well as in the religious sphere. My claim here is that these collective cultural practices represent what Bourdieu has designated as a "universe of belief" that can be understood as symbolic of a historic way of life that pertains to a particular region within the United States. It is precisely through an emphasis on cultural and religious practice that the text functions as a sign of ethnic identity in which the autobiographer "ensures the active presence of past experiences,"[45] particularly in terms of the way they affect the female subject within the family.

Imaginary Formations and the Female Subject

So as to further highlight the female subject and her position within a cultural system, the present section examines the imaginary formations evident within the discourse of the narrative text by focusing on representations made by the autobiographer with respect to herself, others, and specific referents. My intention here is to draw on the theoretical perspective of Michel Pêcheux regarding discourse analysis as a means of understanding the autobiographer as the obvious protagonist of her life story. I am also interested in the "meaning-effect" of the discourse evident within her narrative.

Michel Pêcheux's work focuses on linguistic and textual analysis where he suggests that "texts, like language, function."[46] His study of the function of texts is based on the notion of information schema, which is derived from Roman Jakobson's ideas concerning the *addresser* who sends a message to the *addressee* about a particular referent that is understood by both parties. In his adaptation of Jakobson's ideas, however, Pêcheux uses the term "discourse" rather than "message." Discourse production for Pêcheux involves elements A and B as "something other than the physical presence of individual organisms"; rather they are to be seen as "determinate positions within the structure of a social formation and that sociology can describe [as] the bundle of objective features that characterize them" (85).

The discursive process, therefore, involves the functioning of "imaginary formations" that can be analyzed on the basis of the representations that subject position A (*addresser*) makes about A, about B (*addressee*), as well as those representations made about R (*referent or theme of discourse*). In addition, other positions that may be present as imaginary formations within the text include the representations that position B makes about B, about A, and the representations that position B makes about R. The expressions designating imaginary formations have been represented by Pêcheux in the following way:

A:

IA(A) → Image of position A for the subject placed at A
IA(B) → Image of position B for the subject placed at A
IA(R) → A's "view" of R

B:

IB(B) → Image of position B for the subject placed at B
IB(A) → Image of position A for the subject placed at B
IB(R) → B's "view" of R

These imaginary formations also involve implicit questions formulated by the addresser and addressee that underlie and anticipate the corresponding representations that are formed with respect to the self, the "other," or the referent:

IA(A) "Who am I to speak to her/him like that?"
IA(B) "Who is she/he for me to talk to her/him like that?"
IB(B) "Who am I for her/him to talk to me like that?"
IB(A) "Who is she/he to talk to me like that?"
IA(R) "What am I talking to her/him about like that?"
IB(R) "What is she/he talking to me about like that?" (86)

In his comments regarding elements of the above schema, Pêcheux points out that these formations are derived from "other conditions of production" (88) which correspond to the concepts of *presupposition* and *implication* described by Oswald Ducrot;[47] that is, it is impossible for the speaker to describe or refer to situations strictly in terms of a particular chronology. Rather, as suggested by Ducrot, "the 'knowledges' the speaking subject ascribes to his listener are an integral part of the 'discourse situation' to which the presuppositions refer. It therefore concerns the image the participants in the dialogue have of one another."[48]

Ducrot has also made a clear distinction between two types of audience that receive the speaker or addresser's message. There are those listeners of the general public who happen to hear the addresser's enunciation, and there are specific addressees to whom the speaker or addresser explicitly directs his or her ideas. Because the present corpus of texts is written by women, we can also assume that certain aspects of the narrative are intended for the female reader. Indeed, as noted by Julia Kristeva in her essay "Word, Dialogue and Novel," "dialogism is coextensive with the deep structures of discourse." As a means of understanding the dialogism evident within the written word, she also notes the necessity of turning to "the psychic aspect of writing as a trace of a dialogue with oneself."[49] Thus, I suggest that not only does the autobiographer address other women, the first reader the text is intended for is the writer herself; that is, to a certain extent, the text functions as a space in which the addresser enters into dialogue with herself as a means of questioning and coming to terms with her assigned roles.

As I have commented in the previous section of this chapter, the female writer is immersed within a particular *habitus*, therefore it is through an analysis of imaginary discursive formations that we are able to further observe ideological formations of a system of "structuring dispositions." Here it is important to recall that for Pêcheux "every discursive formation, by the transparency of the meaning constituted in it, conceals its dependence on the complex whole in dominance of discursive formations, itself imbricated with the complex of ideological formations."[50] Therefore, my analysis also includes certain reflections on power relations and those relations of meaning manifested within the "ideological materiality" that is evident in the discourse of the text.[51]

Because of the constraints presented by the hierarchical system of patriarchy evident within Mexican American cultural practice, it is also compelling to examine the way in which the autobiographer enters into dialogue with herself and with the potential female reader. Thus, my discussion, which is based on the notion of imaginary formations, will focus on the autobiographer's perception of self within the patriarchal system, and the discursive means by which she addresses others and presents her perspective with respect to referents such as the female figure, the male figure, the educational system, and authority figures within that system.

"Early Life and Education" and *Dew on the Thorn*

We should recall that the autobiographical subject of "Early Life and Education" presents sequences of information that emphasize her sense of self in the second section of the life story entitled "Education," where the use of "I" occurs thirty-six times. In the passages that follow it is possible to observe examples of this type of usage:

> Previous to our moving to San Antonio, I had attended, for one year, a one-teacher school in English. . . . Even though the English I learned was elemental, it helped me a great deal. This, together with my knowledge of Spanish enabled me to enter the fourth grade at the age of ten. . . . I was able to be promoted at the end of the school year. . . . I finished the high school course when I was eighteen.
>
> The summer of 1925 brought me a far reaching experience. I met J. Frank Dobie. Heretofore the legends and stories of the border were interesting, so I thought, just to me. However, he made me see their importance and encouraged me to write them, which I did, publishing some in the *Folk-Lore Publications* and *Southwest Review*.[52]
>
> After getting a B.A. degree from Our Lady of the Lake in 1927, I became a full-time teacher at Saint Mary's Hall. Two years later . . . I was awarded the Lapham Scholarship. . . . My thesis, "Social Life in Cameron, Starr, and Zapata Counties," is the result of that year's study and a lifetime of love and understanding for my people. . . . As a result of the thesis I was awarded a Rockefeller grant in 1934. (xii–xiii)

In this segment of the text the speaking subject presents positive imaginary formations regarding herself and her intellectual achievements, particularly the fact that she has acquired not only an undergraduate but also a master's degree. However, in the last part of this section of the text she presents a different perspective: "In 1935, Edmundo E. Mireles, whom I had met as a student at the University of Texas, and I were married in San Antonio. . . . For four years we lived in Del Rio where Edmundo was principal of the San Felipe High School and I taught English. . . . My husband

and I collaborated in writing two sets of books. . . . Until my retirement I taught Spanish and Texas History at W. B. Ray High School in Corpus Christi. We have been happy" (xiii). Evident here is a change in the discourse as the narrator presents positive imaginary formations when referring to her husband and his position as principal of San Felipe High School. At this point in the narrative she also presents a description of herself as simply collaborating with her husband and teaching English and then Spanish and Texas history. Ultimately she presents a positive imaginary formation regarding the context of her married life in which she tells the reader, "We have been happy." The phrase "We have been happy" is similar to the ending of a typical fairy tale. I would argue for the significance of this type of ending and the fact that she is silent and does not comment about the changes that take place in her life after her marriage. Indeed, the discourse at the end of the life story emphasizes "Edmundo E. Mireles," "my husband," and "we." Thus, we see an obvious shift in emphasis regarding the female subject, from the speaking "I" and her own achievements to one that places "Edmundo," "my husband," in a dominant position. Ultimately the subject is erased and becomes part of the marital "we."

Particularly relevant is the implicit aspect of the narrator's silence. In chapter 2 I noted the autobiographer's seeming compliance with her husband's life plan, in spite of her own intellectual ability. Furthermore, suggests José Limón, in her letters González expresses her desire for further academic studies; therefore, the final words of her autobiography must be questioned. "We have been happy" can clearly be seen as masking a "taboo on the object of speech," where not all things can be expressed at all times, especially by the female subject who is immersed in a system of patriarchy that can be seen as a diffuse type of social ideology, one that is based on broadly extended beliefs regarding gender roles. Indeed, in this final passage, the autobiographer consistently refers to herself after mentioning her husband, and she is totally silent within her text regarding any difficulty she might have had in adapting to her role within the marriage. It is precisely her silence that functions as an implicit commentary on the constraints placed on her own sense of autonomy. The autobiographer does not explicitly speak of her response to these constraints within her brief life story. However, she uses the narrative space of *Dew on the Thorn* to critique the subjugated position of woman in the patriarchal system. I would argue, therefore, that it is through the fictional narrator and the voices of other female characters such as Doña Margarita and Rosita, as well as through stories and folklore inserted within this autobiographically informed narrative, that this critique takes place.[53]

At various points in the text, for example, the narrator represents Don Francisco within the context of the Olivareño as a "feudal lord," someone who was "feared and respected," a "tyrant," and an "absolute ruler." In this type of discourse we perceive negative imaginary formations in which the narrator would seem to be speaking not only about Don Francisco but about all male heads of family. There are also several references that focus on the marital relation between Don Francisco and Doña Margarita:

> But though he was the master of many he was the slave of one—Doña Margarita, his wife. And as he thundered through the rooms of the house, his spurs echoing through the tile floors, one look from his wife was sufficient to calm him. Often, when he was in one of his dark moods or when angered by the mismanagement of the *caporal*, she would come to him and say:
>
> "Francisco, my Lamb, let me read to you a while." Then the lion, now a lamb, indeed, sat by her while she read to him from the lives of the Saints . . . or from some romantic novel. When her reading was not sufficient to soothe him, she played melodies that both had loved in their youth. (12)

Here we find a discursive process in which the narrator presents a positive image of Doña Margarita, who seemingly has control over her husband's "dark moods"; she has the power to transform the "lion" into a "lamb." However, we also detect an imaginary formation presented by the narrator regarding the negative constraints of the marriage in which Doña Margarita must find various ways to "soothe" her husband when her efforts at reading are not enough to do so. Through discursive formations of this type we find the narrator taking on the role of critic as she addresses the reader regarding the position of the female, who is subject to the moods of the male as the dominant force within the marriage. Once again, as we have seen in "Early Life," there is silence on the part of Doña Margarita, who does not complain about her husband's "dark moods" and her position of having to cajole and manipulate her husband into a more peaceful mood. Here we perceive the implicit suggestion of the woman's power within the home space, yet it is a power that must be used to calm the male. I would argue, therefore, that it is through this type of discursive reference that the writer of the text enters into a dialogue with herself as she contemplates the constraints of marriage.

Dew on the Thorn also focuses on the Rosita-Carlos love story, an important element of the narrative that clearly demonstrates the subjugated position of the female within the system of patriarchy. Rosita and Carlos are in love, but Carlos is accused of stealing cattle. As a result we find that he is punished by his father Don Ramón and sent away, thus leaving Rosita without the man she loves. Rosita too is subject to her father's power. When speaking to her uncle, Tío Patricio, she sobs, "My father commands me to forget him . . . as if love could be ordered away. He told me that Carlos had disgraced himself and his family and that I must never think of him again" (60). It is interesting to note here that Gilbert and Gubar argue that women are often represented in literature as either "angel" or "monster." Those who are angelic tend to be "wholly passive, completely void of generative power" (16–21). Rosita is definitely presented as a passive angel as she waits for the return of Carlos. Her discourse is never directed to her father; she simply accepts his instructions, although we detect her implicit negative imaginary formation, her critique of her father as she notes that love cannot "be ordered away." Ultimately devoid of power, Rosita becomes ill and "a mere shadow of a once carefree girl whose song had echoed through the house" (62).

Through the character of Rosita as a referent of the discourse of the family doctor and Doña Margarita, we also observe a critique of the constraints of patriarchal hierarchy that are evident within the text where we find that Doña Margarita and the family doctor try to convince Don Francisco to give Rosita some hope:

> "Seriously speaking," the doctor told him later, "due to her delicately nervous constitution and the great love she bears the young man, unless she is made to feel the possibility of her marriage, I fear she will not recover."
>
> After the doctor's verdict, Doña Margarita pleaded with Don Francisco, but he remained adamant in his decision. He could not and would not tolerate the marriage of his daughter to one who had brought shame to his family and to his name.
>
> "What is a name to the life of a daughter?" argued the mother.
>
> "A name is family honor, honor comes from the soul, and the soul belongs to God."
>
> "How like a man you reason! I can forget family honor, I can forget

> all, all, to save the life of my daughter. What is a name? A hollow sound easily carried away by the wind. Something that passes; but a daughter, ah, Francisco! A daughter," she continued softly, "is a being so tender and so loving; someone created from our very selves and sent to us by God. Would you sacrifice her? Would you break her heart with your harsh actions and words?"
>
> All of Doña Margarita's eloquence fell on barren soil. With the firmness of conviction that characterized him, Don Francisco vowed he preferred to mourn for a dead daughter than for one living in disgrace. (62-63)

There are a number of imaginary formations within this passage that are of key importance. First of all, the doctor speaks to Don Francisco of Rosita and her health and the possibility of not recovering from her sadness. He is implicitly trying to appeal to Don Francisco's love of his daughter. As we have seen previously, Doña Margarita addresses her husband, whom she knows to be a harsh man, and, using the authority of the doctor's verdict as a shield, she appeals to the importance of saving her daughter's life. Previously Doña Margarita has been able to exercise some power over her husband through the use of cajoling words, songs, and stories, but here we do not find a husband converted into a "lamb." Instead Don Francisco addresses his wife not about the health of his daughter but about the importance of family honor. In response, Doña Margarita presents a negative imaginary formation of her husband as she rebukes his "harsh actions and words" when she tells him, "How like a man you reason!" Not even her questions to him about sacrificing his daughter and breaking her heart are sufficient to change his mind. The narrator reinforces Doña Margarita's response as she presents another negative imaginary formation regarding Don Francisco's unfeeling reply. Noteworthy here is the meaning effect of the text, which is based on a diffuse type of ideology in which the importance of two generally held beliefs—family honor and the importance of children within the family—come into conflict. In the end, the perspective of the male as head of the family, who would prefer his daughter's death rather than the disgrace of the family name, takes precedence over that of the female.

The previous examples present women who are subject to cultural practice that privileges the position of the male's authority over the woman within the marital state. However, *Dew on the Thorn* provides the reader with other types of women who function as a type of commentary within the fictional narrative. In direct contrast to Rosita, who is compliant to her father's will, Nana Chita is not afraid of Don Francisco. This female character is not presented with angelic qualities or as a witch, yet she possesses knowledge of good and evil spirits. She is described as "a small, agile, old woman who, whether walking sprightly or talking tartly with a ready comeback, resembled a little brown bird. Besides being the mother of Pedro, and Don Francisco's old nurse, she was the weaver of fanciful tales" (78–79). Here we find an imaginary formation which presents Nana Chita's capacity to speak; yet her speech is not like the cajoling speech of Doña Margarita who "soothes" her husband, nor is it the silence of Rosita. Instead she speaks "tartly," with an edge and "a ready comeback"; that is, she responds directly to those who address her, even to the patriarch of the Olivareño. This is evident when Nana Chita tells her *comadre* María that she alone is not afraid of Don Francisco: "Yes, I am the only one who is not afraid of him and treats him as though he were not a God."

For example, when Don Francisco and Rosita come to visit her we find the following exchange:

> "The age of miracles has not ceased yet, I see," she called out.
>
> "The saints alone perform them, Nana Chita," replied Don Francisco.
>
> "If you refer to my coming, Margarita is responsible for that."
>
> "Sit down, sit down both of you. How is Margarita?"
>
> "As usual, Nana. I don't have to ask you how you feel; your bright eyes and your sharp tongue tell me you are well."
>
> "Yes, *gracias a Dios*, Francisco, I am always in good health. I was expecting you today."
>
> "Expecting me? I did not know myself I was coming until this noon when Margarita asked me to bring Rosita to see you."
>
> "Not you, particularly, but I knew someone was coming and I told Pedro so this morning."
>
> "Did you have one of your symptoms?" laughed Don Francisco.
>
> "Laugh if you must, but as sure as I get up with a jumpy feeling in my heart, I am sure to see someone I like."
>
> "I bet it almost broke through your ribs this time."
>
> "Don't flatter yourself, Francisco, a mere flutter it was and very indistinct besides," she said winking at Rosita. (82–83)

This dialogue between Nana Chita and Don Francisco presents the reader with one of the only instances in which a female speaker responds directly to Don Francisco. Furthermore, she is also capable of speaking down to him as she tells him not to flatter himself into thinking that the "jumpy feeling" in her heart, which let her know when a visitor was to arrive, was anything more than an indistinct flutter. It is here that we see a positive representation of Nana Chita, who does not have to find ways to pacify Don Francisco. Instead she is presented as a healthy woman who knows what others do not know because she listens to her body and the knowledge it provides her. Furthermore, she refers to Don Francisco as "not a God" and calls him simply Francisco without the title of don. Thus, it is in the character of Nana Chita that we find another example of the way in which the narrator of *Dew on the Thorn* enters into dialogue with herself and other female readers as she presents a fictional character whose voice represents a strong response to the taboo of woman's speech and expression of knowledge about herself and others.

This capacity of the woman to speak out is further emphasized in a folktale that Tío Patricio recounts to Cristobal, who as a child had witnessed his mother being whipped with a rope by her husband as a means of curing her of what was deemed to be her bewitched state. Cristobal's inability to understand his father's cruelty toward his mother and Don Francisco's unbending will with regard to his daughter's relation to Carlos is explained by Tío Patricio through a folktale about a cardinal. Here we are told that a "little gray bird," a male, wanted to sing but could not. Because "beauty and voice" could only be given to one of the two—either the male or the female bird, it was through the sacrifice of the "not very pretty" female bird that the male received his "brilliant red" color and his "clear and triumphant" song. As the story continues the reader finds that the male cardinal "soon forgot his wife's sacrifice, grew overbearing and cruel, and scolded and pecked her because of her ugliness . . . and "she, knowing the vanity of his sex," tossed her little head and flew off laughing at "the stupidity of husbands" (50). Just as we have seen that Doña Margarita is subject to her husband's bad humor and must pacify him, and just as she is unable to convince him to change his mind about forbidding Rosita to see Carlos, Tío Patricio tells a tale that presents a negative image of the male figure as vain and stupid, thereby further emphasizing the nature of man as dominant yet cruel and unfeeling.

Finally, it is through the imaginary formations evident within the narrative that we are able to perceive the embedded commentary that is responsible for the meaning effect of the text. Doña Margarita, Rosita, Nana Chita, and the voice of the female cardinal are not to be understood simply as individual fictive characters; rather they represent the female position within a social formation that is expressed throughout the work as a whole. It is precisely through the voices of the fictional characters of *Dew on the Thorn* that we find a discourse that is dialogical in nature. That is, these multiple voices present a view of a world that is dominated by the power of the patriarchal head of the family, whether he be the father or husband. Furthermore, as Bakhtin has noted, there is a correlation between the author and the character in terms of the total artistic work. The author and the autobiographer cannot be seen as one and the same, but it is the author who directs the characters created.[54] I would argue, therefore, that the autobiographer chose not to speak extensively in "Early Life and Education" about her life after she was married. Instead she directs the "other," or the voice of the female characters within the narrative space of *Dew on the Thorn*, as a means of pronouncing that which she is prohibited from speaking elsewhere. Therefore, it is through the fictional characters of *Dew on the Thorn* that the autobiographer is able to figuratively represent a specific cultural reality that she uses as the basis for her dialogical exchange with the reader and herself.[55]

Romance of a Little Village Girl

As I have noted in the above discussion, within the discourse of both "Early Life and Education" and *Dew on the Thorn*, the reader is able to perceive certain imaginary formations that result in a meaning effect regarding the female subject and her subjugated position in which she must mold her life to her husband's plans, respond to his moods, and accept his dictates. Within the *Romance* text, the reader also discovers passages that focus on the autobiographer's marginalized position within the male-female relationship. For example, after her engagement to Col. Venceslao Jaramillo, the autobiographer presents imaginary formations regarding referents such as her marriage preparations, Venceslao, and her mother-in-law. Interestingly, "Ven" takes a predominant role in preparations, which include a trip to Denver and El Pueblo:

> The trousseau at last finished, we left for El Pueblo. . . . At the jewelry store, Ven bought five silver table sets. My mother-in-law, seeing a four-piece tea set, said she wanted to get me one with my name engraved. "You want this name on the four sets?" the clerk asked. "Yes,"

> Ven answered. On the four pieces, I timidly corrected, but I was not heard, and the four sets, on four round silver platters, came with my name and wedding date engraved on each. By now I was bewildered and said: "How extravagant!" "Oh, well, I intend to be married just once," Ven said. . . . I want a quiet wedding in the capilla, I told the family. Ven answered, "That will never do. The last time I was in Santa Fe I met Governor Otero and he said, Colonel, I and my staff are coming to your wedding. We cannot accommodate those people here. Tomorrow we go to Taos and arrange for rooms at the hotel." . . .
>
> Next day a perfect July day arched the blue heavens. I again sat by my Romeo in timid silence. (74–75)

Within this passage the autobiographer presents imaginary formations about her future husband Venceslao: "Ven bought" and "Ven answered." Although we observe dialogues in which the autobiographer addresses Ven and tells him that his purchases are "extravagant," Ven then addresses his future wife by telling her "Oh, well, I intend to be married just once," thereby appropriating the wedding as his domain. Furthermore, although the autobiographer has told her family that she prefers a small wedding in the capilla, we find a dialogue in which Ven addresses his wife-to-be and insists that a small wedding is impossible.

As I commented at the beginning of this section, imaginary formations often involve an implicit question such as "Who is she/he to talk to me like that?" Therefore the dialogue in which Ven addresses his future wife suggests an attitude in which he minimizes her point of view. For him, she is simply a woman, the "other" who is presumed to have little knowledge of the type of wedding that must be planned; thus, her opinion is to be ignored. Ultimately we find that the autobiographer presents herself as "timidly silent." Like Rosita in *Dew on the Thorn*, who is unable to contest her father's will, the discourse evident within the above passage also presents the autobiographer's assimilation of a diffuse type of ideology in which the woman's negative response to a male directive is considered taboo; instead she demonstrates the expected behavior of this cultural sphere—silence before men.

The silent position of the woman in relation to the male is further emphasized in the narrative as the narrator comments on her role as companion to her husband in his political career. For example, she explains that during her visits to the legislature it was common for the wives of legislators to attend the teas and dinners that were organized during this period. Noteworthy are the imaginary formations she presents of herself in the following fragment: "I very much enjoyed meeting intelligent people, but fresh from nine years of secluded convent life, in my timidity, I encased myself in a quiet reserve before an English-speaking gathering. Not having enough practice in speaking their language fluently, nor being yet schooled in their social ways, I was afraid to make a mistake, and rather profited by my quiet observation; although I felt I was giving people the impression of being stupid, and many times felt dissatisfied with myself because I was not a smarter woman, more able to help my husband more intelligently to carry on his social and political ambitions" (114–15). There are two types of imaginary formations evident in this portion of the text. The narrator first emphasizes her silence before the referent, or "English-speaking gathering." That is, she elaborates on the fact that she did not have sufficient practice to speak English or comply with "their social ways." Ultimately she expresses her sense of timidity, her dissatisfaction with not being "a smarter woman," and her fear of being perceived as "stupid." In addition to representing herself so negatively, she also notes that she preferred "quiet observation" or silence. This clearly demonstrates the autobiographer's perception of her speech as unvalidated and outside a discourse of power that is based on the ability to speak English. Furthermore, as I have mentioned in chapter 2, there is a change in the autobiographer as she is faced with widowhood, the brutal death of her daughter, and having to continue life on her own. In contrast to the silent, timid woman she describes herself as in the beginning of her marriage, we later find an autobiographical subject capable of articulating her sense of autonomy as she presents imaginary formations regarding herself and those activities she considers important for preserving certain cultural practices, especially the Santa Fe Fiesta:

> So far we have been seeing mostly what Americans have arranged. ... I planned a program for the coming fiesta, just two months ahead. The following morning, full of enthusiasm, I called five ladies who I thought would be interested in helping to carry out my plans.... I told them my plan, which was to try to arouse more interest amongst our Spanish-speaking population in taking part in the fiesta in greater numbers....
>
> The Fiesta Council, having heard about my activities, elected me to be a member and sent me an invitation to attend the weekly meetings. A week before the fiesta, the council asked that my group elect

> the Fiesta Queen. In great haste, I called a meeting of my charter members with two others. After much discussion, we elected Miss Espinosa as Fiesta Queen and notified the council of our choice. For political reasons, I imagine . . . the council replied that we would have to choose another. I explained that this would be very embarrassing to the young lady, as she had already ordered her costume and notified her relatives. She was then accepted. (174–75)

This passage projects a marked difference in the imaginary formations that the autobiographer presents with regard to herself as she notes that, "I planned a program"; "I called five ladies"; "I called a meeting of my charter members"; and "I explained that this would be very embarrassing." Here she represents herself discursively in an extremely positive light, as someone who is capable of taking charge of the organization of the Santa Fe Fiesta. Most importantly, however, she acquires her own voice and argues in favor of the young lady, Miss Espinosa, who was initially rejected by the council as the fiesta queen. Of particular importance, then, is the positive result of her argument and the impositions it contests.

This type of discourse clearly demonstrates the narrator's concern with the continuance of what she considers to be genuine social practice that must be preserved. Indeed, as she remarks: "Our mansions have crumbled back to the earth from which they sprung. Nevertheless, if we were to ransack our mothers' old trunks, I believe we would find some fine old-fashioned silk gowns and jewels. So far we have been seeing mostly what Americans have arranged" (174). The discourse in this portion of her life story contrasts greatly with her previous imaginary formations about herself in which she feared being perceived as stupid by the Americans. We now discover a speaking subject who has found her own sense of autonomous power. She presents a view of herself as someone who is able to break the taboo of silence as she contests and corrects Americans who are "deficient" in their knowledge.[56] She then demonstrates her own knowledge as she forms "*La Sociedad Folklórica*," which, she argues, "should be composed of only thirty members, all of whom must be of Spanish descent, and [whose] meetings must be conducted in the Spanish language, with the aim of preserving our language, our customs and traditions" (176). Although she seems to be speaking only of the Sociedad Folklórica, she is implicitly speaking to those Americans who mistakenly think they know something about Spanish customs. Furthermore, she uses the word "must" as the basis of a discourse that sets limits and stipulates that all non-Spanish people were to be excluded from this society. This autonomous voice stands in stark contrast to the "timidly silent" woman we meet at the beginning of the narrative.

A Beautiful, Cruel Country

A Beautiful, Cruel Country is different from the previously mentioned texts as it presents the reader with a life story in which imaginary formations demonstrate the development of a sense of female identity that is contrary to what Gilbert and Gubar have termed traditional sexual ideology, one that stipulates the angelic and passive role of women. These authors have noted, for example, that Goethe's vision of the "Eternal Feminine" has to do with the "ideal of contemplative purity," whereas "the ideal of significant action is masculine."[57] Noteworthy in this life story, therefore, is the manner in which the autobiographer presents herself as a child who is expected to take action and participate in activities traditionally assigned to the male sphere. For example, she explains:

> I decided that I had to determine when I was old enough to do certain things and when too young to attempt to undertake them. I engaged the help of my father. . . . I was his favorite daughter . . . and by that token I chose him as my favorite parent. But my favorite parent was not always the most understanding parent. My father was a hard man. When something had to be done it had to be done on the spot and one had to go about it the right way. Neither man nor beast was spared. How unpleasant, difficult, or painful the task might be was not to be considered. When one of such tasks was assigned to me I was expected to go in shoes and all just like anybody else. Neither my sex, my age, or my sensitivity was ever considered. Consequently, I grew up in emotional upheaval. (46–47)

Initially the autobiographer presents positive imaginary formations about herself and what she perceives as her decision and capacity to take part in certain activities that are guided by her father. She then presents a negative imaginary formation of her father who is referred to as "not always the most understanding" and as "a hard man." Therefore, when she says that "I engaged the help of my father" she is obviously recalling her childlike sense of needing her father in order to comply with those tasks that "had to be done on the spot . . . and in the right way." This is a response that masks a fear of her father and corresponds to an ideological formation in which absolute obedience to the father is assumed by the child.

There is little emphasis in the narrative that points to the autobiographer's sense of femininity. Although she spends time at home and observes her mother in the kitchen as she cooks, sews, and tends to children, the autobiographer presents herself as spending most of her time out on the open range with her father and the ranch hands. Indeed, she notes that "Mother dressed me in the long overalls she had made me from Father's discarded levis. I didn't like to wear them." Her father's response, however, is different: "'Wear them, wear them. . . . Those are your chaps and you'll need them to protect your legs against the brush and the catclaw.'" She then tells the reader: "Well, I like[d] that. If they were chaps that was good enough for me" (49). Here we find that the autobiographer represents her parents as the referents of her discourse. Because the child's mother knows it is impossible to go against her husband's decision to take his daughter up the mountain, she dresses her daughter in overalls, which according to her husband will serve as protection. The autobiographer notes her struggle with this imposition by her father when she says "I didn't like to wear them." Yet because her father calls the overalls "chaps" she accepts the fact that she must wear male clothing in order to venture outside the female sphere of the home to take part in the more significant action of the male world. Thus, early in her text, the autobiographer comments on the patriarchal authority of the father, yet she also represents her tentative, childlike desire to please him and take part in his world.[58]

Another implicit struggle between this young child and the demands placed upon her by her father is also apparent in her discourse as she continues to represent conflicting views of him. First she tells the reader that he was "my favorite parent," yet this view of her father is immediately followed by a description of him as "a hard man" who expected her to do things regardless of her "sex," "age," or "sensitivity." She implicitly suggests that saying no to a particular task was unthinkable; that is, saying no to the task would be tantamount to saying no to her father, an action that is prohibited. Hence, she presents us with a vision of her world—"I was expected to go in shoes and all just like anybody else"—a vision based on a diffuse and seemingly rational ideology in which the father represents a position of power that is part of the established order of this cultural field. Like Rosita in *Dew on the Thorn*, the autobiographer of *A Beautiful, Cruel Country* has assimilated the knowledge that disobedience to the father and questioning his orders is totally unacceptable. It is precisely this struggle to come to terms with the father who imposes his will that results in what she describes as her "emotional upheaval."

Because this text focuses on the early life of the autobiographer, it is interesting to point out those strategies developed by this young girl to cope with her father's demands. The following passage reveals much about her ability to adapt:

> With the work increasing by leaps and bounds, Father was always in a hurry and usually out of sorts. He would often ask me, "Have you seen the team, Eva?"
>
> "Yes, Pa. They were up there." I would point vaguely upward.
>
> "Up where!"
>
> "By the trail, near the cottonwoods."
>
> My inability to be explicit always exasperated Father beyond reason.
>
> One day he came to the house at a gallop. "Eva, did you see Midnight at the water hole?"
>
> "Yes, Pa. He drank and went up the trail."
>
> "What trail?"
>
> "The trail of the mulberries."
>
> Father jumped back on the saddle and disappeared across the creek. He came back within minutes leading Midnight. My description had worked beautifully. That was the way to answer Father. I decided then and there to name every rock, gate, hill, or hole in the ground, and it would be up to Father to remember just which place was Mockingbird Meadow or Lobo's Gulch, or Screech Owl's Hollow Tree.
>
> In such ways I eventually learned to cope with Father's outlandish whims and unreasoning anger. (88–89)

This portion of the text presents positive imaginary formations on the part of the narrator in reference to her capacity for learning to adapt to her father's harsh manner. However, the reader then encounters negative imaginary formations regarding the father as a referent of the narrator's discourse when she speaks of him in terms of "his outlandish whims and unreasoning anger" and as "exacting and severe." Implicit within this type of discourse is a child who is fearful of her father, and her only defense against him is to make a game of finding ways to subvert his harsh manner. Indeed, in reference to herself, she once again tells the reader: "I decided then and there to name every rock, gate, hill, or hole in the ground, and it would be up to Father to remember" (89).

Thus, just as we have seen in "Early Life," *Dew on the Thorn*, and *Romance*, the female subject does not speak back to the father, nor does she speak out against the constraints of her life. In each case, the voice of the autobiographer or the fictional female character is silent and she acts in accordance with the demands and limits placed upon her by the father or husband. However, in the same way the female subject of the *Romance* text ultimately succeeds in becoming an author and organizer of the Sociedad Folklórica, so too does the young girl of *A Beautiful, Cruel Country* learn to excel in ranching activities. Thus, although she presents negative comments regarding her father, she implicitly tells the reader that her way of taking control, of "speaking" back to him, was to name things in her surroundings and force him to discover the meaning she had designated for each one. Furthermore, as I have mentioned in chapter 2, she learns to excel in her capacity to ride Diamante and ride to the top of the Cerro, as well as guard the gap and prevent cattle from escaping. Therefore, she presents an important imaginary formation with regard to herself and her sister as she notes that some of the hired men would quit their job on her father's ranch once they discovered the capacity she and Ruby had for ranch activities.

This capacity is further emphasized as she presents a moment in which she takes part in the dangerous activity of breaking in wild horses:

> Doña Tomaza came and sure enough, before we knew it she was on Diamante and I was with her behind the saddle. Father saddled one of the broncs in the creek bed, stepped into the stirrup, and swung himself into the saddle. He removed the blindfold from the bronc and the horse took off at a dead run.
>
> Tomaza galloped alongside, heading the horse away from the creek slope and said, "Take hold of me, *hija*, and we'll keep him in the creek." Her calling me "daughter" reassured me a little and I held onto her as she asked.
>
> The bronc ran close to the bank and stopped dead. Try as she might, Tomaza just couldn't get him to move one way or the other. She finally took the lead rope from Father, dallied it around the saddlehorn, and gradually pulled the young bronc away from the bank. (89)

In this section of the text the narrator presents her implicit view of Doña Tomaza as an expert rider, but also as someone who is equal to a man in her skills. Because Tomaza calls the autobiographer *hija*, we sense this child's feeling of oneness and identification with Tomaza, who clearly reminds us of Nana Chita in *Dew on the Thorn*. Nana Chita spoke back to Don Francisco, whereas Tomaza, without speaking, takes the rope from the child's father and is able to control the bronc, an action or cultural ritual that is considered to be part of the male sphere. Finally, the autobiographer, who is on the saddle with Doña Tomaza, shares in this achievement, a moment of empowerment. Doña Tomaza, then, is represented as contesting a system that intends to exclude women and "puny girls" from certain types of activity.

By the end of the narrative, the reader encounters a girl who has come to enjoy her freedom. In the chapter entitled "Up at the Cima, Alone, *Olé*" Wilbur-Cruce points to a moment when Grandfather Vilducea questions the fact that his granddaughter takes part in activities with male Indians:

> "Agustín," said Grandfather, "What will your mother think when she sees Eva run down the river with the Indians? I know they are good boys, but it doesn't look nice. What will your mother say, Hijo?"
>
> "My mother doesn't have anything to say, Pa. . . Eva takes care of herself."
>
> "How can you let your five-year-old daughter run off wrangling with a couple of pagans miles away from home?" Grandfather demanded. Then he enlisted Mother's support and she, too, thought it was wrong to go alone with the boys. The argument got bigger and louder. My grandfather raised his voice and Father raised the roof. . . .
>
> Father suddenly dropped the argument, stood up, and said, "If you're going with the boys you'd better get yourself to the corral, Eva." (266–67)

This particular passage reveals an implicit sense of triumph on the part of the autobiographer. Grandfather Vilducea addresses Eva's father as they speak of the young girl who wants to wrangle horses with the Indian boys. Note that Eva's father responds to Grandfather Vilducea, who also represents patriarchal power in the family, by saying that "Eva takes care of herself." His words take on a sense of power that extends beyond those of the child's grandfather as he tells his daughter to go to the corral with the boys. The struggle between the two male heads of the family clearly points to the dominant position of the father's discourse. His word is to be taken as "truth" and accepted unquestioningly by all. These portions of the narrative point clearly to the autobiographer's intention to critique her father's harsh ways. However, this final scene also suggests an attempt on the part of the autobiographer who retrospectively contests a dominant discourse that limits the role of the woman within society. Ultimately we find that *A Beautiful, Cruel Country* is different from "Early Life," *Dew on the Thorn*, and *Romance* as it presents the bold proposition of energetically contesting the confines of the "Eternal Feminine." This text instead suggests the possibility of a woman of action capable of taking part in the same activities as men, and this new type of female subject is represented by the autobiographer as she portrays herself as a young child sitting on the saddle with Doña Tomaza, thereby sharing in the status of a woman who has proven her capacity to stand firmly within the male sphere of activity.

Hoyt Street

Ponce's *Hoyt Street* is a narrative in which the autobiographer as observer presents a number of imaginary formations that have to do with referents such as those women and girls who were part of her life and who have appropriated traditional female roles. Like *Dew on the Thorn* and *Romance*, the text initially involves discursive formations that demonstrate the effect of a diffuse ideology that situates the woman within the domestic sphere. Those women assigned to the domestic space and who participate in traditional female activities include the autobiographer's mother, her sisters, and Doña Luisa, her "adopted grandmother."

As I have mapped out previously, the narrator initiates her life story by focusing on the home built by her father. Through imaginary formations regarding this space as a referent, the kitchen is described as "the place where my mother cooked, ironed, and bathed her many children." It was also a place where "everyone congregated to eat."[59] The autobiographer also presents a view of her mother as a type of ministering "angel" within the home.[60] Indeed, in the third section of the life story entitled "Knowledge," she directs our attention to both her mother and Doña Luisa as referents, as she notes the Monday ritual of washing clothes: "When my mother and Doña Luisa did the family laundry on Monday mornings, Berney's white shirts were set aside to be washed separately from those of my father and other brothers. First the shirts were boiled in Purex bleach, scrubbed until snowy white, then rinsed several times in cool water. In the final rinse my mother added a piece of bluing, which was sold in squares like chocolate candy. Doña Luisa then hung the camisas to dry on the clothesline. The white shirts dancing on the line made a pretty picture, their long arms flapping in the wind" (276–77). The message conveyed in this passage once again points to the woman as a selfless entity in her home, someone dedicated to the work of purifying the laundry, especially the shirts worn by the male members of the family. Indeed, as I have mentioned previously, the home is the site of male authority that is invested in both the autobiographer's father as the head of the household, and Berney as the eldest son. By observing her mother's example, the autobiographer assimilates knowledge of the home as a space in which women minister to and are subservient to the male members of the household.

Although the autobiographer's mother and Doña Luisa model the role to be assumed by women in the home, it is also significant to mention other types of women evident in the narrative. For example, early in the life story the narrator presents positive imaginary formations regarding her sister Elizabet, whom she describes as "my mother's right hand, a girl who helped with both the easy and hard chores. She cooked, cleaned, ironed . . . and spent most of her life catering to our mother" (20). She further points out that "she was a fantastic cook" and an "expert seamstress [who] knew everything about sewing: how to cut on the bias, adjust for fit, sew French seams, and add a sleeve gusset" (20–21). The activities engaged in by this sister highlight a diffuse ideology that dictates certain ministering duties that are naturally to be accepted by female members of the household. Elizabet is also represented as someone who "aspired to something other than a job in a ceramic plant." Indeed, having "learned typing, shorthand, and accounting" in high school, she was like other girls of the 1940s who "yearned to be secretaries or telephone operators, to work in an office, and to wear high heels and white gloves" (21–22).

The autobiographer notes that Elizabet fulfilled this yearning and worked as a legal secretary and "often accompanied her boss to the Los Angeles jail to take depositions" (22). This role is further described as an opportunity "to wear high heels and white gloves" (22). These portions of the text point to a tradition based on gender as an ideological system that differentiates sexual roles in the work space as well, and where the female is expected to help the male. However, her use of high heels and white gloves mark her as a "lady" and thus implicitly incapable of man's work.

Within the narrative the autobiographer continues to make reference to her sister as we discover that "Elizabet worked on the assembly line at Lockheed Aircraft in Burbank, California. Like other Mexican-Americans on our street, she wanted to do her share in the war effort and to earn good money." Here the narrator communicates positive imaginary formations regarding her sister's desire to contribute to "the war effort" but also to earn "good" money. This reference, particularly the linguistic marker "good," suggests the possibility of earning a higher salary in a work sphere normally assigned to men, and which, we can assume, paid more than secretarial positions.

The reader ultimately discovers that in spite of her achievements as a secretary and factory worker, "Elizabet fell from grace; she eloped with R., a handsome young man who wore a snappy uniform" (22). Here the autobiographer creates an imaginary formation about Elizabet's marriage as a referent: "[It was] almost like in the movies, except that there a girl would climb down a ladder from an upstairs window into the waiting arms of her novio, then off they went to get hitched by a judge." This romantic view of her sister's elopement is complemented by another imaginary formation in which the autobiographer tells the reader of her own childlike response to her sister's marriage: "I found it terribly exciting" (22).

Elizabet's experiences, then, highlight the types of choices open to women during the 1940s. Elizabet further represents the way in which the female subject assumes positions limited by the constraints of a dominant ideology that assigns women to certain tasks such as cooking, sewing, "typing, shorthand, and accounting." Indeed, although the autobiographer notes that "women got to wear pants" when they worked on the assembly line—a reference to a first move away from the assigned female clothing of "high heels and white gloves"—Elizabet eventually opts for marriage to a handsome young man in uniform. Hence, she fulfills a prescribed role within the confines of a sexual ideology that deemed marriage the ultimate imperative of a woman's life.

Within other sections of her life story Ponce centers attention on girls like Tina who "hated catechism and the nuns, gave not a whit for Girl Scouts, nor cared to sing in the church choir." Later the reader is told that Tina "was caught up in the many changes that followed the end of the war, a time when everything seemed to change: clothes, hairdos, cars, and attitudes." Ponce further tells us, "It was as teenagers that Trina and I bonded . . . we shared a bedroom and giggled far into the night. We wore the same size clothes and shoes; we shared plaid skirts, pastel sweaters, and saddle oxfords. . . . We scrutinized movie magazines for beauty secrets and spent our money on Max Factor pancake makeup (#2), Tangee lipstick, Maybelline, and rouge" (34). Here the autobiographer presents Tina as someone who shares her "beauty secrets." These references remind us of the *Romance* text and its emphasis on the coquetry girls learned to imitate from a young age. It would seem then that the beauty secrets revealed in movie magazines provided the key to achieving the femininity that was naturally to be assumed by young girls, just as marriage was deemed the ultimate goal to be achieved.

This sense of femininity and emphasis on the physical appearance of the female is also visible in the chapter entitled "La Nancy," where the autobiographer communicates an imaginary formation about her friend:

> The year I was eleven, my best friend was la Nancy. Unlike Concha and Virgie, girls my age who giggled and acted silly, Nancy, at twelve, was quite sophisticated. She walked with a slight swing of her skinny hips and tilted her head to the left when talking to boys. Often she halfway closed her eyes, wanting to look like the movie stars who were supposed to have "bedroom" eyes. . . .
>
> I yearned to be like Nancy; at home I locked myself in the bathroom to imitate her. I put out the lights to create "an atmosphere" (as in the movies), then stood in front of the mirror to tilt my head and close my eyes halfway . . . just like Nancy. (287).

The discourse of these passages reveals much about the way girls learned to attract men, a sexual ideology that is also played out in the movies where film stars such as "María Felix wore tight dresses with huge shoulder pads and draped skirts that skimmed her full hips" (302). Nancy and María Felix stand as referents that suggest a ritualized and symbolic system of education in which girls are subjected to a discourse that fixes roles for the female subject. The narrative clearly draws our attention to young girls who "yearn" to be secretaries or to be seductive like Nancy. Indeed, the only power a woman might have is that of attracting men like Elizabet's handsome man in a "snappy uniform." Thus, Elizabet as well as the autobiographer and her girlfriends demonstrate an assimilation of sexual ideology, which as suggested by Kristeva, points to an acceptance of the position "bequeathed to [them] by tradition."[61] Women, then, are expected to use their bodies as objects to attract the attention of men only to be rewarded in the marital space with the honor of bleaching and ironing their shirts.

In spite of the excitement she expresses over Elizabet's elopement, and her enchantment with a traditional sense of femininity that she shares with Tina and Nancy, the autobiographer then describes her development toward adolescence and a growing sense of the limits of the woman's traditional position. That is, she presents a negative imaginary formation regarding another type of referent as she tells the reader about some of the girls who attended school with her: "these overripe girls, some of whom were very, very pretty, were not the least bit interested in school; some had been put back a grade or two." Furthermore, she speaks of another friend, Elvira, "an *A* student with whom I competed for gold stars."[62] Here the autobiographer implicitly suggests her perception that being "very, very pretty" and "overripe" was not necessarily a formula for success. Thus, by negatively pointing to those "overripe girls" as uninterested in school, she situates herself in opposition to them as she competes with her classmate, an A student, for the prized gold stars.

Along these same lines the narrator also presents negative imaginary formations with regard to Chita and her group of friends, who "were just hanging around until eighth-grade graduation, bored with books they could not read and school assignments that never made sense. . . . Few of them went on to high school. . . . What's more, boys were encouraged to go on to high school, while it was generally thought that girls would not need a diploma to change diapers" (313). We must recall that in the early section of her life story, the autobiographer refers to her sisters. Nora, the "intellectual," the "seeker of knowledge, a buyer of books," passed her knowledge down to her younger sister; Elizabet, described as a "bookworm," a reader of historical novels, bought books for her younger sister for her birthday and Christmas. Thus, in contrast to those who were "bored with books," the autobiographer highlights the fact that "[b]y the time I was twelve, I was steeped in good literature and had read *The Razor's Edge*, *Leave Her to Heaven*, and my favorite romance novel, *Came a Cavalier*. . . . From an early age I could discern good literature from trash. I never did care for comic books" (21). Thus, although the autobiographer presents a view of herself as trying to imitate the dictates of sexual ideology that emphasize the physical aspect of femininity, she demonstrates a capacity for attempting to cross traditional gender boundaries. Indeed, the narrator presents herself as a young girl who competes with the boys on the playground; she "felt free to climb walls and scale fences" (282) as she played hide-and-seek with the boys who called girls "nuthin but sissies" (285). She learned at an early age that men like "la güera['s]" father were capable of beating women, only to try to remedy the act through gifts of jewelry. All of these everday life experiencies would be complemented with what she learned from books that ultimately mark her life with a love for the written word and the knowledge provided therein. *Hoyt Street*, therefore, suggests a female child and pre-adolescent who will follow a different road from that of those "overripe" girls who would not continue their education.

It is precisely this suggestion of a different road to be followed that marks *Hoyt Street* and the other texts analyzed in this project. In "Early Life" the autobiographer emphasizes her academic achievements, and the "I" of the *Romance* narrative represents herself as a woman of strength, capable of creating a life of her own after her husband's death. The autobiographer of *A Beautiful, Cruel Country* also portrays a female subject who follows a different path, someone who is able to run with boys and compete with men as a *vaquerita*. Hence, although each text demonstrates the way in which the female subject is immersed in an ideology marked by the constraints of patriarchy and the limitations of traditional female activities, each autobiographer clearly presents imaginary formations of herself that point to her ability to move beyond those confines.

Conclusions

"I shall speak about women's writing: *about what it will do*," Hélène Cixous says. "Woman must write her self: must write about women and bring women to writing, from which they have been driven away as violently as from their bodies—for the same reasons, by the same law, with the same fatal goal. Woman must put herself into the text—as into the world and into history—her own movement.[1]

The border autobiographies created by Jovita González, Cleofas Jaramillo, Eva Antonia Wilbur-Cruce, and Mary Helen Ponce represent a continuum of information or knowledge that coexist and that can be understood as an attempt on the part of the Mexican American female autobiographer to "put herself into the text" and thus write her experience into existence.[2] Furthermore, each narrative functions as a signifier of a common heritage that emanates from a distinct geographical space in the Southwest and that focuses on a life course during the period prior to the Chicano movement. It is through the study of this corpus of texts that I have attempted to arrive at a more clear understanding of the individual life course that took shape within a particular context and that involves a cultural memory that points to personal and collective history as well as social practices that are reflected within the discourse of the border autobiography.

All utterances involve an indeterminate meaning that must be interpreted. The border autobiography can be considered a type of utterance in which the autobiographical "I" interprets her life and the lives of those who share her cultural experience. Because each autobiographer is an observer of her own life, and because she strives to situate herself as a "new subject of history,"[3] she has chosen certain aspects to set before the reader so as to highlight their value and meaning. Interpretation, then, contributes meaning to texts, and because the corpus of works considered here involves multi-structured or multilayered meanings, they merit a deep analysis of purpose and perspectives concerning the life and the world that is presented within each narrative.

Throughout this study, I have undertaken a process of interpretation that began with a brief survey of the three phases of criticism concerning autobiography. As we have seen, the genre of autobiography has traditionally been limited by notions of gender and the celebration of the lives of "great men." One of the most glaring limits of this phase of criticism is its emphasis on facts and truth telling concerning the life course of model male figures considered to be important because of their contribution to public history. Ultimately this type of perspective, which focuses on autobiography as the highest and most instructive form for understanding the "phenomenal" male life, is responsible for excluding other types of narrative practice, such as letters, journals, or memoirs, especially those written by women. From this viewpoint autobiography is considered useful only in terms of understanding the significance of religious meditation and conversion, self-revelation, or the political deeds of great men. Because autobiography is necessarily representative of a period, any other type of writing, especially that which takes its form from other branches of literature and deals with average, everyday life, is considered inferior or superficial.

The second phase of theoretical perspectives recognizes that the subtleties of the unconscious contribute to an understanding of the genre of autobiography as creative and involving fictive metaphors as well as the use of allegorical language to refer to the autobiographical "I." Here autobiography is perceived as art, yet we still find vestiges of the exclusionary aspect of the first phase of criticism; that is, autobiography is essentially considered to be a Western and Christian literary form where selfhood and individuality are emphasized. On the basis of Derrida's questioning of the limits placed on this genre, as well as Foucault's perspective concerning discursive systems of control and power, we find a viewpoint that contests the "will to truth" that marked the notion of autobiography presented by theorists such as Dilthey and Misch. Derrida's perspective also contests the dominant position of the primary text, or the grand narratives; furthermore, the "I" does not necessarily take on a central role within structures, or, as is the case with the present study, within the border autobiography. Of primary importance in this third phase of criticism are feminist and ethnic studies that focus on the relevance of cultural practice that does not emanate from the dominant sociocultural sphere. This view of autobiography, therefore, has informed the project I have presented here.

Because my discussion has focused on autobiographies written by women of Mexican descent, and because they provide a view of the individual and collective life experience of a marginalized group, I have found the notion of the border autobiography to be extremely useful as a means of classifying and defining the types of narratives under consideration here. Indeed, the border autobiographies of González, Jaramillo, Wilbur-Cruce, and Ponce are narratives that present a female autobiographical subject who is of mestizo origins. The women represented in these four texts harbor and nurture cultural knowledge that is based on life experiences that take place in a space that develops as the result of the intersection of semiotic systems. That is, their texts reaffirm an identity that is not Indian, Spanish, Mexican, or American, but somewhere in between. These texts, then, represent the voice of women in the borderlands. Furthermore, the view of history evident in each text does not correspond to a dominant American perspective. At first glance, this group of narratives seems simply to present a chronology of the autobiographer's development from childhood to adulthood, from the single state to marriage and then widowhood, from life within the mother's space to the open range of the male world, from innocence to knowledge. Upon closer reading, however, we find a group of texts that provide the reader with various levels of meaning concerned with the "I" in relation to others, as well as references to historical and cultural memory and social practice. Each text also presents the life course as it takes shape in relation to the spheres of Mexico and the United States during the first half of the twentieth century. The border autobiographies considered here, then, trespass the limits of traditional notions of autobiography as they include traces of various types of life writing that have been labeled testimonial, memoirs, ethnic life narrative, genealogy, and bildungsroman without fitting completely within the limits of any of these types of writing. Instead, as I have argued, they can be seen as "other" trajectories, as hybrid narrative forms.

Because of the various layers of information registered within each text, my discussion has been guided by an analytic model that is multidisciplinary and that focuses on narrative and descriptive discourse as well as cultural semiotics and ideology. As I have noted, it is possible to interpret the narrative discourse of each text in terms of the time-space dimension of the chronotope as defined by Bakhtin. Therefore, my first approach to the life story involved an analysis of the chronological development of the autobiographer within various symbolic spaces and as a "subject-in-process." The spatial symbolism evident in each narrative makes it clear that the life story is concerned with the development of the autobiographical subject and the way she has been shaped within different spaces as she struggles with the process of "becoming." That is, within each text we have been able to observe the way the autobiographer negotiates the terrain of those master narratives that assign women roles such as those of obedient daughters and submissive wives subject to male authority. We have also observed how each autobiographer has developed her narrative in a way that demonstrates a personal capacity for moving beyond traditionally assigned roles to experience other options—such as becoming a researcher, a writer and organizer of cultural societies, a capable *vaquerita*, or a reader of books, a studious young girl who intends to continue her studies—and therefore go beyond the culturally assigned role of woman as an object of desire, as someone who must not invade spaces where male power is exercised.

Although the autobiographer includes references to herself, another important meaning that emerges from each narrative has to do with family history and an attachment to the land, or to a particular neighborhood, and a sense of home. On the basis of the theoretical perspective of the School of Neuchâtel, which approaches discourse analysis from the perspective of "natural logic" and its relation to schematization and cultural preconstructs, I have examined the hierarchical representation of the descriptive passages that form part of each life story. By looking at descriptive aspects such as "land" and "home," for example, it was possible to arrive at an understanding of implicit arguments presented by the autobiographer regarding land ownership and the loss of the homeland, or a sense of belonging to the space of Arroyo Hondo, the Arivaca Valley, or the barrio. Indeed, it is precisely on the basis of an interpretation of cultural preconstructs related to the discursive objects of "land" and "home" that we are able to perceive the autobiographer's knowledge and worldview regarding historical struggles and belonging to a particular place in the southwestern border regions of Texas, New Mexico, Arizona, and California.

Once again, by referring to specific aspects of family history, the autobiographer is not simply telling an individual story but has constructed a literary narrative that includes the experiences of a cultural collectivity. Indeed, the linguistic markers of "land" and "home" suggest the importance of a cultural community and its relation to a "home" and sense of belonging to a particular geographical space. This is evident, for example, in narrative and descriptive references to those families represented in *Dew on the Thorn* and *Romance of a Village Girl* who have lost their land or have seen it intruded upon by the Americanos. In *A Beautiful, Cruel Country*, on the other hand, this language of community concerns land that has been affected by the historical changing of borders and by those who, like Grandfather Wilbur, have homesteaded the land of others. The barrio of *Hoyt Street* is different from the spaces of the previous texts as it focuses on the representation of a marginalized space where a large number of Mejicano immigrants form their own sense of community within the barrio. Thus, the autobiographer's use of descriptive discourse can be considered as a strategy of signification in which identity is tied to the history and culture of a particular place, such as the Southwest or California.

Another significant facet of the border autobiographies that make up the present corpus has to do with cultural memory and the way it is represented in each text, particularly in terms of its socio-communicative function. As I have argued, each autobiographer speaks from a particular social position and has one or more audiences in mind when she writes. It is to these audiences that she communicates her memories as a means of writing her cultural experience into history. Lotman's theory of cultural semiotics has served as a framework for my interpretation of this group of texts that focuses on the past made present and meaningful within the autobiography as well as the autobiographically informed fictive narrative. For Lotman, memory is central to the individual human as well as to texts and cultures, which he defines as "thinking" semiotic structures. At one level the memories recalled in each text can be understood as the autobiographer's attempt to preserve and reproduce information. Of further relevance is the cultural sense of memory as a dialogue between past and present, and not simply as a mechanism for transmitting information. It is this dialogue between the past and the present, especially the autobiographer's recollection of and reflection on this past, that generates historical meaning within each text.

As I have demonstrated, the memories evident in each narrative focus not only on the "separate self," but also on the self as part of a cultural group. For example, "Early Life" presents personal and family history as it relates to "the border people" (xiii). Furthermore, although the autobiographer leaves behind her desire to continue graduate work, she ultimately decides to join her husband in his endeavors. The fact that she chose to teach Spanish and Texas history reveals her deep commitment to others and her desire to share her sense of connection with Texas Mexican border culture, yet she also communicates a view of the female subject as oppressed and controlled by men. Her text, therefore, stands as a response intended to undercut that very oppression. The autobiographer of *Romance of a Little Village Girl* also presents herself as part of a larger community as she organizes a Sociedad Folklórica with the intention of preserving an ancestral legacy of New Mexico. However, a major aspect of this portion of her text is concerned with her own process of becoming, as she contests Anglo writers who have attempted to write about the cultural practices of New Mexico. Indeed, she speaks out against their claim to that knowledge, which she presents as her own, pertaining to those who are the true cultural descendants of a Spanish past. Furthermore, although she marginalizes the Mexican identity that marks her sphere of existence, her work clearly points to a Mexican past as well.

In *A Beautiful, Cruel Country* we find that the autobiographer points to "my memories" of life in Arizona, but she also notes that these memories are shared by those from the past. That is, her life story refers not only to herself and personal memories, but also to nature, her parents and grandparents, neighbors, *vaqueros*, and Indians. In this way she demonstrates a sense of being part of a complex cultural whole. Of further importance are those moments of her narrative that spotlight her struggle against the oppressive relation she has with her father, yet she ultimately emphasizes her ability to outwit him and to take possession of knowledge that is traditionally reserved for men. This emphasis on others is also apparent in *Hoyt Street*, which centers on life in Pacoima, California, as the autobiographer underscores the importance of her writing about life in the barrio, which is intended to allay negative stereotypes concerning Mexican Americans. She clearly states that it is for the "hard-working, decent, and honorable" Mejicanos that she writes;[4] therefore, her text stands in contrast to Western autobiographical practice with its emphasis on the individual "I." However, she clearly intends to situate herself as different from other girls presented in her text. That is, she chooses to portray herself as someone capable of going beyond those gender and racial boundaries that attempt to limit her.

We also find evidence of a connection to others in the way each text emphasizes social practice, particularly in terms of education and religious institutions. Bourdieu's theory of *habitus* has been a fundamental tool in examining these elements of the text. Each of the works of the corpus can be seen as a cultural field in which the position-taking of the autobiographer becomes evident. Indeed, as we have seen, each autobiographical narrator constructs her own creative project according to her perception and appreciation of the *habitus*. This is particularly notable, for example, in the way she situates herself, her family, and the larger cultural group as Catholic. This position-taking stands as a referent that points to the struggle between those who adhere to Catholic practice and the white Anglo-Saxon Protestant perspective that constitutes the dominant identity of the semiotic system of the United States. By looking at the various types of cultural practices such as Nochebuena, St. John's Day, the *penitente* ceremonies, the Feast of the Holy Cross, and Holy Week observances, I have attempted to highlight the position taken by the autobiographer as she presents her appreciation of these religious practices that mark a specific cultural field, one that is evident during the first half of the twentieth century. The cultural practices presented in each text further demonstrate the interrelatedness of these autobiographical works, each of which functions as a microcosm that points to social origins that contribute to the shaping of the individual as well as a cultural collectivity.

I have also suggested that the autobiographers of these texts reveal themselves as women who must negotiate their way through, and struggle with, the conditions that result from a system of patriarchy that permeates society, particularly in the early years of the twentieth century. Indeed, the individual and the range of her experiences evident in the life story present a scenario that signals the process by which she is shaped within a particular environment. The "meaning-effect" of the discourse evident within each narrative reveals a system of patriarchy, particularly in terms of the role of the father, husband, and eldest brother and the constraints they represent in the autobiographical subject's life. My analysis of this aspect of the life story is informed by the work of Michel Foucault, who asserts that within all societies discourse production is controlled, selected, organized, and redistributed through procedures of exclusion. As I argue in the final section of this study, the border autobiography clearly demonstrates the effect of certain discourses on the female autobiographical subject. Indeed, her discourse responds to various regulative practices evident within the home, religious institutions, and educational spheres. Hence, the life stories created by these women point to the reality of the central role of gender in society and, importantly, to the female's initial appropriation of a subjugated position.

Michel Pêcheux's perspective on the discursive process and the functioning of "imaginary formations" has been fundamental in my arriving at an understanding of those symbolic social positions from which the addresser speaks and expresses her view of the addressee or other referents. Within my discussion I pointed to the importance of subject positions that are the result of discourse formations that display relations of antagonism, alliance, or domination. Therefore, a close analysis of these discursive formations has revealed the ideological positions evident within the text. For example, each narrative presents the reader with evidence of the ideological construction of a gendered self-identity, one that corresponds to a traditional view regarding the designated role of women in the domestic sphere, where they are taught to tend to the needs of men. Indeed, given the female's assigned position of marginality, one of the major concerns of my analysis and interpretation has been the way in which the autobiographical subject has chosen to speak autonomously through her life story.

As I have argued, the autobiographical subject first represents herself as having assumed certain roles assigned to her by a patriarchal system. However, a close analysis of each text reveals a voice that takes on an assertive tone. The autobiographer of "Early Life," for example, would seem to remain silent as she abruptly discontinues her focus on her academic achievements only to speak of her marriage and then tell the reader "We have been happy." However, she does speak out, albeit through the voice of the narrator of *Dew on the Thorn*. Here we discover a voice that brings to light the excesses of a patriarchal system that is represented through Don Francisco, the family patriarch, who exercises firm control over the *peones* and his daughter Rosita. The autobiographical "I" of *Romance of a Little Village Girl* initially represents herself as a compliant daughter and wife, yet her text ultimately presents a female voice that speaks of her assertive role as the organizer of the *Sociedad Folklórica* and of the numerous honors that were bestowed upon her as a result of her activities after she was widowed.

Within *A Beautiful, Cruel Country* the autobiographer brings to light the fact that she grew up in a period when men were unwilling to accept the competence of a woman. As I have demonstrated in my interpretation of this work, the Arivaca Valley is represented textually as a world dominated by Grandfather Wilbur, Grandfather Vilducea, and the autobiographer's father. Indeed, this text is marked by references to the father's cruelty. However, the speaking subject of this narrative also notes that she wore pants and that her hair was cut like a boy's. In addition she ultimately accepted her role as boss over adult men. Thus, we find a writer who recalls the way she was able to participate in activities that crossed the boundaries of gender-specific roles.

Hoyt Street, on the other hand, presents a view of the woman and her role that was limited to the domestic sphere. The autobiographer clearly represents herself as a young girl who has appropriated this discourse. As I have suggested, this is particularly evident in the section of the text that refers to her role as the sister who "ironed best" her brother Berney's shirts. However, once again, careful analysis and interpretation of the text brings to light an autobiographical subject who also speaks of another world, the world of books that opened new horizons for her. In each section of her narrative, for example, she emphasizes her educational development and the importance of books in her life. It was her love of books that distinguished her from girls like Anita, Tina, and Nancy. Ultimately, then, each of these female writers "speaks" through the written word as she includes references within the text that deal with the problematic of an ideology of normative femininity that has been prescribed for her. However, by taking up the pen, each of these women has "put herself into the text, into the world, and into history."

This study, then, represents a view of the border autobiography as a text that is multi-structured and complex. Each text certainly involves a chronology of personal development; most importantly, however, it portrays the process of subject formation in relation to other members of the cultural communities of Texas, New Mexico, Arizona, and California. Imbedded within the life story we also find evidence of a cultural memory that presents a different view of history and therefore a different view of "home." Furthermore, one of the major intentions of these works is the restoration of memory that focuses on social practice derived from the past, specifically from Spain and Mexico. Each text, then, represents a countertradition, one that asserts a way of life that has been excluded from the dominant discourse of the United States. Thus, rather than a conflating of the lives of outstanding male individuals, the border autobiography reminds the reader of those lives that take shape in the margins, especially the lives of women who, although they have taken on the identity of daughters, wives, or mothers, have also demonstrated their capacity to go beyond the confines of the social roles defined for them.

Indeed, if we return to the question of why Jovita González, Cleofas Jaramillo, Eva Antonia Wilbur-Cruce, and Mary Helen Ponce chose the autobiographical genre as a means of expression, perhaps another look at Gloria Anzaldúa's motivation for writing will help in our search for an answer: "I seek our woman's face, our true features, the positive and the negative seen clearly, free of the tainted bias of male dominance. I seek new images of identity, new beliefs about ouselves, our humanity and worth no longer in question."[5] Through a poetic literary journey, the autobiographical texts of the four women I have analyzed here demonstrate an attempt to search for the features of their own faces. Along the way, each has discovered a history of self embedded within a culture tainted by the effects of patriarchy and the subjection of women. This is "the negative seen clearly." However, during this process of self-discovery, each writer expresses her own sense of connection with others. As she comes to grips with the knowledge that her voice and that of the collectivity to which she belongs has been marginalized, she also discovers the positive features of her identity as a woman of strength, one who is capable of resisting the temptation to succumb to those limits that would be imposed upon her. Therefore, narrating the life story of self and community becomes a creative act that allows each writer to enter into dialogue with herself as she embarks on a personal project that allows her to uncover her own sense of worth as a speaking subject.

Finally, although I have attempted to interpret the multiple facets of each text, it is pertinent to note that there are still elements of these narratives that should be addressed in the future. First, I would suggest that *Dew on the Thorn* offers an important opportunity for a more detailed interpretation of the female voice by examining the folkloric references within the text. My analysis only briefly touches on the symbolic importance of the female within each story that is inserted into the major narrative. Therefore, this is clearly an area for future study. The poetic function of each text, especially the way each autobiographer presents the landscape, also merits attention.

This study focuses on the works of four female authors, yet there are a number of early Mexican American texts that would further broaden the scope of my analysis. As I have noted in my discussion, the everyday tasks of going to school, preparing for feasts, and celebrating various customs are some of the key elements of the border autobiography. It is precisely the details and memories of "everyday life" in texts such as *Memorias de mi viaje*, by Olga Beatrice Torres, and *Migrant Daughter*, by Frances Esquibel Tywoniak, that should also form part of future discussions, especially in terms of the way these texts demonstrate a commonality with the works of González, Jaramillo, Wilbur-Cruce, and Ponce. I would suggest that *Memorias de mi viaje* and *Migrant Daughter*, as well as *The*

Rebel and *La rebelde*, written by Leonor Villegas de Magnón, and Norma Elia Cantú's fictionalized memoirs, *Canícula: Snapshots of a Girlhood on La Frontera*, also can be understood as border autobiographies. As such, they provide the reader with an opportunity to come into contact with narratives that include ethnographic elements surrounding the life story of the individual female "I" in addition to aspects such as history, social-cultural practices, and the ideologies that give shape to a community.

Although this book has focused on the works of women writers of Mexican origin, the border autobiography is not limited to this area of textual expression. I would also suggest the importance of taking into account other minority works that represent different perspectives, ones that have resulted from a life experience involving the intersection of two or more semiotic systems. As I have pointed out in the first chapter of this study, the life stories of those who have experienced the effects of a change in geographical boundaries or dislocation and the process of initiation into a new way of life clearly lend themselves to analysis and interpretation of the multifaceted aspects of what I have termed the border autobiography. The experiential elements of this type of text contribute to the inclusion and restoration of those life stories and they provide a means for discovering the multiple elements that link the lives of those who represent "other" or alternative trajectories.

Notes

NOTES TO INTRODUCTION

1. Genaro Padilla uses the term "Chicano," which generally refers to first-generation Americans born to Mexican parents. Although it is a term used to refer to Mexican Americans, as suggested by Bruce-Novoa it is a term associated with the Chicano movement, a sociopolitical struggle that took place as part of the civil rights movement of the 1960s. Use of the term "Chicano" is also related to a sense of ethnic pride. In *My History, Not Yours: The Formation of Mexican American Autobiography*, Padilla focuses on autobiographies that predate what is considered the Chicano period (1943–present). He considers the term "Mexican American" to be "more historically representative" than "Chicano," which is a "recent self-designation" (xi). For the purposes of the present analysis, and because the works under consideration refer to more than one sociocultural system, I have chosen to use the following terms: "Mexican American," "women of Mexican descent," and "women of Mexican origin."

2. Padilla, "Yo sola aprendí," 95.

3. Padilla has noted that of the 150 California narratives in this collection, less than 40 represent the female voice.

4. These time periods refer to the historical development of Hispanic literature in the Southwest and are based on those designated by the Recovering the U.S. Hispanic Literary Heritage Project, which has to do with "locating, rescuing from perishing, evaluating, disseminating and publishing collections of primary literary sources written by Hispanics in the geographic area that is now the United States from the Colonial Period to 1960." See Nicolás Kanellos, "Forward," *Recovering the U.S. Hispanic Literary Heritage* (Houston: Arte Publico Press, 1993), 13.

5. Padilla, *My History, Not Yours,* 44.

6. This text was originally published as a series in the *Laredo Times* between March and June of 1961. It was later recovered and published by Arte Público Press and with the cooperation of coordinators of the Recovering the U.S. Hispanic Literary Heritage Project. It has been classified as part of the early Chicano period of writing. This text has been published in English, as well as in Spanish as *La Rebelde*.

7. Reyna, "Jovita González y su obra folclórico-literaria," 184.

8. Saldívar, *Chicano Narrative*, 172.

9. The Oregon Territory would eventually be organized into the states of Oregon, Washington, and Idaho. This area also included portions of present-day Montana, Wyoming, and Canada.

10. Eisenhower, *So Far from God*, xix.

11. See Nicolás Kanellos, *Thirty Million Strong: Reclaiming the Spanish Image in American Culture* (Golden, CO: Fulcrum, 1998), 74.

12. See Robert A. Divine, et al., *America Past and Present* (New York: Addison Wesley, 1999), 304.

13. Paredes, "Mexican-American Literature," 31.

14. According to the Recovering the U.S. Hispanic Literary Heritage Project, González's narrative can be located in the Interaction period, whereas the works of Jaramillo, Wilbur-Cruce, and Ponce correspond to the early Chicano period. However, each of these autobiographical works focuses on life experiences prior to the Chicano period.

15. Throughout my discussion I will make reference to specific life experiences and social practices in relation to those of Amerindian (or Indian), Spanish, Mexican, and Mexican American descent. Mention of "Amerindians" or "Indians" refers to those first groups or native people who inhabited North America prior to European invasion. I frequently refer to the Spanish influence in North America, or those experiences and cultural practices related to people from the Iberian Peninsula. In speaking of a Mexican heritage I am considering the contact between what Miguel León Portillo calls "ancient Mexico"—those groups such as the Aztecs, Olmecs, Toltecs, Mixtecs, and Mayas—and the conquerors who arrived from Spain (with its Moorish legacy). Mexican identity is complex as it refers to a process of *mestizaje* or, as suggested by Matt Meier and Feliciano Ribera, the intermingling or "physical blending of Europeans and Indians." In referring to "Mexican Americans" I am speaking of those Americans of Mexican origin. See Miguel León-Portillo, *Pre-Columbian Literatures of Mexico* (Norman: University of Oklahoma Press, 1974), 3–5, as well as Matt S. Meier and Feliciano Ribera, *Mexican Americans/American Mexicans: From Conquistadors to Chicanos* (New York: Hill and Wang, 1972), 282.

NOTES TO CHAPTER 1

1. Smith and Watson, *Reading Autobiography*, 1–2.

2. Ricoeur, *Memory, History, Forgetting*, 12.

3. Gilmore, *Autobiographics*, 5.

4. Although the English text was published in 1960, it was translated from *Der Aufbau der geschichtlichen Welt in den eisteswissenschaften* (The Construction of the Historical World in the Human Sciences), pp. 68–106 in *Gesammelte Schriften*, vol. 7, 1927 [1907]).

5. Dilthey, *Pattern and Meaning in History*, 85–86.

6. It is important to note that, given the time when Dilthey's text was published (1927), he was indeed referring only to those autobiographies written by men. Although this represents language usage that is sexist, it was the accepted form during the period in which he wrote.

7. Misch, *A History of Autobiography in Antiquity*, 5.

8. Smith and Watson, *Reading Autobiography*, 124.

9. Freud, "Psychopathology of Everyday Life," 69–95.

10. Olney, "Autobiography and the Cultural Moment," 21.

11. Hart, "Notes for an Anatomy of Modern Autobiography, 221–22.

12. Weintraub, *The Value of the Individual*, 1.

13. Spengemann, *The Forms of Autobiography*, xii.

14. Olney, *Metaphors of Self*, 15.

15. Olney, "Autobiography and the Cultural Moment," in *Autobiography: Essays Theoretical and Critical*, 4.

16. Derrida, "Structure, Sign, and Play," 279.

17. Derrida, "Différance," 3–27.

18. Smith and Watson, *Reading Autobiography*, 133.

19. Foucault, "The Order of Discourse," 52.

20. Bakhtin, *The Dialogic Imagination*, 288.

21. Bruss is referring to Pascal's text, *Design and Truth in Autobiography* (Cambridge: Harvard University Press, 1960). For Pascal, autobiography must conform to certain types of conventions.

22. Bruss, *Autobiographical Acts*, 2.

23. Bruss, "Eye for I: Making and Unmaking Autobiography in Film," 299–300.

24. Renza, "The Veto of the Imagination," 269.

25. Smith, *The Poetics of Women's Autobiography*, 17.

26. Mason, "The Other Voice," 108.

27. Jelinek, *Women's Autobiography*, 8.

28. Varner Gunn, *Autobiography*, 9.

29. Stanton, "Autogynography: Is the Subject Different?," 132.

30. Smith, *The Poetics of Women's Autobiography*, 12.

31. Chodorow, *The Reproduction of Mothering*, 126–27, quoted in Smith, *The Poetics of Women's Autobiography*, 12.

32. Smith, *The Poetics of Women's Autobiography*, *17.*

33. Benstock, "Authorizing the Autobiographical," 21.

34. Gilmore, *Autobiographics*, 42.

35. Lionnet, *Autobiographical Voices*, 112.

36. Lionnet's definition of *métissage* is based on the writings of Edouard Glissant, a Martinican author of poetry, novels, and theoretical works. See *Le Discours antillais* (Paris: Seuil, 1981), 60–71.

37. Cantú, *Canícula*, xi.

38. Anzaldúa. *Borderlands/La Frontera*, 77.

39. Mendoza, *Historia*, 6.

40. Padilla, *My History, Not Yours*, 6.

41. Velasco, "Automitografías," 321.

42. Here Velasco is referring to Gloria Anzaldúa's use of transformation of the "small 'I' into the total Self." See Anzaldúa, *Borderlands/Fronteras*, 82.

43. Elenes, "Chicana Feminist Narratives," 106.

44. Derrida, "The Law of Genre," 56.

45. Lejeune. *On Autobiography*, 5.

46. Derrida, "The Law of Genre," 57.

47. Lotman uses the term "semiotic system" as well as the term "structure" in his paper "Dinamicheskaia model semioticheskoi sistema," published in Moscow in 1974. However, my reference is taken from *La Semiosfera II: Semiótica de la cultura, del texto, de la conducta y del espacio*, a collection of his essays published by Ediciones Cátedra in 1998. Lotman, "Un modelo dinámico del sistema semiótico,"

64. Unless otherwise stated, all translations throughout are mine.

48. Evan-Zohar, "Polysystem Studies," 11.

49. Lotman, "Un modelo dinámico del sistema semiótico," 68.

50. Evan-Zohar, "Polysystem Studies," 18.

51. Dimic, "Las literaturas canadienses de menor difusión," 207–19.

52. Van Gennep, *The Rites of Passage*, 26.

53. Kanellos, *Thirty Million Strong*, 75–76.

54. For in-depth treatment of various topics related to border theory, see Anzaldúa, *Borderlands/La Frontera*; Maciel and Herrera-Sobek, *Culture across Borders* (Tucson: University of Arizona Press, 1998); Mendoza, *Historia*; and Saldívar-Hull, *Feminism on the Border: Chicana Gender Politics and Literature* (Berkeley: University of California Press, 2000).

55. Limón. *American Encounters*, 3.

56. Dilthey, *Pattern and Meaning in History*, 89.

57. Klahn, "Literary [Re]Mappings," 116.

58. I am referring to Pierre Bourdieu's *The Logic of Practice* in which he presents the notion of *habitus*, something that acts as "a system of cognitive and motivating structures." An analysis and application of *habitus* as evidenced in the corpus of this project forms part of the content of chapter 4.

59. Renza, "The Veto of the Imagination," 290.

60. Mignolo, "Entre el canon y el corpus," 24.

61. For a more complete definition of each of these categories, see Appendix A of *Reading Autobiography: A Guide for Reading Life Narratives* (Minneapolis: University of Minnesota Press, 2001), 183–207.

62. As suggested by José Limón in his introduction to Jovita González's text *Dew on the Thorn*, there are three perspectives concerning folklore. The first approach is an anthropological one, as suggested by Franz Boas who saw folklore as "imbedded in culture and as a kind of mirror of that culture that reflected society's fundamental values and beliefs" (xix). A second perspective is that of Stith Thompson who perceived of folkloric narratives as "literary artifacts," especially in the way they are distributed over time and in particular geographical spaces. The third approach is that of J. Frank Dobie who also looked at the literary and cultural aspects of the narrative, but placed more emphasis on "an aesthetic appreciation of what [he] often called 'flavor' in a text" (xx). Of primary importance for Dobie was the appreciation of the folkloric text and, as he notes, the way it revealed the "folk who nourished the lore" (qtd. in González, xx).

63. Derrida, "Living On," 101.

64. My focus here is on the discursive functions or language functions of these texts, as suggested by Jakobson's work "Linguistics and Poetics," in which he refers to six functions of language: poetic, emotive, conative or appellative, referential, phatic, and metalingual. See Roman Jakobson, *On Language*, eds. Linda R. Waugh and Monique Monville-Burston (Boston: Harvard University Press, 1995) 70–77.

65. Arte Público Press was founded in 1979 by Nicolás Kanellos for the purpose of providing for the possibility of publication of Hispanic literature which was often not considered by mainstream presses. Upon accepting a position at the University

of Houston, Kanellos was invited to take the press with him to the university, where it continues to publish Hispanic works.

66. González, "Early Life and Education," vii.

67. González, *Dew on the Thorn*, 3.

68. Jaramillo, *Romance of a Little Village Girl*, ix.

69. Wilbur-Cruce, *A Beautiful, Cruel Country*, xiii.

70. I would like to mention that Juan Bruce-Novoa has suggested that "in generic terms, Wilbur-Cruce has written a true autobiographical *Bildungsroman*." See Juan Bruce-Novoa, "Eva Antonia Wilbur-Cruce: la autobiografía como *Bildungsroman*," in *Mujer y literatura mexicana y chicana: culturas en contacto* (México: El Colegio de México, 1990), 219.

71. Wilbur-Cruce's text refers to the Papago Indians who are now called Tohono O'odham. Throughout my discussion, I will retain her usage when referring to this cultural group. For a discussion of the Tohono O'odham, see Allan J. McIntyre and the Arizona Historical Society, *The Tohono O'odham and Pimeria Alta* (Charleston, SC: Arcadia Publishing, 2008), 9.

72. Dust jacket of the 1987 edition.

73. Ponce, *Hoyt Street*, ix.

74. Moya, *Learning from Experience*, 4.

75. Quintana, *Home Girls: Chicana Literary Voices*, 2.

NOTES TO CHAPTER 2

1. Benveniste, *Problems in General Linguistics*, 208.

2. Foucault, *The Archaeology of Knowledge*, 80.

3. Foucault, "The Order of Discourse," 62-66.

4. Barthes, *Roland Barthes*, 79, 167.

5. Fraisse, "A Philosophical History of Sexual Difference," 51.

6. Foucault, *The History of Sexuality*, Volume 1, 101-102.

7. From a poststructuralist point of view Sara Mills notes a movement away from the Cartesian subject to the subject-in-process, a term that I find useful for my discussion. See *Discourse* (London and New York: Routledge, 1997), 30.

8. My use of the notion of assumed or appropriated discourse is based on Foucault's "The Order of Discourse," in which he discusses "societies of discourse" that "function to preserve or produce discourses" and which demonstrate "forms of appropriation" of certain doctrines, truths, or rules that underlie validated discourses.

9. Prince, *Narratology*, 1.

10. Bal, *Narratology*, 5.

11. Barthes, "Introduction to the Structural Analysis of Narration," 79.

12. Martin, *Recent Theories of Narrative*, 76.

13. Genette, *Narrative Discourse*, 168.

14. Barthes, "Introduction to the Structural Analysis of Narration," 111-12.

15. Bakhtin, "Autor y personaje en la actividad estética," 22. Unless otherwise stated, all translations are mine.

16. Genette distinguishes between a narrator who is a character in the story—

a homodiegetic narrator, and a narrator who is not a character in the story yet is aware of everything concerned with it—a heterodiegetic narrator. Genette uses the term "autodiegetic narrator" to define the homodiegetic narrator who is also the protagonist of the narrative. I find the term "autodiegetic" appropriate for referring to a narrator who is the protagonist of the life story she is telling.

17. Foucault, "Texts/Contexts of Other Spaces," 22–27.

18. Bakhtin, "The Bildungsroman and Its Significance," 22.

19. Bakhtin, *The Dialogic Imagination*, 248.

20. Both Betty Bergland, "Postmodernism and the Autobiographical Subject," and Ramón Saldívar, "Ideologies of the Self" present chronotopic analyses of ethnic autobiographies. See Laura Marcus, *Auto/biographical Discourses: Criticism, Theory, Practice* (Manchester: Manchester University Press, 1994).

21. Smith and Watson, *Reading Autobiography*, 65.

22. Jovita González, "Early Life and Education," ix.

23. Jovita González, *Dew on the Thorn*, 3.

24. Jovita González, "Early Life and Education, x.

25. Jovita González, *Dew on the Thorn*, 4.

26. Jovita González, "Early Life and Education,' x.

27. It is important to note that the "fantastic tales" about la infanta doña Urraca and Delgadina referred to by the autobiographer point to stories concerned with women as objects of a phallocentric system. Urraca is a key player in the fighting that took place between Alfonso and Sancho over the lands they had inherited from their father, Fernando I de León y Castilla. Although Fernando divided his kingdom between Sancho, Alfonso, and the Infante García, Sancho as the eldest son deemed himself the legitimate heir to León, Castilla, and Galicia. Fighting over these lands between Sancho and Alfonso took place, and Alfonso, in an attempt to limit Castillian expansion, gave his sister Urraca the area of Zamora. As the story goes, Urraca received these lands as payment for certain sexual favors bestowed upon her brother. "Delgadina," one of the most widely known romances in the Spanish language, involves a crude theme regarding the obsessive sexual harassment of an abusive paternal hierarch intent on raping his daughter. Both of these themes, loss of land and excessive paternal strength are critiqued in *Dew on the Thorn*.

28. González, *Dew on the Thorn*, 179.

29. González, "Early Life and Education," xi–xii.

30. Limón's comment is based on correspondence in the E. E. Mireles and Jovita González de Mireles Papers, Special Collections & Archives, Texas A&M University–Corpus Christi Bell Library.

31. Chodorow, Psychoanalysis and the Society of Gender, 169.

32. González, *Dew on the Thorn*, 173.

33. Beauvoir, "Interroge Jean-Paul Sartre," 12, quoted in Miller, "Writing Fictions: Women's Autobiography," 50.

34. In her introduction to *Romance of a Little Village Girl*, Tey Diana Rebolledo uses the term "Nuevo Mexicanos" to refer to the people of New Mexico and she uses the term "Hispano" to refer to Jaramillo's perspective concerning this particular area of the Southwest.

35. Jaramillo, *Romance of a Little Village Girl*, 1.

36. See Anzaldúa, *Borderlands/La Frontera*.

37. Jaramillo, *Romance of a Little Village Girl*, 70.

38. It is important to note that *Shadows of the Past/Sombras del Pasado* was originally published by Ancient City Press in 1941 and reprinted in 1971. The *Genuine New Mexico Tasty Recipes* text was originally published by Seton Village Press in 1942 and then reprinted in 1982 by Ancient City Press. *Cuentos del Hogar* (Spanish Fairy Tales) was published in El Campo, Texas, by Citizen Press in 1939.

39. Juan Bruce-Novoa has classified the Wilbur-Cruce text as a bildungsroman based on Bakhtin's definition, which has to do with the process of a man's emergence during the life course. See Bakhtin, "The Bildungsroman and Its Signifiance," (25). I would argue, however, that rather than classify *A Beautiful, Cruel Country* as a bildungsroman, this text can be defined as a border autobiography because in addition to dealing with key moments of development in a child's life, it also involves recollections regarding personal moments of emergence and a life story in relation to the narrator's ancestors, history, and social practice. I would agree with Bruce-Novoa that this border autobiography involves elements of the bildungsroman such as the process of education that this young female child undergoes. However, given the brief life period referred to in this text, it is difficult to speak of the total emergence of the autobiographical subject. Instead we find the beginning moments of this emergence, which is amplified in the text "Eva Antonia Wilbur-Cruce" that forms part of the text *Songs My Mother Sang to Me*. See Martin, *Songs My Mother Sang to Me*.

40. Those elements of the text that refer to cultural memory will be dealt with in chapter 3.

41. Wilbur-Cruce, *A Beautiful, Cruel Country*, 1.

42. As noted by Wilbur-Cruce in Martin, *Songs My Mother Sang to Me*, 173, "Grandfather Wilbur's wife, my grandmother, was Rafaela Salazar, from Altar, Sonora. Her family had already moved to Arivaca, where he met and married her."

43. The narrator's grandmother is focusing on important family ancestors: Salvador Moraga was the last to govern at the presidio (military outpost) of Tubac, the oldest European settlement in this area; Moraga's daughter Juana married Bartolomé Suástegui and they settled in Altar, Sonora, Mexico. Their son, Reverend Bartolomé Suástegui, was a priest in Altar. The mention of Samaniego is most probably a reference to Manuel de Samaniego del Castillo, a colonel and first Count of Samaniego, who was one of the early settlers of New Spain. See Miguel Tinker Salas, *In the Shadow of the Eagles* (Berkeley: University of California Press, 1997).

44. Fraisse, "A Philosophical History of Sexual Difference," 61.

45. Wilbur-Cruce, *A Beautiful, Cruel Country*, 51.

46. Fraisse, "A Philosophical History of Sexual Difference," 50.

47. Wilbur-Cruce, *A Beautiful, Cruel Country*, 217.

48. *A Beautiful, Cruel Country* ends with a note, "About the Author," which states, "Eva Antonia Wilbur-Cruce has lived most of her life in Arizona. She inherited her family's ranch in 1933 and has owned it ever since" (319). However, in Martin, *Songs My Mother Sang to Me*, Wilbur-Cruce clarifies that she bought the ranch and later sold it to the Nature Conservancy, keeping only the house and ten acres (192–94).

49. Norma Cantú has classified this text as "strictly autobiographical." However, as I have suggested in my discussion of chapter 1, this narrative can instead be understood as a border autobiography as it deals not only with the autobiographical "I" but also aspects such as family history, cultural practice, and ideological formations. See Cantú. "The Writing of Canícula," 98.

50. Ponce's emphasis on the space of the barrio echoes Ernesto Galarza's *Barrio Boy* where he describes it as "a colony of refugees." He notes that in spite of their contact with the "Americans," this was a space where people "remained Mexican." See *Barrio Boy* (Notre Dame: University of Notre Dame Press, 1971), 200–205.

51. Ponce, *Hoyt Street*, 5.

52. Wilbur-Cruce, *A Beautiful, Cruel Country*, 58.

53. Ponce's emphasis on the value of books in her life coincides with José Antonio Villarreal's *Pocho* and the reference to Richard, who would lose himself in books, as he focused on reading and studying. Just like Ponce, Richard expresses his desire to learn. See José Antonio Villarreal, *Pocho* (New York: Anchor Books, 1959).

54. Ponce, *Hoyt Street*, 122.

55. Wilbur-Cruce, *A Beautiful, Cruel Country*, 243.

56. Ponce, *Hoyt Street*, 326

57. Genette, *Narrative Discourse*, 26

58. Jean-Blaise Grize defines schematization as a discursive representation of an object or concept that is communicated by the Interlocutor A and that is in turn reconstructed by Interlocutor B. See *Logique et Langage*, 29.

59. Adam and Petitjean, *Le Texte descriptif*, 131.

60. For a more detailed discussion of "descriptive networks," see Phillipe Hamon, *Introduction à l' analise de descriptif* (Paris: Hachette, 1981).

61. According to Mieville, cultural preconstructs involve a set of knowledge, notions, desires, and opinions that are necessary for communication to take place. See Denis Mieville, "Prelude a l'analise du descriptif," Centre de Rechereches Semiologiques, Cahier #52 (Neuchâtel: U. de Neuchâtel, 1986), 119–146.

62. Compan and Pieprzak, "Introduction," 7.

63. "Land," *Webster's New World College Dictionary*.

64. Friedman, *Mappings*, 19.

65. González, "Early Life and Education," ix.

66. González, *Dew on the Thorn*, 3. González was born in 1904, but as suggested by José Limón in his introduction to the text, this date also points to a period of historical change when large numbers of Anglo Americans from the Midwest arrived and settled in South Texas.

67. See "General State of the Foundation of the Colony of Nuevo Santander," Volume I, http://archives.cclibraries.com/cdm/compoundobject/collection/odf/id/1296, which documents the inhabitants of the Spanish settlements.

68. González, "Early Life and Education," xvii.

69. González, *Dew on the Thorn*, 178.

70. Jaramillo, *Romance of a Little Village Girl*, 1.

71. Gonzales-Berry and Maciel, "Introduction," *The Contested Homeland*, 5.

72. Jaramillo, *Romance of a Little Village Girl*, 2.

73. González, *Dew on the Thorn*, 178.

74. Jaramillo, *Romance of a Little Village Girl*, 9.

75. "Country," *Webster's New World College Dictionary*.

76. Wilbur-Cruce, *A Beautiful, Cruel Country*, 1.

77. Initially Sonora included what is known today as Arizona. The geographic area of Pimeria Alta, for instance, was first settled by Spaniards in 1687, and after Mexico gained its independence from Spain in 1821, large Mexican ranches in southern Arizona were established. As suggested by Manuel Gonzales, most of the new settlers in the Sonora frontier were ranchers and miners. See Gonzales, *Mexicanos: A History of Mexicans in the United States*.

78. It is interesting to note that Napoleon's Grand Army invaded Russia in 1812. The invasion was a failure and by 1814 his empire was destroyed.

79. In referring to the history of social classes and particularly the nobility, Maurice Halbwachs notes, "When a noble looks at the portraits of his ancestors in a gallery of his castle or looks at the walls and towers built by them, he strongly feels that what he is today depends on events and persons of which these are only vestiges." See *On Collective Memory*, 128.

80. There were a number of Indian groups that had inhabited this area, but this text emphasizes the Papagos, a Piman tribe, now called Tohono O'odham. The original territory settled by this group was south of the Gila River and south of Tucson, Arizona. See David J. Weber, *The Mexican Frontier 1821–1846: The American Southwest under Mexico* (Albuquerque: University of New Mexico Press, 1982), 51.

81. Ponce, *Hoyt Street*, 3.

82. Gupta and Ferguson, "Beyond 'Culture'," 6.

NOTES TO CHAPTER 3

1. Lotman, *Universe of the Mind*, 3.

2. It is important to note that Lotman's use of the term "space" is metaphorical. Also, for Lotman, language is not simply the natural or common language used in communication. He uses the term "languages" to point to the many different languages expressed within semiotic space: the language of history, the language of music, the language of literature, the language of art, etc.

3. Lotman, *La semiosfera I*, 35.

4. See Harold Bloom, *The Western Canon: The Books and School of the Ages* (New York: Riverhead Books, 1994), 247.

5. Here author Cleofas Jaramillo offers an apology in the preface to her autobiography: "I feel an appalling shortage of words, not being a writer, and writing in a language almost foreign to me. May I offer an apology for my want of continued expression in some parts of my story" (ix). The author obviously feels uncomfortable writing in English, yet for this text to reach a broad reading public, English was the required language.

6. Lotman, *La semiosfera I*, 27.

7. In the English translation of Lotman's text, the word "boundary" is used. However, in the Spanish translations of the three anthologies—*Semiosfera I*, *Semiosfera II*,

and *Semiosfera III*—the translators have used the word "frontera." "Frontera" has multiple meanings: confín de un Estado; límite; linde; marca. I would like to suggest that the concept of boundary as well as border are of importance for my discussion here; therefore, I will use the words "boundary" and "border" interchangeably.

8. Lotman, *Universe of the Mind*, 131.

9. Lotman, "La semiótica de la cultura y el concepto de texto," 24.

10. For Bhabha, interstices involve "the overlap and displacement of domains of difference" and they are spaces in which "the intersubjective and collective experiences of nationness, community interest, or cultural value are negotiated." See Homi Bhabha. *The Location of Culture* (London: Routledge, 1994), 2.

11. Bhabha, "DissemiNation," 2.

12. Lotman, *Universe of the Mind*, 142. Italics are mine.

13. See Lotman's "El texto y el poliglotismo de la cultura," in *La semiosfera I*, for a more extensive discussion of the term "poliglotismo" that focuses more on the cultural sense of the term than the notion of simply speaking a number of natural languages.

14. For a more extensive discussion of the text as a meaning generator, see Lotman's essay "La semiotica de la cultura y el concepto de texto," 77–81.

15. Lotman, "La memoria a la luz de la culturología," 157.

16. Rebolledo, *Women Singing in the Snow*, 46.

17. Wilbur-Cruce, *A Beautiful, Cruel Country*, viii.

18. Ponce, *Hoyt Street*, ix.

19. Lotman, *Cultura y explosión*, 19.

20. Lotman, *Universe of the Mind*, 219.

21. I would like to remind the reader again that references to history from a semiotic perspective can be seen as a type of language.

22. Saldívar, *Chicano Narrative*, 5.

23. Quintana, *Home Girls*, 11.

24. Moyano Pahissa, *México y Estados Unidos*, 31.

25. Lotman, *Cultura y explosión*, 159.

26. Brinkley et al., *American History*, 154.

27. Moyano Pahissa, *México y Estados Unidos*, 32.

28. "The Monroe Doctrine (1823)," 304–305.

29. John O'Sullivan was cofounder and editor of the *United States Magazine and Democratic Review* (later titled *United States Democratic Review*), which published political and literary essays. See "Annexation" in the *United States Democratic Review* 17, no. 85 (July/August 1845), http://digital.library.cornell.edu/

30. Gonzales, *Mexicanos*, 61.

31. Alcaraz et al., *Apuntes para la historia de la guerra*, 2–5.

32. Gonzales, *Mexicanos*, 70.

33. Here Moyano is referring to history prior to the war between Mexico and the United States. President Polk sent John Slidell to negotiate with the Mexican government. The US proposal included Mexico's acknowledgment of the Rio Grande as the boundary for Texas, the cession of New Mexico (for which the United States would

pay $5 million), and the cession of California (for which the United States offered to pay up to $25 million). Brinkley et al., *American History*, 380).

34. Bernal et al., *Historia General de México*, 577.

35. Limerick, *The Legacy of Conquest*, 232.

36. Kanellos, *Thirty Million Strong*, 64-65.

37. Weber, "Editor's Introduction: Cultures Collide," 97.

38. Brinkley et al., *American History*, 381.

39. Divine et al., *America Past and Present*, 362.

40. Moyano Pahissa, *México y Estados Unidos*, 122.

41. Weber, "Editor's Introduction: Cultures Collide," 97-99.

42. Divine et al., *America Past and Present*, 364.

43. Maciel and Gonzales-Berry, "The Nineteenth Century: Overview," 14.

44. Divine et al., *America Past and Present*, 364.

45. Moyano Pahissa, *México y Estados Unidos*, 247.

46. Brinkley et al., *American History*, 382-83.

47. Arteaga, "An Other Tongue," 27.

48. Weber, "Editor's Introduction: Cultures Collide," 140.

49. Padilla, *My History, Not Yours*, 4. For further information, see David Weber's *Foreigners in Their Native Land: Historical Roots of the Mexican Americans* (Albuquerque: University of New Mexico Press, 2003), 140-60.

50. González, "Early Life and Education," xi.

51. Padilla, *My History, Not Yours*, 42.

52. González, "Early Life and Education," ix.

53. De la Teja, "Discovering the Tejano Community in 'Early' Texas," 39.

54. For references to the Treaty of Guadalupe Hidalgo see, "Treaty of Guadalupe Hidalgo," Avalon Project, http://avalon.law.yale.edu/19th_century/guadhida.asp.

55. Alonzo, "Mexican-American Land Grant Adjudication," 65.

56. Limón, "Introduction," in González, *Dew on the Thorn*, xxv.

58 González, *Dew on the Thorn*, 3.

59. González, "Early Life and Education," x.

60. González, *Dew on the Thorn*, 11. Editor José Limón suggests that "powerful man" may be a reference to the King Ranch in Texas.

61. In her introduction to *Romance*, Tey Diana Rebolledo uses the term "New Mexican Hispano" to refer to Jaramillo's sense of identity. David R. Maciel and Erlinda Gonzales-Berry also use the term "Hispano" to refer to Nuevomexicanos; therefore, I will continue to use this term.

62. Maciel and Gonzalez-Berry, *The Contested Homeland*, 5.

63. Jaramillo, *Romance of a Little Village Girl*, ix.

64. Maciel and González-Berry, *The Contested Homeland*, 12.

65. Jaramillo, *Romance of a Little Village Girl*, 2.

66. Kearny, quoted in Weber, "Editor's Introduction: Cultures Collide," 161.

67. Kearny, quoted in Padilla, *My History, Not Yours*, 47.

68. Jaramillo, *Romance of a Little Village Girl*, 2.

69. I would also argue that the autobiographer was keenly aware of the American

perspective regarding miscegenation. For example, as noted by Kanellos in *Thirty Million Strong*, "[d]uring 1846 and 1847, there was much controversy in Congress and in the popular press as to the decision to annex all of Mexico to the United States. People were concerned about 'debasing' the American form of government by making Mexico a colony and/or having its mongrelized people become citizens of the United States" (75). Therefore, the autobiographer's portrayal of herself and her family as descendants of Europeans is a clear example of her dialogue with the Anglo reader.

70. Divine et al., *America Past and Present*, 365.

71. Jaramillo, *Romance of a Little Village Girl*, 9.

72. Maciel and Gonzales-Berry, *The Contested Homeland*, 15.

73. Arteaga, "An Other Tongue," 19.

74. As Tey Diana Rebolledo has mentioned in her introduction to the text, "there is an explicit critique of Anglo inroads into culture" (xxv).

75. Wilbur-Cruce, *A Beautiful, Cruel Country*, 4.

76. Tinker Salas, *In the Shadow of the Eagles*, 5.

77. Poston was one of the first explorers of Arizona and was instrumental in persuading the US government to grant territorial status, which was granted in 1863. He was appointed superintendent of Indian affairs and would ultimately become the first delegate to Congress in 1864.

78. See *A History of Mining in Arizona, the Mission, Means and Memories of Arizona Miners*, Arizona Mining Association, http://www.azmining.com/images/HISTORY_FULL.pdf.

79. Wilbur-Cruce, *A Beautiful, Cruel Country*, 3.

80. So as to understand more clearly the practice of fencing in the land, David Montejano's discussion of the relations between Mexicans and Anglos in Texas is relevant here: "the barbed-wire fence movement of the 1880s becomes not just a sign of progress but an enclosure movement that displaced landless cattlemen and maverick cowboy." Montejano, *Anglos and Mexicans in the Making of Texas*, 2.

81. A desire on the part of the United States to attain the right to transit across the Isthmus of Tehuantepec resulted in conversations between the US government and President Santa Anna. Ultimately the Gadsden Purchase resulted in American payment of $10 million for a total of 29,142,000 acres of territory ceded by Mexico in 1853. This land comprised part of Arizona and New Mexico. See Richard Griswold del Castillo, *The Treaty of Guadalupe Hidalgo: A Legacy of Conflict* (Norman: University of Oklahoma Press, 1990), 59–60.

82. Tinker Salas, *In the Shadow of the Eagles*, 79.

83. Wilbur-Cruce, *A Beautiful, Cruel Country*, 301.

84. Ponce, *Hoyt Street*, ix.

85. Gonzales, *Mexicanos*, 113.

86. Gonzales (ibid.) notes that although "every decade has witnessed a significant influx of Mexican immigrants into the United States" (113), the first thirty years of the twentieth century stands as a period marked by the immigration of more than a million Mexicans into the United States.

87. Ponce, *Hoyt Street*, 3.

88. Gonzales, *Mexicanos*, 119.

89. Haas, *Conquests and Historical Identities in California*, 165.

90. Ponce, *Hoyt Street*, 3.

91. Although his work focuses on Texas Mexican border cities, Daniel Arreola's discussion is relevant here. He notes that, "barrios (e.g. the colonias and fraccionamientos) have remained distinct residential entities characterized by a sense of community." See Arreola and Curtis, *The Mexican Border Cities*, 49.

92. Lotman, *Cultura y explosión*, 230.

93. Schütz, "Transcendences and Multiple Realities," 245-62.

94. González, "Early Life and Education," x.

95. Velasquez comments that "the description of the way of life in the border communities that are established along the Río Grande Valley and of their inhabitants becomes a predominant theme in the prose fiction of Jovita González" (80). In her discussion Velasquez also mentions two collections of sketches by González, "America Invades the Border Towns" and "Among My People." Velasquez Treviño, "Cultural Ambivalence in Early Chicana Prose Fiction," 81.

96. González, *Dew on the Thorn*, 5.

97. Montejano, *Anglos and Mexicans in the Making of Texas*, 88.

98. González, *Dew on the Thorn*, 12.

99. Montejano. *Anglos and Mexicans in the Making of Texas*, 75.

100. Velasquez Treviño, "Cultural Ambivalence in Early Chicana Prose Fiction," 87.

101. González, *Dew on the Thorn*, 3.

102. Jaramillo, *Romance of a Little Village Girl*, 2.

103. Vélez-Ibañez, *Border Visions*, 37.

104. Jaramillo, *Romance of a Little Village Girl*, 2.

105. Vélez-Ibañez, *Border Visions*, 38. The use of the term "segundos pobladores" refers to those like General De Vargas who returned and recaptured Santa Fe during what has been considered the second conquest, or the reconquest, of New Mexico in 1692.

106. Jaramillo, *Romance of a Little Village Girl*, 17-18.

107. The autobiographer is referring to New Mexican and Indian resistance to Colonel Sterling Price, who was placed in command of American troops during the occupation of New Mexico in 1847. In reality she is referring to the leadership of Hispanic Pablo Montoya and an Indian known as Tomasito in this revolt.

108. Padilla, *My History, Not Yours*, 220-22.

109. Jaramillo, *Romance of a Little Village Girl*, 103.

110. Vélez-Ibañez, *Border Visions*, 41.

111. Wilbur-Cruce, *A Beautiful, Cruel Country*, 20.

112. This particular commentary by the narrator points to the history of Father Kino, who was responsible for conversion of great numbers of the Papago at the beginning of the eighteenth century. See Gonzales, *Mexicanos*, 40-42.

113. I am referring to Homi Bhabha's use of the term "mimetic" in "Of Mimicry and Man," 85-92.

114. Bhabha, "DissemiNation," 86.

115. Wilbur-Cruce, *A Beautiful, Cruel Country*, 100.

116. Also relevant here is Frantz Fanon's comment, "As painful as it is for us to have to say this: there is but one destiny for the black man. And that is white." See Fanon, *Black Skin, White Masks* (New York: Grove Press, 1952), xiv.

117. A "catrín" is someone who is well dressed. Thus, Wilbur-Cruce's use of "catrines" refers to those who, like members of her family, were of a higher socio-economic level. See *Diccionario de la lengua española*, 22nd ed., Real Academia Española, http://www.rae.es/rae.html.

118. Ponce, *Hoyt Street*, 3-5.

119. Spivak, "Can the Subaltern Speak?," 24.

120. Ponce, *Hoyt Street*, 5.

121. Lotman, "Acerca de la semiosfera," 29.

122. Ponce, *Hoyt Street*, 122.

123. "Ensconce," *Webster's New World Dictionary*, 3d ed.

NOTES TO CHAPTER 4

1. Said, *Culture and Imperialism*, xiii.

2. Foucault, "The Order of Discourse," 52.

3. Saldívar, *Chicano Narrative*, 3.

4. Fowler, "Power," 63.

5. Foucault, *The Archaeology of Knowledge*, 138.

6. Foucault, "The Order of Discourse," 52.

7. Foucault's earlier work, *Madness and Civilization: A History of Insanity in the Age of Reason*, also deals with the concept of madness as that which is constructed by society on the basis of certain cultural as well as intellectual and economic structures. That is, society develops its own "formulas of exclusion."

8. Rebolledo, *Women Singing in the Snow*, x-xi.

9. Said, *Culture and Imperialism*, xiii.

10. Foucault, "The Subject and Power," 212.

11. Thompson, *Ideology and Modern Culture*, 123.

12. For a more detailed definition of the terms presented by Thompson, see ibid., 61-65.

13. Reboul, *Lenguaje e ideología*, 11-22.

14. I present definitions of these terms in the introduction, note 15.

15. Webb, Schirato and Danaher, *Understanding Bourdieu*, 21-22.

16. Lotman, "El texto y el poliglotismo de la cultura," 83-90.

17. Corse, *Nationalism and Literature*, 1.

18. Bourdieu, *Language and Symbolic Power*, 38-39.

19. Ibid., 57.

20. For Bourdieu, *habitus* concerns "systems of durable, transposable dispositions, structured structures predisposed to function as structuring structures, that is, as principles which generate and organize practices and representations." See *Logic of Practice*, 53.

21. Limón, "Introduction," in González, *Dew on the Thorn*, xx.

22. González, *Dew on the Thorn*, 13.

23. The word "albahaca" has its origin in the Hispanic Arabic word "alhabáqa," which in turn is derived from the Arabic word "habaqah." See *Real Academia Española Diccionario de la lengua española*, 22d ed., http://buscon.rae.es/draeI.

24. Bacon, *History of American Christianity*.

25. Jaramillo, *Romance of a Little Village Girl*, 24.

26. Gilbert and Gubar, "The Madwoman in the Attic," 816.

27. Jaramillo, *Romance of a Little Village Girl*, 25.

28. Gilbert and Gubar, "The Madwoman in the Attic," 816.

29. Jaramillo, *Romance of a Little Village Girl*, 35.

30. Bourdieu, *The Logic of Practice*, 53.

31. Jaramillo, *Romance of a Little Village Girl*, 48–49.

32. Bourdieu, *The Field of Cultural Production*, 30.

33. Wilbur-Cruce, *A Beautiful, Cruel Country*, 3.

34. Bourdieu, *Language and Symbolic Power*, 111.

35. See Gonzales, *Mexicanos*, 40–47.

36. Wilbur-Cruce, *A Beautiful, Cruel Country*, 10.

37. Paula Moya's *Learning from Experience* presents an interesting discussion of identity and the way it is related to social and political discursive domains.

38. As noted by Paul L. Allen, *tesguin* is "[a] home-brewed beer that is . . . made by mixing cracked corn, brown sugar and occasionally fruit with water and allowing it to ferment for several days. . . . Determined consumption would produce intoxication, a hangover and a thorough 'cleansing' experience." "Tucson Honors Rainy Day Saint," *Tucson Citizen*, June 24, 2006, http://tucsoncitizen.com/morgue/2006/06/24/16987-tucson-honors-rainy-day-saint.

39. This pilgrimage to Magdalena de Kino, an old mission town, is one of the most important religious rituals that take place in the area of the Sonoran Desert. Thousands make the pilgrimage as a sign of devotion to St. Francis Xavier.

40. Ponce, *Hoyt Street*, 7.

41. Etymologically, "oikos" is the Greek root of both economy and ecology. It means "house," and over time this term has come to mean household management.

42. Foucault, *Historia de la Sexualidad 2*, 82.

43. Kristeva, "Word, Dialogue and Novel," 142.

44. Ponce, *Hoyt Street*, 276.

45. Bourdieu, The *Logic of Practice*, 55.

46. Pêcheux, *Automatic Discourse Analysis*, 68.

47. Ducrot has established that language involves both presuppositions ("Peter stopped smoking" presupposes that he smoked) and implications ("Peter stopped smoking" might imply "you should follow his example"). Thus, a presupposition is any background assumption that enters into the discursive structure, thereby establishing a link between what is said and what stands as background information not explicitly stated. Implication or implicature is most often embedded in discourse and must be inferred from what the speaker says since this information is not explicitly stated. Thus, implicatures are generated via inferences that are the consequence of an act of saying something. See Oswald Ducrot, *Decir y no decir: principios de semántica lingüística* (Barcelona: Editorial Anagram, 1982) 19–33.

48. Pêcheux, *Automatic Discourse Analysis*, 89. In this reference Pêcheux is citing O. Ducrot, "Logique et linguistique," *Langages* 2 (1966), 3–30. Pêcheux and Paul Henry, however, use the term "preconstruct" as an alternative term to Ducrot's "presupposition," which refers to a trace of an utterance which has been pronounced elsewhere.

49. Kristeva, "Word, Dialogue and Novel," 44.

50. Pêcheux, *Language, Semantics and Ideology*, 113.

51. Pêcheux, *Automatic Discourse Analysis*, 89–90, 127.

52. González, "Early Life and Education," xi–xii.

53. As I mentioned in chapter 1, Spengemann has suggested that the "fictive metaphor" and the use of allegorical language in the poetic autobiography is a literary means of referring to the "I."

54. Bakhtin, "Actitud del autor hacia el héroe," 18–28.

55. Leigh Gilmore argues, "Autobiography represents the real through extended figurations of continuums, through chronology and the implied continuities in places and persons." Because *Dew on the Thorn* is an autobiographically informed narrative—and as José Limón has clarified in his footnotes to the recovered text, González often drew on personal family history in the fictional text—it is difficult not to perceive the characters presented within the text as another type of representation of the "real."

56. Jaramillo is clearly critical of those Anglo-American writers such as Mary Austin and Mabel Dodge Luhan, who are not really "of" New Mexico and therefore could not possibly capture the true spirit of this space.

57. Gilbert and Gubar, "The Madwoman in the Attic," 21.

58. Juan Bruce-Novoa has indicated that "la función de ambos padres es diferente desde el primer recuerdo de Eva . . . Los padres colaboran, pero es sobre todo el padre quien siempre la dirige hacia fuera, hacia el mundo exterior, siempre como representante de la imposición de cierto sistema de control y orden sobre la naturaleza." See "La autobiografía como Bildungsroman," *Mujer y literatura mexicana y chicana: culturas en contacto*, eds. Aralia López González, Amelia Malagamba y Elena Urrutia (México, D.F.: Colegio de México, 1990), 219–32.

59. Ponce, *Hoyt Street*, 9–10.

60. According to Gilbert and Gubar, "The ideal woman that male authors dream of generating is always an angel." They also postulate that "from the eighteenth century on, conduct books for ladies had proliferated, enjoining young girls to submissiveness, modesty, selflessness; reminding all women that they should be angelic." Indeed, they point to the writings of Abbé d'Ancourt, *The Lady's Preceptor*, published in 1745, in which we find the following: "if Woman owes her Being to the Comfort and Profit of man, 'tis highly reasonable that she should be careful and intelligent to content and please him" (20–23).

61. Kristeva, "Women's Time," 199.

62. Ponce, *Hoyt Street*, 310.

NOTES TO CONCLUSIONS

1. Cixous, "The Laugh of the Medusa," 347.

2. As I have mentioned, the importance of the works created by González, Jaramillo, Wilbur-Cruce, and Ponce resides in the documentation they provide regarding life experiences that precede the Chicano movement. We can say, therefore, that their life writing sets the stage for Chicana authors such as Gloria Anzaldúa, Cherríe Moraga, Pat Mora, and Norma Cantú, who have also chosen the autobiographical form as a means of expression, as a way of placing their lives into history and into the world. See Anzaldúa, *Borderands/La Frontera*; Moraga, "La Guera"; Moraga, *Loving in the War Years*; Cantú, *Canícula*; Mora, *House of Houses.* Each of these works deals with elements concerned with the personal "I" as well as the collective "we" in relation to border experiences. Moreover, these texts cross the boundaries of genre as they present use of hybrid literary styles that include prose, poetry, proverbs, recipes, and prayers.

3. Moraga, *Loving in the War Years,* 127.

4. Ponce, *Hoyt Street*, x.

5. Anzaldúa, *Borderands/La Frontera*, 87.

Works Cited

Adam, Jean Michel, and Andre Petitjean. *Le Texte descriptif: Poétique, historique et linguistique textuelle*. Paris: Nathan, 1989.

Alcaraz, Ramón, et al. *Apuntes para la historia de la guerra entre México y los Estados-Unidos*. Mexico: Siglo Veintiuno Editores S.A, 1848.

Alonzo, Armando C. "Mexican-American Land Grant Adjudication." *En Aquel Entonces: Readings in Mexican American History*. Edited by Manuel G. Gonzalez and Cynthia M. Gonzalez. Bloomington: University of Indiana Press, 2000. 64–71.

Anzaldúa, Gloria. *Borderlands/La Frontera: The New Mestiza*. San Francisco: Aunt Lute Books, 1987.

———. *Interviews/Entrevistas*. New York: Routledge, 2000.

Arnold, Matthew. *Culture and Anarchy*. (1882). University of Toronto English Library, http://www.library.utoronto.ca/utel/nonfiction_u/arnoldm_ca/ca_titlepage.html (accessed June 7, 2012)

Arreola, Daniel D., and James R. Curtis. *The Mexican Border Cities: Landscape Anatomy and Place Personality*. Tucson: University of Arizona Press, 1993.

Arteaga, Alfred. "An Other Tongue." *An Other Tongue: Nation and Ethnicity in the Linguistic Borderlands*. Edited by Alfred Arteaga. Durham, N.C.: Duke University Press, 1994. 9–33.

Bacon, Leonard Woolsey. *History of American Christianity*. New York: Christian Literature, 1897. *Christian Classics Ethereal Library*, Calvin College. http://www.ccel.org/ccel/bacon_lw/history.html (accessed June 7, 2012)

Bakhtin, M. M. "Actitud del autor hacia el héroe." *Estética de la creación verbal*. México: Siglo Veintiuno Editores, 1982. 13–27.

———. *The Dialogic Imagination: Four Essays*. Austin: University of Texas Press, 1981.

———. "The Bildungsroman and Its Significance in the History of Realism (Toward a Historical Typology of the Novel)." *Speech Genres and Other Late Essays*. Austin: University of Texas Press, 1986. 10–59.

———. "Autor y personaje en la actividad estética." *Estética de la creación verbal*. México: Siglo Veintiuno Editores, 1982.

———. "La forma especial del personaje." *Estética de la creación verbal*. México: Siglo Veintiuno Editores, 1982. 28–91.

———. "Forms of Time and Chronotope in the Novel." *The Dialogic Imagination: Four Essays*. Austin: University of Texas Press, 1981. 84–258.

Bal, Mieke. *Narratology: Introduction to the Theory of Narrative*. Toronto: University of Toronto Press, 1999.

Barthes, Roland. "Introduction to the Structural Analysis of Narration." *Image, Music, Text*. New York: Hill and Wang, 1977. 79–124.

———. *Roland Barthes*. Translated by Richard Howard. New York: Noonday, 1977.
Benstock, Shari. "Authorizing the Autobiographical." *The Private Self: Theory and Practice of Women's Autobiographical Writings*. Edited by Shari Benstock. Chapel Hill: University of North Carolina Press, 1988. 150-90.
Benveniste, Émile. *Problems in General Linguistics*. Coral Gables: University of Miami Press, 1971.
Bergland, Betty. "Postmodernism and the Autobiographical Subject." *Autobiography and Postmodernism*. Edited by Kathleen Ashley, Leigh Gilmore, and Gerald Peters. Amherst: University of Massachusetts Press, 1994. 130-66.
Bernal, Ignacio, et al. *Historia General de México*. D.F., México: El Colegio de México, 2000.
Bhabha, Homi. "DissemiNation." *Nation and Narration*. Edited by Homi Bhabha. New York: Routledge, 1990. 139-70.
———. *The Location of Culture*. London: Routledge, 1994.
Bourdieu, Pierre. *The Field of Cultural Production*. Edited by Randal Johnson. New York: Columbia University Press, 1993.
———. *Language and Symbolic Power*. Edited by John B. Thompson. Translated by Gino Raymond and Matthew Adamson. Cambridge, Mass.: Harvard University Press, 1991.
———. *The Logic of Practice*. Translated by Richard Nice. Stanford, Calif.: Stanford University Press, 1990.
Bourdieu, Pierre, and Jean-Claude Passeron. *The Inheritors: French Students and Their Relation to Culture*. Chicago: University of Chicago Press, 1979.
Brinkley, Alan, et al. *American History*. 8th ed. New York: McGraw-Hill, 1991.
Bruss, Elizabeth. *Autobiographical Acts: The Changing Situation of a Literary Genre*. Baltimore: Johns Hopkins University Press, 1976.
———. "Eye for I: Making and Unmaking Autobiogrpahy in Film." *Autobiography: Essays Theoretical and Critical*. Edited by James Olney. Princeton, N.J.: Princeton University Press, 1980. 296-320.
Cantú, Norma. *Canícula: Snapshots of a Girlhood en la Frontera*. Albuquerque: Unversity of New Mexico Press, 1995.
———. "The Writing of 'Canícula': Breaking Boundaries, Finding Forms." *Chicana Feminisms*. Edited by Gabriela F. Arredondo, Aída Hurtado, Norma Klahn et al. Durham, N. C.: Duke University Press, 2003. 97-108.
Chacón, Ramon D. "Labor Unrest and Industrial Agriculture in California: The Case of the 1933 San Joaquín Valley Cotton Strike." *En Aquel Entonces: Readings in Mexican American History*. Edited by Manuel G. Gonzalez and Cynthia M. Gonzalez. Bloomington: University of Indiana Press, 2000. 142-49.
Chodorow, Nancy. *Psychoanalysis and the Sociology of Gender*. Berkeley: University of California Press, 1978.
Cixous, Hélène. "The Laugh of the Medusa." *Feminisms: An Anthology of Literary Theory and Criticism*. Edited by Robyn R. Warhol and Diane Price Herndl. New Brunswick, N.J.: Rutgers University Press, 1991. 347-62.
Compan, Magali, and Katarzyna Pieprzak. "Introduction." *Land and Landscape in*

Francographic Literature: Remapping Uncertain Territories. Edited by Magali Compan and Katarzyna Pieprzak. London: Cambridge Scholars, 2007. 1-9.

Corse, Sarah M. *Nationalism and Literature: The Politics of Culture in Canada and the United States*. Cambridge: Cambridge University Press, 1997.

"Country." *Webster's New World College Dictionary*. 3rd ed. 1997.

De la Teja, Jesús E. "Discovering the Tejano Community in 'Early' Texas." *En Aquel Entonces: Readings in Mexican American History*. Edited by Manuel G. Gonzalez and Cynthia M. Gonzalez. Bloomington: University of Indiana Press, 2000. 38-44

Deleuze, Gilles, and Felix Guattari. *A Thousand Plateaus: Capitalism and Schizophrenia*. Translated by Brian Massumi. Minneapolis: University of Minnesota Press, 1980.

De Man, Paul. *The Rhetoric of Romanticism*. New York: Columbia University Press, 1984.

Derrida, Jacques. "Différance." *Margins of Philosophy*. Translated by Alan Bass. Chicago: University of Chicago Press, 1982. 3-27.

———. "The Law of Genre." Translated by Avital Ronell. *Critical Inquiry* 7.1 (1980): 55. http://dx.doi.org/10.1086/448088

———. "Living On." *De-Construction and Criticism*. New York: Continuum, 1999. First published 1979. 62-142.

———. "Structure, Sign, and Play in the Discourse of the Human Sciences." *Writing and Difference*. Translated by Alan Bass. Chicago: University of Chicago Press, 1978. 278-93.

Dilthey, Wilhelm. *Pattern and Meaning in History: Thoughts on History and Society*. New York: Harper and Row, 1962.

Dimic, Milan V. "Las literaturas canadienses de menor difusión: observaciones desde un punto de vista sistémico." *Teoría de los polisistemas*. Compiled by Montserrat Iglesias Santos. Madrid: Arco/Libros, S.L., 1999. 207-22.

Divine, Robert A., et al. *America Past and Present*. Vol. 1. New York: Longman, 1999.

Dorchester, Daniel. *Christianity in the United States*. New York: Phillips and Hunt, 1888.

Eagleton, Terry. *The Idea of Culture*. Malden, Mass.: Blackwell, 2000.

———. *Literary Theory*. Minneapolis: University of Minnesota Press, 1983.

Eakin, Paul John. *Touching the World: Reference in Autobiography*. Princeton, N.J.: Princeton University Press, 1992.

Eisenhower, John S. D. *So Far from God: The U.S. War with Mexico 1846-1848*. New York: Anchor Books, 1989.

Elenes, C. Alejandra. "Chicana Feminist Narratives and the Political Self." *Frontiers: A Journal of Women Studies* 21.3 (2000): 105-23. http://dx.doi.org/10.2307/3347113

"Ensconce." *Webster's New World College Dictionary*. 3rd ed. 1997.

Evan-Zohar, Itamar. "Polysystem Studies." *Poetics Today* 2, no. 1 (1990): 1-86.

Foucault, Michel. *The Archaeology of Knowledge and the Discourse on Language*. Translated by A. M. Sheridan Smith. New York: Pantheon Books, 1972.

———. *Historia de la Sexualidad 2: El uso de los placeres*. México: Siglo veintiuno editores, 1986.

———. *The History of Sexuality: An Introduction*. Vol. 1. Translated by Robert Hurley. New York: Vintage Books, 1990.

———. "The Order of Discourse." *Untying the Text: A Post-Structuralist Reader*. Edited by Robert Young. Boston: Routledge and Kegan Paul, 1981. 48–78.

———. "The Subject and Power." *Michel Foucault: Beyond Structuralism and Hermeneutics*. Edited by Hubert L. Dreyfus and Paul Rabinow. Chicago: University of Chicago Press, 1983. 208–26.

Fowler, Roger. "Power." *Handbook of Discourse Analysis, Volume 4: Discourse Analysis in Society*. Edited by Teun van Dijk. London: Academic Press, 1985. 61–82.

Fraisse, Geneviève. "A Philosophical History of Sexual Difference." *A History of Women: Emerging Feminism from Revolution to World War*. Edited by Geneviève Fraisse and Michelle Perrot. Cambridge, Mass.: Belknap Press of Harvard University Press, 1993. 48–79.

Freud, Sigmund. *An Outline of Psychoanalysis*. Translated by James Strachey. New York: W. W. Norton, 1949.

———. "Psychopathology of Everyday Life." *The Basic Writings of Sigmund Freud*. Translated and edited by A. A. Brill. New York: Modern Library, 1938. 69–95.

———. "The Structure of the Unconscious." *The Basic Writings of Sigmund Freud*. Translated and edited by A. A. Brill. New York: Modern Library, 1938.

Friedman, Susan Stanford. *Mappings: Feminism and the Cultural Geographies of Encounter*. Princeton, N.J.: Princeton University Press, 1998.

Genette, Gérard. *Narrative Discourse: An Essay in Method*. Ithaca, N.Y.: Cornell University Press, 1980.

Gilbert, Sandra, and Susan Gubar. "The Madwoman in the Attic." *Literary Theory: An Anthology*. Malden, Mass.: Blackwell, 2004. 812–25.

Gilmore, Leigh. *Autobiographics: A Feminist Theory of Women's Self-Representation*. Ithaca, N.Y.: Cornell University Press, 1994.

Gonzales, Manuel G. *Mexicanos: A History of Mexicans in the United States*. Bloomington: Indiana University Press, 2000.

Gonzales-Berry, Erlinda, and David R. Maciel. "Introduction." *The Contested Homeland: A Chicano History of New Mexico*. Edited by Erlinda Gonzales-Berry and David R. Maciel. Albuquerque: University of New Mexico Press, 2000. 1–9.

González, Gilbert G. "Women, Work, and Community in the Mexican *Colonias* of the Southern California Citrus Belt." *En Aquel Entonces: Readings in Mexican American History*. Edited by Manuel G. Gonzales and Cynthia M. Gonzales. Bloomington: Indiana University Press, 2000. 150–57.

González, Jovita. *Dew on the Thorn*. Edited by José Limón. Houston: Arte Público Press, 1997.

Grize, Jean-Blaise. *Logique et langage*. Paris: Ophrys, 1990.

Gupta, Akhil, and James Ferguson. "Beyond 'Culture': Space, Identity, and the Politics of Difference." *Cultural Anthropology* 7.1 (1992): 6–23. http://dx.doi.org/10.1525/can.1992.7.1.02a00020

Gusdorf, Georges. "Conditions and Limits of Autobiography." *Autobiography: Essays*

Theoretical and Critical. Edited by James Olney. Princeton, N.J.: Princeton University Press, 1980. 28–48.

Gutierrez, Ramón A. *When Jesus Came, the Corn Mothers Went Away: Marriage, Sexuality, and Power in New Mexico, 1500–1846*. Stanford, Calif.: Stanford University Press, 1991.

Haas, Lisbeth. *Conquests and Historical Identities in California*. Berkeley: University of California Press, 1995.

Halbwachs, Maurice. *On Collective Memory*. Edited and translated by Lewis A. Coser. Chicago: University of Chicago Press, 1992.

Hart, Francis R. "Notes for an Anatomy of Modern Autobiography." *New Directions in Literary History*. Edited by Ralph Cohen. Baltimore: Johns Hopkins University Press, 1974. 221–47.

Hennesey, James J. *American Catholics: A History of the Roman Catholic Community in the United States*. New York: Oxford University Press, 1982.

Herrera, Carlos R. "New Mexico Resistance to U.S. Occupation." *The Contested Homeland: A Chicano History of New Mexico*. Edited by Erlinda Gonzales-Berry and David R. Maciel. Albuquerque: University of New Mexico Press, 2000. 23–42.

A History of Mining in Arizona: The Mission, Means and Memories of Arizona Miners. Phoenix: Arizona Mining Association, n.d. http://www.azmining.com/images/HISTORY_FULL.pdf

Jakobson, Roman. "The Speech Event and the Functions of Language." *On Language*. Edited by Linda R. Waugh and Monique Monville-Burston. Cambridge, Mass.: Harvard University Press, 1995. 69–79.

Jaramillo, Cleofas M. *Romance of a Little Village Girl*. Albuquerque: University of New Mexico Press, 2000.

———. *Shadows of the Past / Sombras del Pasado*. Santa Fe: Ancient City Press, 1941.

Jelinek, Estell C. "Introduction: Women's Autobiography and the Male Tradition." *Women's Autobiography: Essays in Criticism*. Edited by Estelle C. Jelinek. Bloomington: Indiana University Press, 1980. 1–30.

Kanellos, Nicolás. *Thirty Million Strong: Reclaiming the Hispanic Image in American Culture*. Golden, Colo.: Fulcrum, 1998.

Klahn, Norma. "Literary [Re]Mappings: Autobiographical [Dis]Placements by Chicana Writers." *Chicana Feminisms*. Durham, N.C.: Duke University Press, 2003. 114–45.

Kristeva, Julia. "About Chinese Women." *The Kristeva Reader*. Edited by Toril Moi. New York: Columbia University Press, 1986. 138–59.

———. "Women's Time." *The Kristeva Reader*. Edited by Toril Moi. New York: Columbia University Press, 1986. 187–213.

———. "Word, Dialogue and Novel." *The Kristeva Reader*. Edited by Toril Moi. New York: Columbia University Press, 1986. 34–61.

"Land." *Webster's New World College Dictionary*. 3rd ed. 1997.

Lejeune, Philippe. *On Autobiography*. Minneapolis: University of Minnesota Press, 1989.

Limerick, Patricia Nelson. *The Legacy of Conquest: The Unbroken Past of the American West*. New York: W. W. Norton, 1987.

Limón, José E. *American Encounters: Greater Mexico, the United States, and the Erotics of Culture*. Boston: Beacon Press, 1998.

Lionnet, Françoise. *Autobiograhical Voices: Race, Gender, Self-Portraiture*. Ithaca, N.Y.: Cornell University Press, 1989.

Lotman, Yuri. "Acerca de la semiosfera." *La semiosfera I: Semiótica de la cultura y del texto*. Translated by Desiderio Navarro. Madrid: Ediciones Cátedra, S.A., 1996. 21–42.

———. *Cultura y explosión: Lo previsible y lo imprevisible en los procesos de cambio social*. Translated by Delfina Muschietti. Barcelona: Editorial Gedisa S.A, 1999.

———. "La memoria a la luz de la culturología." *La semiosfera I: Semiótica de la cultura y del texto*. Translated by Desiderio Navarro. Madrid: Ediciones Cátedra, S.A., 1996. 157–61.

———. "La memoria de la cultura." *La semiosfera II: Semiótica de la cultura, del texto, de la conducta y del espacio*. Translated by Desiderio Navarro. Madrid: Ediciones Cátedra, S.A., 1998. 157–62.

———. "Un modelo dinámica del sistema semiótico." *La semiosfera II: Semiótica de la cultura, del texto, de la conducta y del espacio*. Translated by Desiderio Navarro. Madrid: Ediciones Cátedra, S.A., 1998. 63–80.

———. "La semiótica de la cultura y el concepto de texto." *La semiosfera I: Semiótica de la cultura y del texto*. Translated by Desiderio Navarro. Madrid: Ediciones Cátedra, S.A., 1996. 77–82.

———. "Sobre el mecanismo semiótico de la cultura." *La semiosfera III: Semiótica de las artes y de la cultura*. Translated by Desiderio Navarro. Madrid: Ediciones Cátedra, S.A., 2000. 168–94.

———. "El texto y el poliglotismo de la cultura." *La semiosfera I: Semiótica de la cultura y del texto*. Translated by Desiderio Navarro. Madrid: Ediciones Cátedra, S.A., 1996. 83–91.

———. *Universe of the Mind: A Semiotic Theory of Culture*. Translated by Ann Shukman. Bloomington: Indiana University Press, 2000.

Lotman, Yuri M., and Boris A. Uspenskii. "Binary Models in the Dynamics of Russian Culture." *The Semiotics of Russian Cultural History*. Ithaca, N.Y.: Cornell University Press, 1985. 30–66.

Maciel, David R., and Erlinda Gonzales-Berry, eds. *The Contested Homeland: A Chicano History of New Mexico*. Albuquerque: University of New Mexico Press, 2000.

Martin, Patricia Preciado. *Songs My Mother Sang to Me: An Oral History of Mexican American Women*. Tucson: University of Arizona Press, 1992.

Martin, Wallace. *Recent Theories of Narrative*. Ithaca, N.Y.: Cornell University Press, 1987.

Mason, Mary G. "The Other Voice: Autobiographics of Women Writers." *Autobiography: Essays Theoretical and Critical*. Edited by James Olney, Princeton, N.J.: Princeton University Press, 1980. 207–35.

Mendoza, Louis. *Historia: The Literary Making of Chicana & Chicano History*. College Station: Texas A&M University Press, 2001.

Mignolo, Walter. "Entre el canon y el corpus: Alternativas para los estudios literarios y culturales en y sobre América Latina." *Nuevo Texto Crítico* 14/15 (1994-1995): 23-36.

Miller, Jean Baker. "The Development of Women's Sense of Self." *Women's Growth in Connection*. New York: Guilford Press, 1991. 11-26.

Miller, Nancy K. "Writing Fictions: Women's Autobiography in France." *Life/Lines: Theorizing Women's Autobiography*. Edited by Bella Brodzki and Celeste Schenck. Ithaca, N.Y.: Cornell University Press, 1988. 45-61.

———. "Writing (from) the Feminine: George Sand and the Novel of Female Pastoral." *Representations of Women in Fiction: Selected Papers from the English Institute*. Edited by Carolyn G. Heilbrun and Margaret R. Higonnet. Baltimore: Johns Hopkins University Press, 1983. 124-51.

Mills, Sara. *Discourse*. New York: Routledge, 1997.

Misch, Georg. *A History of Autobiography in Antiquity*. Westport, Conn.: Greenwood Press, 1973.

Moi, Toril. "Feminist, Female, Feminine." *The Feminist Reader: Essays in Gender and the Politics of Literary Criticism.* Edited by New York: Blackwell, 1988. 117-32.

Molloy, Sylvia. *At Face Value: Autobiographical Writing in Spanish America*. Cambridge: Cambridge University Press, 1991. http://dx.doi.org/10.1017/CBO9780511553844

"The Monroe Doctrine (1823)." *Basic Readings in U.S. Democracy*. Edited by Melvin I. Urofsky. Washington, D.C.: United States Information Agency, 1994. 302-5.

Montejano, David. *Anglos and Mexicans in the Making of Texas 1836-1986*. Austin: University of Texas Press, 1987.

Mora, Pat. *House of Houses*. Tucson: University of Arizona Press, 2008.

Moraga, Cherríe. "La Guera." *This Bridge Called My Back: Writings by Radical Women of Color*. Edited by Cherríe Moraga and Gloria Anzaldúa. New York: Kitchen Table Women of Color Press, 1981. 27-34.

———. *Loving in the War Years: Lo Que Nunca Paso por Sus Labios*. Edited by Gloria Anzaldúa. Berkeley: Third Woman Press, 2002.

Moya, Paula. *Learning from Experience: Minority Identities, Multicultural Struggles*. Berkeley: University of California Press, 2002.

Moyano Pahissa, Angela. *México y Estados Unidos: Orígenes de una relación 1819-1861*. D.F., México: Secretaría de Educación Pública, 1987.

Olney, James. "Autobiography and the Cultural Moment: A Thematic, Historical, and Bibliographical Introduction." *Autobiography: Essays Theoretical and Critical*. Edited by James Olney. Princeton, N.J.: Princeton University Press, 1980. 3-27.

———. *Memory and Narrative: The Weave of Life-Writing*. Chicago: University of Chicago Press, 1998.

———. *Metaphors of Self: The Meaning of Autobiography*. Princeton, N.J.: Princeton University Press, 1972.

O'Sullivan, John. "Annexation." *United States Magazine and Democratic Review* 17, no. 1 (July-August 1845): 5-10. http://digital.library.cornell.edu/

Padilla, Genaro M. *My History, Not Yours: The Formation of Mexican American Autobiography*. Madison: University of Wisconsin Press, 1993.

———. "'Yo sola aprendí': Contra Patriarchal Containment in Women's Nineteenth-Century California Personal Narratives." *Americas Review*, Fall/Winter 1988: 91–108.

Paredes, Raymund A. "Mexican-American Literature: An Overview." *Recovering the U.S. Hispanic Literary Heritage*. Edited by Ramón Gutiérrez and Genaro Padilla. Houston: Arte Público Press, 1993. 31–51.

Pascal, Roy. *Design and Truth in Autobiography*. Cambridge, Mass.: Harvard University Press, 1960.

Pêcheux, Michel. *Automatic Discourse Analysis*. Edited by Tony Hak and Niels Helsloot. Amsterdam: Editions Rodopi B.V, 1995.

———. *Language, Semantics, and Ideology*. New York: St. Martin's Press, 1982.

Polkinghorne, Donald E. *Narrative Knowing and the Human Sciences*. New York: State University of New York Press, 1988.

Ponce, Mary Helen. *Hoyt Street: An Autobiography*. Albuquerque: University of New Mexico Press, 1993.

Prince, Gerald. *Narratology: The Form and Functioning of Narrative*. New York: Mouton, 1982. http://dx.doi.org/10.1515/9783110838626

Quintana, Alvina E. *Home Girls: Chicana Literary Voices*. Philadelphia: Temple University Press, 1996.

Rapport, Nigel. *Social and Cultural Anthropology*. London: Routledge, 2000. http://dx.doi.org/10.4324/9780203451137

Rebolledo, Tey Diana. "Tradition and Mythology: Signatures of Landscape in Chicana Literature." *The Desert Is No Lady: Southwestern Landscapes in Women's Writing and Art.* Edited by Vera Norwood and Janice Monk. New Haven: Yale University Press, 1987. 96–124.

———. *Women Singing in the Snow: A Cultural Analysis of Chicana Literature*. Tucson: University of Arizona Press, 1995.

Reboul, Olivier. *Lenguaje e ideología*. México: Fondo de Cultura Económica, 1986.

Renza, Louis A. "The Veto of the Imagination: A Theory of Autobiography." *Autobiography: Essays Theoretical and Critical.* Edited by James Olney. Princeton, N.J.: Princeton University Press, 1977. 268–95.

Reyna, Sergio. "Jovita González y su obra folclórico-literaria: Reconstrucción de la historia cultural méxico-americana." *Recovering the U.S. Hispanic Literary Heritage*, Vol. 4. Edited by José F. Aranda, Jr., and Silvio Torres-Saillant. Houston: Arte Público Press, 2002. 184–200.

Ricoeur, Paul. *From Text to Action: Essays in Hermeneutics, II*. Translated by Kathleen Blamey and John B. Thompson. Evanston, Ill.: Northwestern Unversity Press, 1991.

———. *Memory, History, Forgetting*. Chicago: University of Chicago Press, 2004.

Rimmon-Kenan, Shlomith. *Narrative Fiction: Contemporary Poetics*. New York: Routledge, 1989.

Rosaldo, Renaro. *Culture and Truth: The Remaking of Social Analysis*. Boston: Beacon Press, 1993.

Ryan, Michael. *Literary Theory: A Practical Introduction*. London: Blackwell, 1999.

Said, Edward W. *Culture and Imperialism*. New York: Vintage Books, 1994.

Saldívar, José David. *Border Matters: Remapping American Cultural Studies*. Berkeley: University of California Press, 1997.

Saldívar, Ramón. *Chicano Narrative: The Dialectics of Difference*. Madison: University of Wisconsin Press, 1990.

Sánchez Martínez, Alicia Verónica. "La macro-operación descriptiva: Sus operaciones lógico-discursivas." *Revista de Humanidades Tecnológico de Monterrey* 8 (2000): 221–40.

———. "Semiótica y Arqueología del Gusto Culinario: Análisis Discursivo/Textual." PhD diss., Tecnológico de Monterrey, 2003.

Schütz, Alfred. "Transcendences and Multiple Realities." *On Phenomenology and Social Relations: Selected Writings*. Edited by Helmut R. Wagner. Chicago: University of Chicago Press, 1970. 245–62.

Smith, Barbara Herrnstein. *On the Margins of Discourse: The Relation of Literature to Language*. Chicago: University of Chicago Press, 1978.

Smith, Sidonie. *The Poetics of Women's Autobiography: Marginality and the Fictions of Self-Representation*. Bloomington: Indiana University Press, 1987.

Smith, Sidonie, and Julia Watson. *Reading Autobiography: A Guide for Interpreting Life Narratives*. Minneapolis: University of Minnesota Press, 2001.

Spengemann, William C. *The Forms of Autobiography*. New Haven: Yale University Press, 1980.

Spivak, Gayatri Chakravorty. "Can the Subaltern Speak?" *The Post-Colonial Studies Reader*. Edited by Bill Ashcroft, Gareth Griffiths, and Helen Tiffin. New York: Routledge, 1995. 66–111.

Stanton, Domna C. "Autogynography: Is the Subject Different?" *Woman, Autobiography, Theory: A Reader*. Edited by Sidonie Smith and Julia Watson. Madison: University of Wisconsin Press, 1998. 3–20.

Swartz, David. *Culture and Power: The Sociology of Pierre Bourdieu*. Chicago: University of Chicago Press, 1998.

Tatum, Charles. "Voces únicas: Trends in Contemporary Chicana/o Autobiography." Presentation at the V International Conference on Chicano Literature. Alcalá de Henares, Spain, May 24, 2006.

Thompson, John B. *Ideology and Modern Culture*. Stanford, Calif.: Stanford University Press, 1990.

Tinker Salas, Miguel. *In the Shadow of the Eagles: Sonora and the Transformation of the Border during the Porfiriato*. Berkeley: University of California Press, 1997.

"Treaty of Guadalupe Hidalgo." *Treaties and Conventions between the United States of America and Other Powers Since July 4, 1776*. Washington, DC: Government Printing Office. Lillian Goldman Law Library, Avalon Project, http://avalon.law.yale.edu/19th_century/guadhida.asp (accessed June 8, 2012)

Tylor, Edward B. *Primitive Culture*. New York: Brentano's, 1924. First published 1871.

Van Gennep, Arnold. *The Rites of Passage*. Chicago: University of Chicago Press, 1960.

Varner Gunn, Janet. *Autobiography: Toward a Poetics of Experience*. Philadelphia: University of Pennsylvania Press, 1982.

Velasco, Juan. "Automitografías: The Border Paradigm and Chicana/o Autobiogrpahy." *Biography* 27.2 (2004): 313–38. http://dx.doi.org/10.1353/bio.2004.0048

Velázquez Treviño, Gloria. "Cultural Ambivalence in Early Chicana Prose Fiction." PhD diss., Stanford University, 1985.

Vélez-Ibañez, Carlos G. *Border Visions: Mexican Cultures of the Southwest United Status*. Tucson: University of Arizona Press, 1997.

Villanueva de Cavazos, Lilia E. *Familias de Nuevo León: Su limpieza de sangre*. Monterrey: Talleres de Grafo Print Editores, S.A., 1993.

Watson, Julia. "Toward an Anti-metaphysics of Autobiography." *The Culture of Autobiography*. Edited by Robert Folkenflik. Stanford, Calif.: Stanford University Press, 1993. 57–79.

Webb, Jen, Tony Schirato, and Geoff Danaher. *Understanding Bourdieu*. London: Sage, 2002.

Weber, David J. "Editor's Introduction: Cultures Collide." *Foreigners in Their Native Land: Historical Roots of the Mexican Americans*. Edited by David J. Weber. Albuquerque: University of New Mexico Press, 2003. 87–100.

Weintraub, Karl Joachim. *The Value of the Individual: Self and Circumstance in Autobiography*. Chicago: University of Chicago Press, 1978.

Wilbur-Cruce, Eva Antonia. *A Beautiful, Cruel Country*. Tucson: University of Arizona Press, 1987.

Williams, Raymond. *The Sociology of Culture*. New York: Schocken Books, 1981.

Index

Other Titles in the Rio Grande / Río Bravo Borderlands Culture and Traditions Series:

Mexican Brick Culture in the Building of Texas, 1800s–1980s
Howard S. Cook

Mexican Coal Mining Labor in Texas and Coahuila, 1880–1930
Roberto R. Calderón

Chicano Timespace
López and Lomeli

El Mesquite: A Story of the Early Spanish Settlements Between the Nueces and the Rio Grande
O'Shea and Falcón

Santa Barraza, Artist of the Borderlands
Barraza and Herrera-Sobek

Medieval Culture and the Mexican American Borderlands
Kearney and Medrano

Historia: The Literary Making of Chicana and Chicano History
Louis G. Mendoza

Voices in the Kitchen: Views of Food and the World from Working-Class Mexican and Mexican American Women
Meredith E. Abarca

The Legacy of Américo Paredes
José R. Morín

Remembering the Hacienda: History and Memory in the Mexican American Southwest
Vincent Pérez

Capturing Nature: The Cement Sculpture of Dionicio Rodríguez
Patsy P. Light

Latina Legislator: Leticia Van de Putte and the Road to Leadership
Sharon A. Navarro

Wealth of Selves: Multiple Identities, Mestiza Consciousness, and the Subject of Politics
Edwina Barvosa

Claiming Rights and Righting Wrongs in Texas
Emilio Zamora

They All Want Magic: Curanderas and Folk Healing
Elizabeth De La Portilla

Moctezuma's Table: Rolando Briseño's Mexican and Chicano Tablescapes
Norma E. Cantú

CPSIA information can be obtained
at www.ICGtesting.com
Printed in the USA
BVHW052248100719
553140BV00014B/112/P

9 781623 498191